MW00892891

Salem's Forgotten Stories

A series of books from the
Nelson Dionne Salem History Collection
Archives & Special Collections
Salem State University
Salem, Massachusetts

salemsforgottenstories.com
facebook/salemsforgottenstories

Part of the proceeds from all of our books benefit the
Nelson Dionne Salem History Fund
at Salem State University.
We invite you to contribute funds and material as well!

★ SALEM SERVES ★

Sites and Stories from the
Military and Patriotic Heritage of
Salem, Massachusetts, 1626–WWII

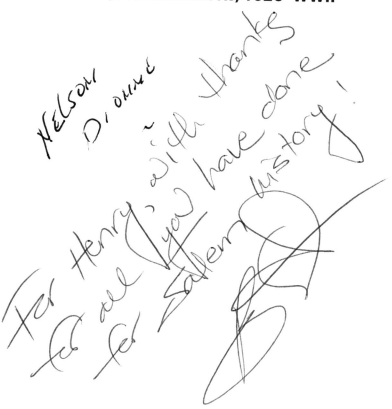

Bonnie Hurd Smith *for the*
Nelson Dionne Salem History Collection

2019 © Bonnie Hurd Smith *for the* Nelson Dionne Salem History Collection
ISBN: 978-1703165906
Design: Bonnie Hurd Smith, bonniehurdsmith.com
Publishing: KDP/Amazon via Hurd Smith Communications

This book is part of *Salem's Forgotten Stories*, a series of books from the
Nelson Dionne Salem History Collection, Archives & Special Collections,
Salem State University, Salem, Massachusetts. Salemsforgottenstories.com
and Facebook/salemsforgottenstories.

*If you use information in this book, please cite it as your source! And if you
would like to use any of the photographs—or if you have your own Salem
photographs to donate—please contact Susan Edwards, Archivist, Archives
& Special Collections, Salem State University, sedwards@salemstate.edu.*

Also by Nelson Dionne

U. S. Coast Guard Air Station Salem, Massachusetts, 1935-1970
    (with Bonnie Hurd Smith, 2015)
Salem Through Time (with Jerome Curley, 2014)
Legendary Locals of Salem (with Jerome Curley and Dorothy V. Malcolm, 2013)
Salem in Stereo: Victorian Salem in 3-D (2012)
Salem Then and Now (with Jerome Curley, 2011)

Also by Bonnie Hurd Smith

*We Believe in You: 12 Stories of Courage, Action, and Faith from
    American Women's History* (2015, 2017)
U. S. Coast Guard Air Station Salem, Massachusetts, 1935-1970
    (for the Nelson Dionne Salem History Collection, 2015)
The House That Love Built: The History of the Franklin Square House
    (with Beth Hinchliffe, for the Franklin Square House Foundation, 2012)
Margaret Fuller's New England (2010)
Letters of Loss & Love: Judith Sargent Murray Papers, Letter Book 3 (2009)
Boston Women & The Law: Four Centuries of Boston Women's Legal History
    (for New England Law, 2008)
*Mingling Souls Upon Paper: The 18th-Century Love Story of Judith Sargent
    and John Murray* (2007)
The Letters I Left Behind: Judith Sargent Murray Papers, Letter Book 10 (2005)
The Living Legacy of Ralph Waldo Emerson
    (for the Unitarian Universalist Association, 2003)
Salem Women's Heritage Trail
    (for the Salem Chamber of Commerce, 2000)
*From Gloucester to Philadelphia in 1790: Observations, anecdotes and thoughts
    from the letters of Judith Sargent Murray* (1998)

Cover: Samuel Dalton (in front), The Adjutant General of Massachusetts, in
1883 (the year he was appointed). He was the only Salem native to hold this
position. *Back cover:* Postcard of Fort Pickering and Winter Island Light, 1905.

For Nelson.

For Len, Al, Tom and "my guys" at the Second Corps.
Thank you for everything. This is *our* book.
Love you all.

Sic itur ad astra!

And for Salem veterans, past and present,
and all who support them.

Acknowledgements

Many friends and colleagues helped make this book better than it otherwise would have been. We are so grateful to the following people, with apologies for inadvertently forgetting a name.

Brig. Gen. Leonid Kondratiuk, the expert on military history in Massachusetts, was always an email, phone call, or visit away. We wouldn't have dared to do this book without him.

John Hardy Wright's vast knowledge of Salem history, editing, and his personal story improved the manuscript on many levels.

Barry Swift's genius with Photoshop made all of the images exponentially sharper. He even had the courage to colorize the cover photo, with expert advice and smashing results.

Iris Weaver's assistance with editing and proofreading was a blessing.

Mary Ellen Lapionka's groundbreaking work on Native Americans on Cape Ann and the North Shore came along just in time.

Denise Kent of Wicked Good Books in Salem is a tireless promoter of local history and a real partner in book design and marketing.

Susan Edwards, as Salem State University's Archives, is in charge of the Nelson Dionne Salem History Collection. She could not have been more helpful, patient, and encouraging. Her second-in-command, Jen Ratliff, stepped in at just the right moment to help with final details.

The Salem Public Library Reference Department, to a person, is always engaged, thorough, and good-natured.

These wonderful friends contributed stories, leads, or physical material to the book: J. L. Bell (boston1775.com), Thomas Brophy (Chief, Salem Fire Department, ret.), Thaddeus Buczko (veteran and First Justice, Essex Probate and Family Court, ret.), Kim Emerling (Director of Veterans Services for Salem—and his work-study students), George E. Gagnon (long-time Salem native and raconteur), Diana Korzenik (art historian and invaluable networking resource), Elizabeth LeBrun (Francois LeBrun, WWI), Christine Lutts (Friends of Greenlawn Cemetery), D. Michel Michaud (Franco-American Institute of Salem), and John Hardy Wright (Assistant Curator, Essex Institute, ret.).

Published here for the first time, with huge gratitude for their generosity, is material from Ben Arlander (on Capt. Henry C. Nichols), George Ford (on Nancy Remond Shearman and the Remond family), Racket Shreve (on William Shreve), Ruth Stearns and the Stearns family (on Joseph Oliver's Civil War service on Winter Island).

Finally, our thanks to James A. Ayube Sr., beloved father of the late James A. Ayube Jr., Salem's most recent casualty of war, for letting us publish his son's photograph. The brave and selfless are among us in every generation, and he was one.

★ Contents ★

Foreword
    by Kim Emerling, CSM, U. S. Army   iv
    Director of Veteran Services, City of Salem

Introduction   v

**Salem, Massachusetts is the Birthplace
of the United States National Guard**   vi
    Origin of the Name "National Guard"   vii

Titles in italic indicate special sections on a specific topic. Content labeled **Exclusive** contains images from private collections published here for the first time.

Salem During Wartime: Colonial Wars–World War II
    Wars Between the Colonists and Native Americans   1
    Revolutionary War   4
        Loyalists in Salem   8
    Quasi-War with France   12
    War of 1812   12
    Mexican-American War   15
    Civil War   16
        Exclusive: *Widow's pension request from*
           Nancy Remond Shearman   20
        The Salem Leg Company   22
    Spanish-American War   24
        Exclusive: *Letter on the death of William Sanders*   26
        The Parker Brothers "At War"   27
        Food Will Win the War   28
    World War I   29
        Liberty Bond Drives   32
    World War II   41
        Port Security and Civil Defense   42
        Auxiliary Police and the Salem Police Department   54
        Massachusetts Women's Defense Corps   57
        Salem Teachers College and the Collegiate
           Defense Committee   68

World War II (cont.)
Air-Sea Rescue Station Designation for
U. S. Coast Guard Air Station Salem 69
Exclusive: *William H. Shreve, and the Fred J. Dion*
Yacht Yard 71
Sylvania Earns "E" Award 78
How Salem Lost its WWII Bomber Memorial 83

Sites to Visit by Neighborhood
Relational Map 86

Salem Common and Downtown 87
President Washington in Salem (1789) 90
Military Bands and Band Music in Salem 97
Salem Names on the Walkway of Heroes 113
Salem's Medal of Honor Recipients 137
McIntire Historic District 153
Exclusive: *Captain William Driver Memorial Park* 156
The True Story of Old Glory 158
Marquis de Lafayette in Salem (1784, 1824) 176
The National Guard and the Salem Fire 187
North Salem 192
Leslie's Retreat 192
Waterfront and Derby Street 214
How Salem's "Sea-fencibles" Saved the
USS Constitution 216
Jonathan Haradan, Privateer 218
The Three Ships Named USS Salem 224
Three Salem Inventors Who Helped "Win the War"
at Sea 234
Early Merchant Marines of Salem 244
Salem's Coastline Defense:
Winter Island, Juniper Point, Salem Neck 245
Fort Pickering 247
Exclusive: *Civil War Service at Fort Pickering:*
Images from the Stearns Family Collection 254
Building the USS Essex 276
Fort Juniper 280
Fort Lee 281

Salem Military Units

Salem Company	291
East Regiment, Massachusetts Volunteer Militia	293
1st Essex Regiment, "Regular Militia," Minutemen, and the Continental Army	295
Salem Independent Cadets/Second Corps of Cadets	296
Massachusetts Militia Law of 1840	298
Salem Light Infantry, Salem Zouaves, and the 8th Regiment Infantry, MVM	309
Salem Mechanic Light Infantry	314
Salem City Guard	315
Fitzgerald Guards and Andrew Light Guard	316
Short-lived Units	317

Salem Veterans Organizations

American Legion, Post 23	319
American Veterans / AMVETS, Post 53	320
Disabled American Veterans / DAV, Chapter 84	321
Franco-American War Veterans, Post 10	322
Grand Army of the Republic / GAR, Post 34	322
Harriet M. Maxwell Auxiliary, U. S. Women Veterans / USWV, No. 27	324
Polish Legion of American Veterans / PLAV, Post 55	325
Salem Light Infantry Veterans Association / SLIVA	326
Second Corps of Cadets Veterans Association / SCCVA	329
United Spanish War Veterans / USWV Capt. Jacob C. R. Peabody Camp, No. 22	330
Veterans of Foreign Wars / VFW, Post 1524	333

Veterans' Squares	335
Veterans' Memorials and Parks	343
About the Nelson Dionne Salem History Collection and the "Salem's Forgotten Stories" Book Series	348
About Nelson Dionne	349
Appendix: Was Salem the *Real* Birthplace of the American Navy?	355
Bibliography	359
Index	367

★ Foreword ★

Since moving to Salem over thirty years ago, I have been fascinated by the engaging stories and characters that make up the City's rich and diverse history. We've had daring seafarers, great architects, staunch military men and women, and the high drama of the witch hysteria. This intricate tapestry of characters firmly secures a definitive place for Salem in American history.

Retired Salem Police Officer Nelson Dionne—a fifth generation Salemite and published author—has a passion for keeping Salem's history alive. His numerous articles, interviews, and books on our local heritage have popularized him as one of our premier amateur historians and collectors. Those who are long past are fortunate to have such an excellent keeper of their history.

This collection of stories about veterans and civic duty, from colonial days through World War II, serves as a reminder of Salem's lasting contributions to community and country. As the recognized "Birthplace of the U. S. National Guard," our City has contributed fighting men and women to every conflict since the Guard's founding in 1636.

Many made the ultimate sacrifice; they are remembered in plaques, markers, memorials, grave sites, ceremonies, and organizations described in this book. And there are many who returned home to start families, work hard, and enjoy the peace they had built. The contributions, family connections, and community relationships made by these veterans are a lasting tribute to our City's success and eminence.

It is said that we live as long as we are remembered. This book helps keep the remarkable story of Salem's military and patriotic history alive and enduring. Read it, reflect upon the stories, and honor the memories and sacrifices of the men and women of Salem who helped shape the community we so enjoy today.

We will always be a community rich in history and rich in sacrifice to our country. May we also always be a community rich in remembering.

Kim F. Emerling, Command Sergeant Major, U. S. Army
Director of Veterans' Services, City of Salem, Massachusetts
June 2019

★ Introduction ★

This book started as a self-guided walking trail of military sites in downtown Salem. I had taken very rough notes during my work for the Peabody Essex Museum's Armory Park Dedication Day project. But then life and more pressing books intervened. That turned out to be a good thing! While collaborating on a new book series about Salem history, Nelson Dionne shared some of his vast personal knowledge on the subject. He also provided the collection of images that dovetailed with my research, and this book was born.

Friends came forward with stories that were new to me, additional research ballooned my rough notes into many pages, and as the number of images we "had to include" grew daily, the book became something unexpected. At some point, I realized that it would be a real gift to Salem veterans, past and present, to their family and friends, to the veterans I have worked with, and Salem's residents and guests who might not otherwise know of our rich military history.

Please don't be put off by the length of the book! It is written to be picked through according to your interests. The table of contents and index can guide you. You may also wish to take it with you to follow the trails (or other Salem walking trails!). For that reason—and as a warning to those who do read chronologically—I have sometimes used an image twice or restated the same information in different places.

And here's my request of YOU. In this age of on-demand printing, it is easy to make corrections and re-upload the book file. I have done my absolute best to use reliable resources, to fact-check, and to present the most accurate information I could. I have also run the draft past several knowledgeable people. But if you see *any* error at all, please contact me so I can fix it!

Finally, in spite of the book's length, this is just a beginning. I hope many of you will choose a specific subject and write a book! Or, if you have material about a veteran, please contact Kim Emerling at the Salem Veterans Services Office. They are building a massive website. And, last but not least, please donate any "paper" you have to the Nelson Dionne Salem History Collection at Salem State University's Archives & Special Collections. Preserving and sharing our history must be a shared goal. Thank you, and enjoy!

Bonnie Hurd Smith, October 2019

Salem, Massachusetts is the Birthplace of the United States National Guard

In 1983, then-Major Leonid Kondratiuk, Chief, Historical Services, National Guard Bureau, Department of the Army, Washington, D. C. proposed a new poster for the National Guard Heritage Series—a poster history of the National Guard. In preparation for the National Guard's 350th anniversary in 1986, he approached Don Troiani, a budding military artist, to paint a scene depicting the first muster of one of the three Massachusetts militia regiments authorized by the Massachusetts Bay General Court on December 13, 1636.

The painting was completed in 1984 and depicts the first muster of the East Regiment on what is now Salem Common in the spring of 1637. The painting was reproduced as a National Guard poster and is displayed in thousands of National Guard armories and installations all over the United States. The original is in the Office of the Chief, National Guard Bureau, in the Pentagon. In 1986 the painting was used as the stamp portion on a postcard issued by the U. S. Postal Service.

In 2002, with the dedication of Armory Park, the City of Salem learned that, because the East Regiment first mustered in Salem in 1637, that, in effect, the city was the birthplace of the Massachusetts National Guard. The establishment date of a military force is determined by the date of its first permanent regiment.

The East Regiment's muster in Salem made the city the birthplace of the National Guard of the United States as well.

—*BG Leonid Kondratiuk, Director*
Massachusetts National Guard Museum and Archives
Commonwealth of Massachusetts

The First Muster by Don Troiani. Salem men became part of the formalized East Regiment of the Massachusetts Militia, created on December 13, 1636, by the General Court of the Massachusetts Bay Colony. Following the English militia system, all men between sixteen and sixty years of age were now required by law to be armed and prepared to defend their community. The following spring, the East Regiment held the first muster in the colonies.

Origin of the Name "National Guard"

On July 14, 1825, the American Revolutionary War hero the Marquis de Lafayette visited New York City on his grand tour of the United States. Lafayette had commanded the French "Garde National de Paris" during the early days of the French Revolution and in honor of that fact the 2nd Battalion of the 2nd Regiment of Artillery of the New York State Militia decided to adopt the name National Guard in Lafayette's honor. The name stuck, and in 1862 the New York State Militia became known as the National Guard New York. Throughout the 19th century other state militias took that name and in 1903 the Dick Act* made that name official.
—*NationalGuard.mil*

* The Dick Act of 1903 is named for Congressman Charles Dick of Ohio, a Major General in the Ohio National Guard, whose bill standardized the name in all states and defined the circumstances under which the National Guard could be called up for federal service.

In 1930, to celebrate the 300th anniversary of Governor John Winthrop's arrival at Salem, the City created promotional items like this postcard. Officials also commissioned a replica of Winthrop's flag ship, the *Arbella*, and built a "colonial village" to demonstrate what Salem might have looked like at the time.

Today, Pioneer Village is managed by the City of Salem and open to the public. The tour tells a more balanced story about the early "contact" between Native people and English colonists.

In 1630, because the colonists encountered hunger and disease in Salem, they sailed on to Charlestown where they endured a gruelling winter. They continued on to Boston the following spring.

Governor Winthrop Arrives at Salem on the "Arbella"

★ 1630 ★

Left: Replica of the ship *Arbella*; Below: "Pioneers' Village, 1930." Note the masts of the *Arbella* in the background.

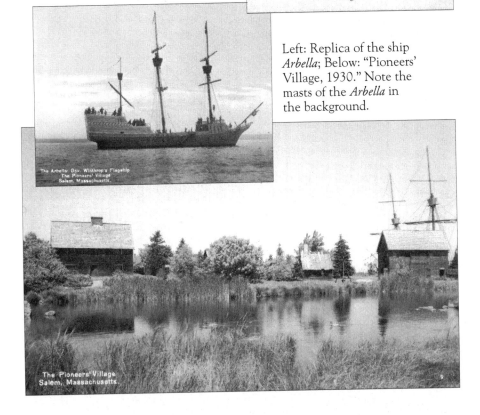

The Arbella: Gov. Winthrop's Flagship
The Pioneers' Village
Salem, Massachusetts

The Pioneers' Village
Salem, Massachusetts

★ Salem During Wartime ★
Colonial Wars–World War II

What was going on in Salem during each war?

Armed military conflicts on land really ended with the Revolutionary War, but coastline defense activities in Salem continued with the War of 1812 through World War II—and, it could be argued, up to today. Years ago, when Salem citizens went far away to serve, what was happening on the home front? Material from Nelson Dionne's Salem History Collection provides wonderful images that give us a "picture" of life in Salem during wartime—and how earlier (pre-photography) times were commemmorated and depicted many years later.

Along with information from Dionne's collection, sources for this general overview include Charles A. Benjamin's essay on Salem military history published in D. Hamilton Hurd's *History of Essex County, Massachusetts* (1888), James Duncan Phillips' *Salem in the Eighteenth Century* (1937), Joseph B. Felt's *The Annals of Salem* (1845, 1849), Frances Diane Robotti's *Chronicles of Old Salem* (1948), essays by Robert S. Rantoul Jr., G. L. Streeter, and others from the Essex Institute Historical Collections, and the Park Service's *Maritime Salem in the Age of Sail* (2009). I consulted newspapers of record from Salem and Boston, many topic-specific secondary sources and websites (with verification), and vertical files and reference books in the Salem Public Library's Salem Room (see *Bibliography*).

I encourage you to "go deeper" with the stories in this book, and delve even further into American history to learn more about the causes and outcomes of each war—and, especially, the costs.

★ Wars Between the Colonists (English and French) and Native Americans — *1637-ca. 1763*

The Massachusetts Bay colonists from England who settled at Naumkeag in 1626 (the Native American name for Salem at the time) did so on land that was already occupied. And because the economy and way of life for these Puritans (in contrast to the "Pilgrims" of Plimoth) revolved around land ownership, they came into conflict with Native Americans whose relationship with the land and Nature was completely different. At the same time, conflicts between England and France played out in their North American colonies—each empire wanting to control more land.

Captain John Endecott (or Endicott) organized the Salem company in 1629. Drilling, or training, commenced in the spring of that year, and continued thereafter. In 1630, Salem contributed three pounds toward the defense of the colony. "Several cannon were brought to Salem at about this time" (April 1631), writes military historian Charles A. Benjamin in *History of Essex County*. Concurrently, Salem constructed its earliest fort, Fort Naumkeag, at the corner of present-day Lynde and Sewall Streets.

Salem men became part of the East Regiment of the Massachusetts Militia, created on December 13, 1636, by the General Court of the Massachusetts Bay Colony. Following the English militia system, all men between sixteen and sixty years of age were now required by law to be armed and prepared to defend their community. The following spring, the East Regiment held the first muster in the colonies. Salem is federally recognized as the Birthplace of the U. S. National Guard because they trace their lineage back to this spring day in 1637, when the (volunteer) East Regiment mustered (drilled) for the first time on Salem Common. That same year, the East Regiment provided a provisional company to fight the Pequots in Connecticut.

On May 10, 1643, the Court created the County of Essex (or Essex County) and the number of militia units grew. The Massachusetts colonists' long series of battles with Native Americans and the French continued. Years of suspicion, fear, and hostility on both sides erupted in 1675 when Philip, Sachem of the Wampanoags ("King" is an English word and concept), led an uprising to take back their land. The Massachusetts General Court ordered fortifications to be erected throughout the colony. In Salem, according to historian Frances Robotti: "Long defenses constructed of palisade and stone are built at the western end of Essex Street. Extending from the North River to the Mill Pond, they cut off all approach by land from the surrounding country to the principal part of the settlement."

The Salem men who were not away fighting in King Philip's War "strengthened the main fort here and built garrisons (blockhouses), for the protection of the farm people outside of the town. These were all garrisoned, and the military of Salem must have been nearly all on duty during this time, at home or with the active forces," according to Charles A. Benjamin.

At sea, Salem merchants and fishermen "were much harassed by [the French] in the fisheries and by their Indian allies in the Eastern settlements," Benjamin writes. Salem vessels were seized, and their sailors were kidnapped, jailed, or impressed (forced) into service. To cite just one example from Joseph B. Felt's *Annals of Salem*:

1695, Sept. 23. As a French privateer had captured shallops at the Isles of Shoals, another in our bay, and it is said that Major Brown's ketch, which was taken, and other booty, are in a harbor in or near Casco bay, a commission is requested for a ketch and shallop, with 40 or 50 fishermen of Marblehead and Salem, to sail from this place, in pursuit of the enemy. The petition was allowed, and funds were granted for the enterprise.

All-out war between England and France for control of the North American continent officially commenced in 1702, and Salem's militia participated. Pirates from the "Spanish main" began to appear off the coast of Salem as well, and in 1703 Massachusetts Governor Joseph Dudley assigned twenty men "for the 'Flying Horse,' an armed cruiser of Salem" to kill or capture these intruders," Benjamin explains.

The fight for land continued in the North, and for roughly three decades Salem men fought at Louisburg, Quebec, and Montreal. Two Salem men in Captain Giddings' 14th Provincial Regiment, Gibson Clough, a private, and Capt. John Tapley, kept journals of their ordeal in Canada. At the end of the war, when Clough returned to Salem, he noted that they were possessed of "great joy and contentment," according to Benjamin.

Decades of war with France were costly for Great Britain. They needed to raise money, and the colonies could provide revenue. Charles Benjamin explains:

The French wars were now ended. The people of the colonies while impoverished by the aid rendered the mother-country (England), had nevertheless learned their strength; and the presence among them of a large body of trained soldiers, just returned from efficient service in the field where they had often proved themselves fully the equals of the British regulars, did not tend to make them tolerant of any tyrannical measures of the Crown.

So for the next fifteen years the people of Salem, in common with their neighbors, were warming up in their quarrel with the mother-country.

★ Revolutionary War — *1775-1783*

By 1768, hostilities between Great Britain and its American colonies were escalating. That year, King George III sent war ships to Boston Harbor and points North to enforce British trade laws. When the HMS *Rose* captured an American ship bound for its home port of Marblehead, local seamen were furious. The loyalists who had alerted the British, Thomas Row and Robert Wood, were tarred and feathered on Salem Common, "set in a cart with the word Informer on their breasts and backs, and ridden out of town with a wild goose continuously thrown at them," writes Beverly historian and statesman Robert S. Rantoul Jr.

The colonists had successfully petitioned the King for the removal of Governor Hutchinson due to growing conflicts, and Salem loyalists hosted a grand farewell for him on April 27, 1774. While the colonists might have thought they had prevailed, Salem historian James Duncan Phillips explains, "With the departure of Hutchinson and the appointment of Gage, the royal government had clearly shown its hand so far as the enforcement of its decrees was concerned and the patriot party in America as promptly accepted the challenge."

Lieut. General Thomas Gage arrived in Boston in 1774 to become the first military governor of Massachusetts, just months after what has become known as the "Boston Tea Party" of December 13, 1773. Under the Boston Port Bill (part of the Coercive Acts of 1774), Gage closed the Port of Boston until reparations were made for the loss of the tea "and as a reprimand to the Province of Massachusetts for its independent attitude since 1646." Boston's trade and shipping shifted to Marblehead and Salem. Salem was "the rendezvous for the custom-house officials who resided in Boston," according to Rantoul.

As Boston became increasingly hostile to the presence of British troops, General Gage moved the General Court (legislature) to Salem where he had the support of many Salem merchants. He was welcomed and feted (by some). But when Gage tried to reconvene the General Court at Salem's Court House, his secretary was refused entrance and Gage was unable to conduct business. In July, Gage sent two companies of the 64th Regiment to Salem to assert British power.

Ninety representatives of the earlier Massachusetts General Court met secretly in Salem on October 5, 1774, to form an Assembly. Bostonian John Hancock was made president. On October 7, they voted to become a Provincial Congress with "sovereign powers" and quickly adjourned for meetings in Cambridge and Concord as Salem was becoming overrun with those who opposed independence from Great Britain. As a result, Rantoul believes:

October 7th then was the birthday and Salem Town House the birthplace of the Commonwealth of Massachusetts.

Bicentennial first day cover, observing Oct. 5, not 7.

Salem was now a hotbed of tension between "patriots" and "loyalists," leading to the events of February 26, 1775, when General Gage dispatched Col. Alexander Leslie and the 64th Regiment to North Salem. They were in search of the cannon and gunpowder hidden there. Salem patriots had been warned in advance, and Col. Leslie's loyalist friends alerted him as he approached Salem. An armed stand-off at the North Bridge was the result, leading to a negotiated agreement for Col. Leslie and his troops to retreat in peace—but news of the event circulated. Americans, for the first time, believed that independence was possible (see pp. 192-201 for more on "Leslie's Retreat").

On March 25, Salem voted to raise two companies of "Minutemen" from the militia. They marched toward Lexington on April 19, and suffered casualties during the fierce fighting in Menotomy (now Arlington) as the British retreated to Boston. Their names appear on the Armory Park Walkway of Heroes (see p. 113).

It was Capt. John Derby who brought the news to London that we were at war, sailing the ship *Quero* from his family's wharf (p. 219).

Salem men participated in the pivotal Battle of Bunker Hill on June 17 where Lieut. Benjamin West was killed, and in battles throughout the colonies until the war was over. John Glover, born in Salem, and his sea-worthy men famously helped General George Washington cross the Delaware River (p. 117). Col. Timothy Pickering "'made a plan of exercise' (or, tactics) … that the Congress ordered to be used by officers of the Massachusetts Militia in 1776," according

THE BATTLE OF BUNKER HILL, JUNE 17, 1775, CHARLESTOWN, MASS.

Color postcard of an artist's rendition of the Battle of Bunker (Breed's) Hill, 1975. Salem's Leiut. Benjamin West lost his life that day.

to Charles Benjamin, before becoming Quartermaster General of the Army and Adjutant General (see pp. 184-86). General Washington called Salem's Col. Samuel Carleton "one of the most intrepid officers who served under him."

At sea, over 150 Salem ship owners become licensed as privateers to harass and seize British ships. Salem's loyalists were subject to taunting, mob violence, and the seizure of property. Some died (see p. 167); others left for Halifax or England rather than take up arms against their country. On June 9, 1780, delegates from Salem and other Massachusetts towns approved the state constitution written by John Adams. The colonies were governed under Articles of Confederation until a federal constitution could be approved.

The war ended in September of 1783, and while many privateers/ merchants profited from the war, most people struggled through a post-war depression. Massachusetts towns west of the coast fared even worse, and they resented the legal and economic demands placed on them by the government in Boston.

In 1787, Daniel Shay led a rebellion in the Springfield area with 4,000 supporters. A small Salem company helped put down "Shay's Insurrection" against the idea of a federal constitution. Then, on June 23, 1788, Salem celebrated the adoption of the U.S. Constitution.

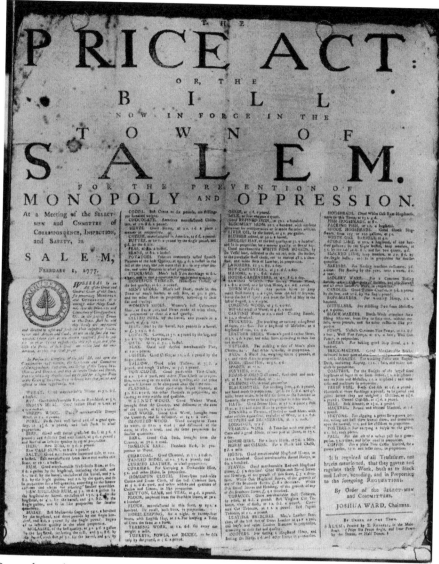

Press photo from an April 28, 1918, article in the *Salem Evening News* titled, "How Salem Regulated Prices 141 Years Ago." It appeared during World War I, when many food items were being rationed, to offer historical perspective. The caption reads: "Few persons realize that price-fixing at the present time is nothing new, for 141 years ago 'committees of public safety' in the various towns were forced to try experiments now being tried by our national government. Every community dealt with its own particular problem, for in some communities certain articles were cheaper, while others were higher priced, owing to the varying ability to supply the demand. Many of these 'price acts' have been discovered, but the Salem 'price act' is quite rare, only one being actually known to be in existence at the present time."

Loyalists in Salem

All of [them] were sincere in their convictions, never bore arms against their country, and simply retired to avoid insult and persecution. They regretted the Revolution rather than opposed it.

—James Duncan Phillips

We Americans tend to forget or dismiss the "other side" of the Revolutionary War story, but this really does a disservice to our understanding of what happened and devalues the men who wished to avoid war. In fact, the Revolutionary War was America's first Civil War as families, congregations, and communities were torn apart by differing views.

As the Salem historian James Duncan Phillips elegantly puts it: "In any great division of opinion there are always two sides to the question, and, forgetting for the moment the impulsive, vindictive, arrogant, and ignorant, there are always kindly, calm, wise men who simply cannot see alike." Salem, he notes, was "almost purely English" at the time, "with a slight tinge of French Huguenot … both those people are famous for personal loyalty rather than loyalty to an idea, and the king meant more to them than the Puritans."

James H. Stark points out in his book *The Loyalists of Massachusetts:* "Because the Revolution had its origin in Massachusetts, and the old Bay State furnished a large part of the men and the means to carry it to a successful issue, it seems to have been taken for granted that the people embraced the popular side in a mass. A more mistaken opinion of this has seldom prevailed."

The Massachusetts Loyalists were men of high political, economic, civic, and social standing, but as tensions between the Crown and the colonists grew their communities became increasingly dangerous places to live. Salem was among them, but the town's loyalists (or tories) held out hope for reconciliation, peace, and continued prosperity. Mob violence was on the rise after the Boston Tea Party of December 1773, including in Salem. While attacking the home of (royal government-appointed) Superior Court Judge Nathaniel Ropes in March 1774, he died from the trauma (see pp. 167-68).

Stark explains: "The persecution of the Loyalists by the Sons of Despotism, or the 'Sons of Liberty,' as they called themselves, was mercilessly carried out; every outrage conceivable was practiced upon them. Freedom of speech was suppressed; the liberty of the press destroyed; the voice of truth silenced, and throughout the colonies was established a lawless power … When this ostracism was approved by a large majority of the inhabitants of a town the victim was practically expelled from the community. None dared give him food or comfort. He was a pariah, and to countenance him was to incur public wrath."

The colonists had successfully petitioned the King for the removal of Governor Thomas Hutchinson due to growing animosity, and Salem loyalists hosted a grand farewell for him on April 27, 1774, culminating in a ball at the Assembly House on Cambridge Street (now Federal).* Many Salem loyalists addressed letters to Hutchinson "expressing their approbation of his conduct," James Duncan Phillips writes. These letters later became public, and were used to identify and persecute loyalists.

Loyalists' optimism must have increased with the arrival of General Thomas Gage, the new, military Governor of Massachusetts. As Phillips writes: "With the departure of Hutchinson and the appointment of Gage, the royal government had clearly shown its hand so far as the enforcement of its decrees was concerned." Salem loyalists feted General Gage on June 2. Two days later, on King George's birthday, Assembly Hall was the site of a "brilliant ball" and for a brief time "things began to be gay in town for the Tory element," writes Phillips. Forty-eight Salem loyalists signed an open letter to Gage, "commending to him the trade and welfare of the port of Salem." This was published in the *Essex Gazette* of June 14.

But the situation changed rapidly, as Phillips continues. General Gage's August 1774 effort "to prevent the town meeting called to choose delegates to the Ipswich convention," led to widespread mob violence against loyalists—smashing windows, setting fires, tarring and feathering. Some loyalists left Salem for England or Halifax, Nova Scotia (Canada). Others stayed put and tried to keep a low profile. As the violence and suspicion worsened, some families departed for Boston where they could live under the protection of British troops.

On February 26, 1775, General Gage ordered Lieut. Colonel Alexander Leslie and the 64th Regiment of Foot to Salem to confiscate the cannon and gunpowder hidden there. He had been tipped off by loyalists. As Col. Leslie approached Salem, loyalists told him where to look and warned him that he would be met with resistance at the North Bridge (see pp. 192-201 on "Leslie's Retreat").

The "real troubles of the loyalists came in the hard, bitter days of 1777 and 1778, when the provincial government was well established and was fighting for its life," writes Phillips. The 1778 Banishment Act prevented loyalists who had left to return—or face death if they did. The 1779 Conspiracy Act and Confiscation Act made matters worse. Phillips writes, "As the pressure on the tories grew, they were arrested and thrown into prison, bound over to keep the peace, and some-times obliged to live in the inland towns."

Phillips divides Salem's loyalists into four categories:

1) "Very able men who had served their province and city faithfully and well. They refused in most cases to change their opinions, and for that reason the patriots could not allow them to remain. They were the leaders of the type

that every country needs." Among them was the Honorable William Browne (appointed "Mandemus Counsellor" by the King in August 1774 in his attempt to replace all government and judicial officials with royal appointments), Judge Samuel Curwen, Colonel Benjamin Pickman, Colonel Peter Frye, Colonel Thomas Poynton, and John Sargent, to name just a handful.

2) Phillips describes the second group as "shop keepers and others not so conspicuous in public life who were forced to leave the town and never return." Among them were George Deblois (small merchant and shopkeeper), Andrew Dalglish (shopkeeper), Nathaniel Dabney (apothecary), and John Prince (physician).

3) "Salem men who became real enemies of their country" —men who joined the British forces. They included James Grant, Francis Cox, Peter Pickman Frye, and Peter Oliver.

4) "Loyalists who stayed in Salem," or, "the passive sort," many of whom retracted the letters they had signed in support of Hutchinson and/or Gage. Among them were the Honorable Benjamin Lynde, William Pynchon, Francis Cabot, Timothy Orne, Nathan Goodale, and Dr. Edward Augustus Holyoke.

Interestingly, Phillips notes, most of the tories who had departed Salem left their wives behind. These women continued to live in their homes, socialize, visit the sick, and shop without fear because "even the mob—and a mob of hoodlums there was … did not commit violence against women … When peace finally came, many of the emigrants returned and took up their old ways."

*This Assembly House was built in 1766 on land absorbed by the laying out of Cambridge Street (now Federal); the building no longer stands.

★ Quasi-War with France — *1797-1798*

Salem merchant ships experienced "various aggressions on our commerce by the English and French" in 1797/98, writes Joseph B. Felt, leading Salem to fortify its forts along the coastline (see pp. 245-89).

Charles A. Benjamin explains the impact of the quasi-war on Salem:

In 1798, it being obvious that the United States needed a navy, and the government having no facilities for ship-building, a request was made that the citizens of certain maritime localities loan funds to aid in the equipment of the navy. In Salem a large sum was subscribed, and the frigate 'Essex,' afterward to become a very famous vessel, was built by Salem ship-builders on Winter Island, rigged and turned over to the government. It was a patriotic task for a little town of nine thousand inhabitants to undertake [see 275-79 for more on the USS Essex*].*

★ War of 1812 — *1812-1815*

This war was not at all popular in Salem. Salem merchants had suffered economically during the Revolutionary War, and again during President Jefferson's trade embargo of 1807. England and France were in conflict again, forcing the British to "impress" (kidnap) thousands of American sailors into their navy. Charles Benjamin explains:

During the years that preceded the War of 1812, the Salem merchantmen in common with others lost men by the high-handed impressments of the British men of war, that exercised a pretended right to take from the ship of any nation met on the high seas, such seamen as their officers chose to consider English subjects; and as they were in need of sailors they were by no means nice in drawing distinctions.

Therefore, while opposed on general principles to the embargo and subsequent declaration of war against England, these unwarrantable acts had left sufficient sting in the minds of the Salem merchants and seamen to render them very ready to again sweep the seas with their privateers to the serious detriment of the British merchant marine ... The daring with which these fine vessels were fought and the brilliant seamanship that so fully utilized their admirable sailing qualities, were the wonder and exasperation of the English navy, and caused British merchants many hours of painful reflection."

It was during this war that "Salem boys" were credited with saving the USS *Constitution*—although Marbleheaders may disagree (see p. 216). Benjamin concludes:

It is to be regretted that a list of those who served in the army during the war of 1812 from Salem cannot be given, as in that existing at the State house the residences of the men are not given. The number was, it is understood, not large, as the war was not over-popular in this neighborhood, and the tastes of a maritime people led them to seek the enemy on their proper element.

One of the more memorable events at this time took place on the early evening of June 1, 1813, when Salem citizens witnessed the battle between the American frigate USS *Chesapeake* and the British warship RMS *Shannon* from the top of Leggs Hill off the coast of the Salem-Marblehead line (below). As Salem historian Jim McAllister tells the story, "At approximately 6 p.m., after a few hours of tactical maneuvering, the two vessels began firing at each other. Within twelve minutes, [they] stood yardarm to yardarm as the crew of one of the ships was preparing to board the other. Then, as thousands of spectators watched from Legg's Hill and along the shore, the *Chesapeake* exploded. Both vessels were enveloped in smoke, and by the time it cleared,

ENGAGEMENT BETWEEN THE CHESAPEAKE AND SHANNON, 1813

From a drawing in the Peabody Museum.

the British had boarded and taken control of the American vessel." It was during this battle that Capt. James Lawrence of the *Chesapeake*, while severely wounded, famously told his second in command, Lieut. Augustus C. Ludlow and his men, "Don't give up the ship!"

Learning that the British had transported the bodies of the captured sailors to Halifax—many of whom were Salem natives—the wealthy ship owner and adventurer George Crowninshield Jr. sailed his brig *Henry* to retrieve them. Salem's massive funeral for Lawrence and Ludlow took place at the congregational Branch Church on Howard Street (later, Howard Street Church). Elbridge Gerry, a Marblehead native and Vice President of the United States, attended; the Honorable Justice Joseph Story of Salem delivered the oration.

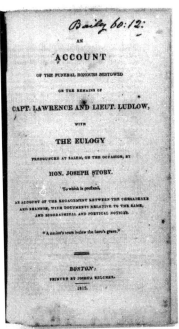

The bodies of Lawrence and Ludlow were interred temporarily in the Crowninshield tomb in the Howard Street Cemetery until they could be moved to their permanent resting place in Manhattan. An account of the battle, biographical sketches, and Judge Story's eulogy were published in Boston in 1813 (see image, left).

Lawrence's friend and fellow officer, Oliver Hazard Perry, ordered the creation of a blue ship's battle flag with Lawrence's famous words in large white lettering. Perry flew the flag from his flagship, the *Lawrence,* and went on to earn the title of "Hero of Lake Erie" in 1813. Capt. Lawrence's words have lived on ever since!

> **Navy Department, July 28, 1813.**
>
> Sir,
> In compliance with your request of the 19th instant, I have the pleasure to enclose the passport and letter from the Secretary of State which you desired, and to express my high sense of the patriotic and honourable motives by which yourself and companions are actuated.
>
> I am, very respectfully,
> your obedient servant,
> (Signed) WILLIAM JONES.
>
> George Crowninshield, Jr. Esq. }
> Salem, Massachusetts. }

Note from the U. S. Secretary of the Navy to George Crowninshield Jr. that appeared in the *Account* (pictured above).

The Mohican Company of Salem's annual outing at Asbury Grove, Hamilton, in 1916. Lower right: a man holds a sign listing Salem men who had not yet returned from the Mexican War: James Ward, Henry Tyburn, and Scott Berry.

★ Mexican-American War — *1846-1848*

In 1844, most of Salem opposed the annexation of Texas fearing it would expand slavery and lead to war with Mexico—which it did. The United States declared war against the Republic of Mexico on April 24, 1846, and Salem, like much of New England, participated only minimally.

The few Salem men who served in this war did so as part of the 1st Regiment Infantry, MVM (Massachusetts Volunteer Militia), under Col. Caleb Cushing of Newburyport. Charles A. Benjamin reports: "This regiment served in the army commanded by General Scott, and took part in the engagements that signalized its resistless march from Vera Cruz to Mexico. If any men from this place joined the so-called New England regiment, it has been impossible to obtain their names." Some Salemites *were* enthusiastic about the hero of the Mexican War, Gen. Zachary Taylor, "Old Rough and Ready," the presidential candidate of the Whig Party who promised to end the expansion of slavery.

★ Civil War — *1861-1865*

With the death of President Taylor in 1850 while in office, Millard Fillmore became president. Under Fillmore, the Compromise of 1850 passed, supported by Salem's former Congressman, Rufus Choate, among others, to end "sectional disputes" over slavery in newly acquired land (from the Mexican War) in favor of business interests. Many Salem merchants at this time were benefiting from slavery.

The North, in general, protested vehemently against the compromise, which included a much harsher Fugitive Slave Law. This 1850 law made it illegal and punishable for anyone to help an escaped slave. In addition, any slave caught would be returned to the South. Salem's active abolitionist community, including the Salem Female Anti-Slavery Society—the first such bi-racial organization in the country—was furious (p. 121). In 1854, Nathaniel Hawthorne's college friend, President Franklin Pierce, signed the Kansas-Nebraska Act to open up the territory for development and for the locally controlled expansion of slavery. Salem's abolitionists pressed on. As Frances Robotti explains, by then the Whig Party had split into North (Republican) and South (Democratic). Northerners demanded the repeal of the Fugitive Slave Law and declared slavery "a great moral, social and political evil."

John Brown's raid on Harper's Ferry on October 16, 1859, and his subsequent hanging, were extensively reported in local newspapers. Salem condemned the secession of Southern states from the Union following Abraham Lincoln's election to the presidency in 1860. They viewed it as an illegal act, joining the cries for "The Union, the Constitution, and the Enforcement of the Law."

Menu cover from the Salem Lowe Restaurant, ca. 1940.

When Confederate troops seized Fort Sumter, South Carolina (federal property), Salem men responded immediately to Lincoln's call for volunteers to protect the capital. Patriotic speeches were delivered at Mechanic Hall,

Civil War-era mail depicting George Washington.

where money was raised by Salem's "well-known gentlemen," Charles Benjamin explains. The City of Salem voted $15,000 "for the aid of the families of absent soldiers," he continues, and as troops prepared to leave, "the town was simmering with the excitement of their approaching departure." The first units to go included the Salem Light Infantry/Salem Zouaves, the Mechanic Light Infantry, and the Salem City Guard (see *Salem Military Units*). Benjamin continues:

They were bid God-speed, and urged to remember the high duty they were called upon to perform, while at every step of their march through the streets they were cheered by enthusiastic crowds, many of whom only regretted that circumstances prevented their being also in their ranks. The city was a unit in their enthusiasm, and while there was plenty of "gush," if the word may be pardoned, and an exaltation of sentiment greater than our national temperament has been usually given to, the occasion justified it, and it was hearty and genuine to the last degree. In these companies over two hundred men left Salem for Washington within five days from the call of the President.

It was soon clear that more troops would be needed for whatever lay ahead, and Salem men enlisted throughout the duration of the war. In its early days, Benjamin notes:

Perhaps never in the history of any country was there seen such an outburst of disinterested enthusiasm so well sustained as marked the first few months of the war in the entire North. And it was fully shared in Salem. Everyone was desirous of doing something in aid of the cause. Men and women seemed for the time to lose sight of the petty aims and thoughts of every-day life, and were dignified by a common love of their country and a desire to serve it.

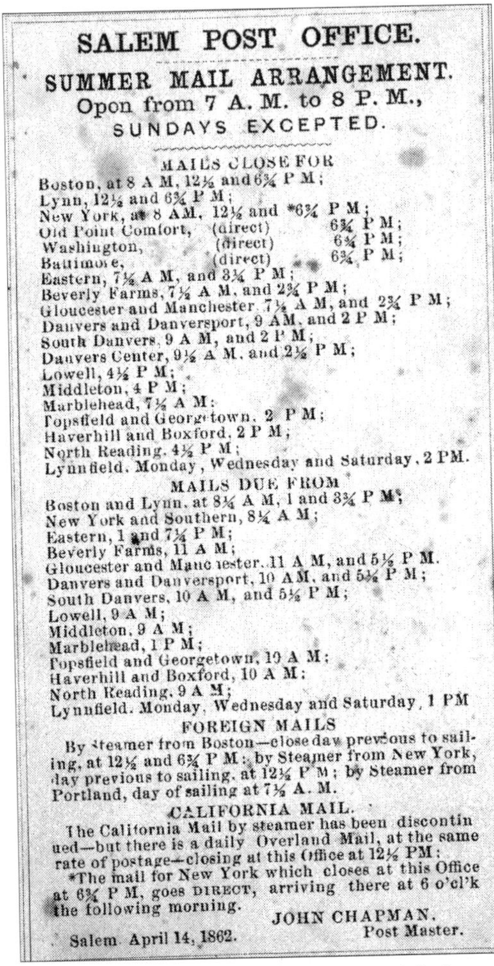

SALEM POST OFFICE.

SUMMER MAIL ARRANGEMENT.
Opon from 7 A. M. to 8 P. M.,
SUNDAYS EXCEPTED.

MAILS CLOSE FOR
Boston, at 8 A M, 12½ and 6¾ P M;
Lynn, 12½ and 6¾ P M;
New York, at 8 AM, 12½ and *6¾ P M;
Old Point Comfort, (direct) 6¾ P M;
Washington, (direct) 6¾ P M;
Baltimore, (direct) 6¾ P M;
Eastern, 7½ A M, and 3¾ P M;
Beverly Farms, 7½ A M, and 2¾ P M;
Gloucester and Manchester 7½ A M, and 2¾ P M;
Danvers and Danversport, 9 AM, and 2 P M;
South Danvers, 9 A M, and 2 P M;
Danvers Center, 9½ A M, and 2½ P M;
Lowell, 4½ P M;
Middleton, 4 P M;
Marblehead, 7½ A M:
Topsfield and Georgetown, 2 P M;
Haverhill and Boxford, 2 P M;
North Reading, 4½ P M;
Lynnfield, Monday, Wednesday and Saturday, 2 PM.

MAILS DUE FROM
Boston and Lynn, at 8¼ A M, 1 and 3¾ P M;
New York and Southern, 8¼ A M;
Eastern, 1 and 7¼ P M;
Beverly Farms, 11 A M;
Gloucester and Manchester, 11 A M, and 5½ P M.
Danvers and Danversport, 10 AM, and 5½ P M;
South Danvers, 10 A M, and 5½ P M;
Lowell, 9 A M;
Middleton, 9 A M;
Marblehead, 1 P M;
Topsfield and Georgetown, 10 A M;
Haverhill and Boxford, 10 A M:
North Reading, 9 A M;
Lynnfield, Monday, Wednesday and Saturday, 1 PM

FOREIGN MAILS
By Steamer from Boston—close day previous to sailing, at 12½ and 6¾ P M; by Steamer from New York, day previous to sailing, at 12½ P M; by Steamer from Portland, day of sailing at 7½ A. M.

CALIFORNIA MAIL.
The California Mail by steamer has been discontinued—but there is a daily Overland Mail, at the same rate of postage—closing at this Office at 12½ PM;
*The mail for New York which closes at this Office at 6¾ P M, goes DIRECT, arriving there at 6 o'cl'k the following morning.

JOHN CHAPMAN,
Post Master.

Salem April 14, 1862.

Broadside, Salem Post Office, 1862. Mail was conveyed over land or by steamer out of Boston, New York, and Portland for "foreign mails."

Civil War-era mail from Salem.

By 1861, American women had been organizing benevolent and political societies for decades and Salem was no different. Through sanitary fairs, church committees, and aid societies, Salem women sewed, knitted, raised money, wrote letters, and helped soldiers' families.

One Salem woman, Kate Tannat Woods, went to the battlefield with her husband, Lieut. Col. George H. Woods, to serve as his nurse (see p. 206).

As the war progressed, enthusiasm gave way to sober reality. This would not be a brief war. The numbers of war dead and wounded listed in local newspapers was staggering.

The year 1861 was also when Salem's Rev. G. W. Wildes "raised a Field Hospital Corps of 60 volunteers from Salem and vicinity which became the first ambulance department in the United States Army," Frances Robotti writes, quoting T. J. Hutchinson's and Ralph Childs' book, *Roll of Honor of Officers and Enlisted Men during the Civil War from Salem, Mass.*

PROVOST MARSHAL'S OFFICE.

Fifth District, State of Massachusetts,
54 Washington St., Salem, July 14, 1863.

To David N. Bridges

Meeting House Georgetown

SIR:

You are hereby notified that you were, on the 10th day of July, 1863, legally drafted in the service of the United States for the period of three years, in accordance with the provisions of the act of Congress, "for enrolling and calling out the national forces, and for other purposes," approved March 3, 1863. You will accordingly report for duty, at such a time as I shall hereafter designate, at the place of rendezvous, in Salem, Mass., or be deemed a deserter, and be subject to the penalty prescribed therefor by the Rules and Articles of War.

Daniel H. Johnson Jr

Captain, and Provost Marshal, Fifth Dist. of Massachusetts.

Draft notice sent to David N. Bridges in 1863 from the Provost Marshal's office at 54 Washington Street. If he did not report to the designated place, Bridges would face consequences as a deserter.

In 1862, two military funerals flooded Salem streets: those for Brig. Gen. Frederick Lander (see pp. 154-55) and Lieut. Col. Henry Merritt (see pp. 122-24) that reminded people, if it had been necessary to do so, "that war was not all pomp and glitter, but meant death and sorrow," writes Robotti.

That Fall, Charlotte Forten, a teacher at Salem's Higginson Grammar School and the first African American graduate of the Salem Normal School (now, Salem State University) traveled to St. Helena Island, South Carolina, to teach recently freed slaves.

President Lincoln's Emmancipation Proclamation went into full effect on January 1, 1863. His executive order freed enslaved persons in all of the states that had seceded from the Union, and it allowed African American men to join the Union forces. In Massachusetts, Governor John Andrew initiated the 54th Massachusetts Volunteer Infantry Regiment—the first all-black unit organized in the North.

Three Salem men were centrally involved in the 54th: Charles Lenox Remond and Robert Morris helped recruit soldiers, and Luis F. Emilio signed up as one of the white officers (see p. 211). The 54th filled up so quickly the 55th Massachusetts was organized from the overflow of recruits.

Exclusive!

In 1866, Nancy (Remond) Shearman of Salem petitioned the Essex County Probate Court for her widow's pension. Her husband, James L. Shearman, had served in the U. S. Navy. Their son William served in the Navy and the 55th Massachusetts. Nancy was the sister of Sarah Parker Remond and Charles Lenox Remond. *Courtesy of George Ford, Remond/Shearman family descendant.*

Above: Unidentified members of the 54th Massachusetts.

Right: Charles Lenox Remond, abolitionist speaker, writer; far right: Robert Morris, the first black attorney to argue a jury case; he also helped desegregate Boston public schools.

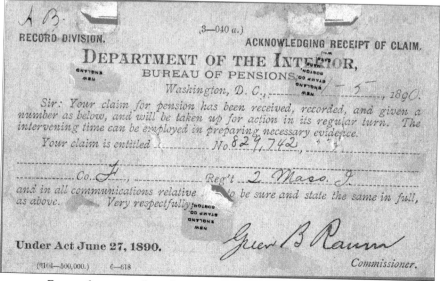

Front of a postcard confirming Jeremiah Connors' pension claim for serving in Co. F, 2nd Massachusetts Infantry Regiment.

All told, writes Charles Benjamin, Salem "responded to all calls upon her for men, about three thousand entering the Army and Navy during the war out of an entire population of a little over twenty-one thousand."

After the war, in 1866, the Grand Army of the Republic (GAR) was founded—the earliest veterans group in the country. Salem's GAR post, General Phil Henry Sheridan, Post 54, opened in 1867 (see pp. 115-17 and pp. 322-24). Abolitionists in Salem, including members of the Remond family, now directed their energy toward Freedmen's Aid Societies. A number of freed slaves settled in Salem, joining a small but thriving African American community.

Wounded soldiers were cared for and some, like Salem's colorful Mayor John "Silk Hat" Hurley, survived for many years. But many died at home from their injuries or lingering disease. Their children founded Sons of Union Veterans and Daughters of Union Veterans, and worked with City officials to erect memorials to honor the war dead.

The Salem Leg Company

In 1856, Rev. George Baker Jewett of Barton Square, while horseback riding with his wife and son one day, survived a terrible accident when his horse panicked and backed into an oncoming train. Jewett's injuries were serious, including the partial loss of one leg. Not wanting to remain immobile, Jewett invented an artificial leg for himself. The leg was so effective compared to others on the market, Jewett patented his "Improvement in Artificial Legs" for the first time on June 24, 1862. A report at the time praised his invention for its "mechanical perfection and simplicity of arrangement." The wearer could also disassemble and repair his leg with ease.

1862 was the same year that the federal government established a program to provide amputees with articial limbs at no cost. In 1866, the state of North Carolina created a similar program and contracted with Jewett to manufacture his "leg" in Raleigh. Jewett's shop stayed in business until June 18, 1867, when the demand for his product diminished.

In Salem, Jewett's neighbor in Barton Square, Dr. Edward Brooks Peirson, helped him establish the Salem Leg Company. Peirson was president, Jewett was superintendent and a director. The shop was located at 22 High Street.

In his younger years, Jewett was a professor of Latin, modern languages, and literature at Amherst College, and he held a divinity degree from Andover Theological Seminary. He served briefly as pastor of the First Congregational Church in Nashua, New Hampshire, but after his accident and subsequent return to Salem, Jewett lived the life of a "missionary at home."

THE SALEM LEG,

PATENTED

June 24th and July 22d, 1862; October 4th, 1864; August 22d (two patents), and December 19th, 1865.

MANUFACTURED BY

THE SALEM LEG COMPANY,

NO. 22 HIGH STREET,

SALEM, MASS.

Promotional brochure.

Stationery from the Salem Leg Company, showing their office location as 26 Lynde Street.

SALEM LEG COMPANY,
OFFICE, NO. 26 LYNDE STREET,
SALEM, MASS.

★ Spanish-American War — *1898*

Francis D. Cahill of Salem was among the survivors of the mysterious explosion of the USS *Maine* in Havana Harbor, Cuba, on February 15, 1898. At the time, Cubans were rebelling against Spanish rule and some Americans—now re-unified after the bloody Civil War—wanted to help them and blamed Spain for the explosion. Others, in this era of imperialism, saw defeating Spain as an opportunity for American empire building. Frances Robotti quotes an interview in the *Salem Evening News* with local Civil War veterans in March who told them that "their unanimous opinion is that America is not prepared for war." But Congress declared war on April 25, and Salem men signed up.

Wartime trade card.

Spanish-American War-era mail.

Lieut. Josephine Raymond was sent to Port-au-Prince, Haiti, as a Sanitary Engineer. There, she helped establish a sanitary training school for women.

Even though Cuba was many miles away, Salem's Mayor David P. Waters had received reports that "Spanish raiders" were "on their way to destroy Gloucester's fishing fleet and to bombard the factories from Lynn to Newburyport," according to Robotti; "considerable nervous tension [was] felt along the whole of the Atlantic Coast of the United States as Admiral Cervera assembl[ed] the Spanish fleet at Cape Verde Islands before sailing for the west."

Company H, 8th Infantry Regiment, MVM headed out in April. Of the 300 Salem men who signed up with the Navy, John Philip Riley, Edward Copson, and Samuel Larivee were on board the USS *Nashville* when she captured a Spanish mail steamship (see pp. 136, 141-42 on John Riley and Riley Plaza).

In Salem, two batteries of the 1st Regiment Heavy Artillery were stationed at Fort Pickering on Winter Island during the three-month war, "serving as Infantry during that short struggle," according to an account in the *Salem Evening News* of October 5, 1925. It was the "first Massachusetts Militia Organization to be mustered into service."

The first Salem man to die in the war was William H. Sanders (or, Saunders) who joined Teddy Roosevelt's Rough Riders and eventually succumbed to yellow fever (see next page).

1st Regiment Heavy Artillery camp at Fort Pickering (detail).

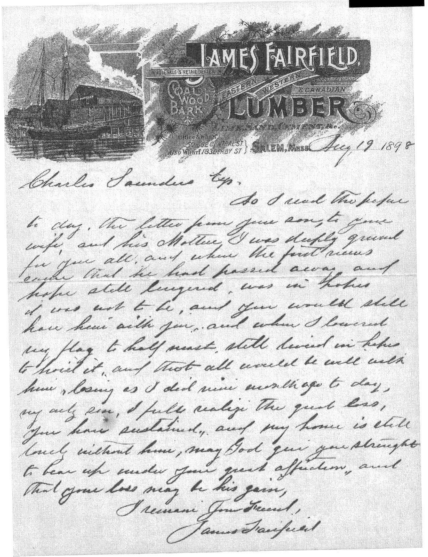

Exclusive!

The first casualty of the war from Salem was William H. Sanders of 43 Chestnut Street. After graduating from Harvard in 1897, according to the historian Donna Seger, "he enlisted a few days after the declaration along with several like-minded friends, foresaking the (local) 8th Regiment Infantry, MVM for Teddy Roosevelt's Rough Riders, which attracted a curious mix of south-western cowboys and Ivy Leaguers like Sanders. Off they went to Texas for training, and then to Cuba, where Sanders saw action with Troop B, and served as Roosevelt's orderly during the Battle of San Juan Hill. He is referenced by Roosevelt in his various regimental memoirs for his service, but also for his death [from Yellow Fever], which came six weeks after San Juan on a hospital boat in Santiago Harbor." This letter of condolence was written to William's father. *Courtesy of Racket Shreve.*

The Parker Brothers "At War"

Founded in Salem in 1883 by George S. Parker, Parker Brothers is best known for creating and manufacturing the board games *Monopoly*, *Clue*, *Sorry!*, and dozens more from their factory on Bridge Street.

But, as George Parker's biographer Phillip Orbanes wrote in his book *The Game Makers: The Story of Parker Brothers from Tiddley Winks to Trivial Pursuit*, "George Parker viewed both war and business as ideal themes for games." As calls for war with Spain intensified with the explosion of the USS *Maine* in Havana Harbor, Cuba, in 1898, and as Teddy Roosevelt's exploits with his Rough Riders dominated the newspapers once America declared war on Spain, Parker Brothers created the games *War in Cuba*, *The Siege of Havana*, *The Battle of Manila*, and *The Philippine War*.

Orbane continues: "All made money and cemented the identity of Parker Brothers as 'America's game company.'" Although Parker was a pacifist, once America entered the World War, some of these games were updated and more were added. These included *Conflict*, *Risk*, and *Civil War Game*.

See p. 80 for photos of a Parker Brothers World War II-era game.

Food Will Win the War

Excerpted or paraphrased from *Food in the American Military: A History* by John C. Fisher and Carol Fisher.

The Spanish-American War has become almost synonymous with bad beef products being issued to soldiers in the U.S. Army. "Fresh beef" was riddled with chemicals; "canned beef" was, in fact, pulp—what was left after the extract had been boiled out of it. The soldiers reported that "the canned beef was nauseating. If swallowed it could not be kept in the stomach." Secretary of War Russell A. Alger observed, "I doubt if the war with Spain will be referred to in this generation without the odious hue and cry of 'rotten beef.'" In 1898, President McKinley convened a commission to investigate. They learned that "the wagons assigned to carry the beef were sometimes not clean, and often there was no protection from sun and rain; but the most serious mistake seems to have been due to a failure to arrange systematically for rapid conveyance and prompt delivery."

With the significant supply problems of the Spanish-American War still fresh in mind and two investigations of the problems completed, major reorganization of the War Department and Army occurred between 1900 and America's entry into World War I.

As American forces prepared for combat in France, the Subsistence Division developed specialized rations to meet varying needs. The <u>reserve ration</u> was for the individual soldier to carry and use when meals were not available: 1-lb. can of meat (corned beef or bacon), two 8-oz. tins of hard bread, 2.4 oz. of sugar, 1.12 oz. of roasted and ground coffee, and .16 oz. of salt. The <u>trench ration</u> fed 25 men for one day in the midst of trench warfare. Items included corned beef, salmon, sardines; salt, sugar, soluble coffee, solidified alcohol, and cigarettes; later additions included chocolates and hard candies, dried prunes, figs, and apples; jam, cheese and macaroni, Vienna sausages, and an increase in the milk allowance.

★ World War I — *U. S. involved 1917-1918*

As early as 1901, America was suspicious of Germany. The *Salem Daily Gazette* of April 27 reported that "Kaiser William II is strengthening his navy against us. The expansion of the German navy is more in preparation for a contest with the United States than with Great Britain because the readiest causes for future naval conflicts will be found in the struggle for the partition or the exploitation of the great South American continent," according to Frances Robotti. Any naval attack by the Germans on or near Salem would involve Fort Pickering.

In 1915, Salem residents joined other Americans in calls for war after a German U-boat sank the British ocean liner RMS *Lusitania*. German submarines were attacking "merchant and passenger ships in the North Atlantic," writes Gerry Tuoti in a recent *North Shore Sunday* story, and a telegram revealing a German plot against the U. S. had been intercepted. In exchange for Mexico's help, the telegram read, Germany pledged to help Mexico reclaim the land it had lost during its recent war with America.

In 1917, Germany announced "a policy of unrestrained submarine warfare," according to Robotti. But Fort Pickering was not activated. After training at Camp Devens, Massachusetts, the Salem men who signed up to fight in The Great War were transported to France to join the British and French fighting forces. Most of these soldiers were National Guardsmen—the 26th Division—the first full division to deploy overseas after the United States entered World War I on

Sylvania employees hang out of their windows to watch Salem soldiers march to the Train Depot and off to war; 3,632 Salem men were eligible to go.

April 6, 1917," Tuoti explains. And because the unit "was nearly entirely composed of guardsmen from Massachusetts and the other New England states," it became known as the Yankee Division—the "YD." "It was the Guard's finest hour," says Brig. Gen. Leonid Kondratiuk, chair of the World War I Centennial Commission and historian of the Massachusetts National Guard. "They were available, organized quickly and went over there quickly." Tuoti describes what the YD faced:

...brutal fighting conditions and horrific new weapons of war ... The war was nearly three years old when the United States joined its French and British allies, and the conflict was mired in a bloody stalemate. Locked in trench warfare across much of Western Europe, opposing forces suffered huge casualties for minimal territorial gain ... When they saw combat, troops in World War I were exposed to the latest military technology of the day. They faced new weapons such as tanks, airplanes, machine guns, heavy artillery and poison gas.

The YD was a "vital cog in the U. S. war effort," Tuoti concludes. The 104th regiment of the YD "went on to receive the rare distinction of being awarded the French Croix de Guerre medal."

Draft Boys, leaving Sep. 21-17 by Leland Tilford for the *Salem Evening News.*

At home in Salem, everyone—including young people—sacrificed some of the comforts of life or helped with the war effort by raising money, volunteering for the Red Cross, writing letters, and more. Frances Robotti notes: "By July [1917], 7,000 Salem women were enrolled in the Food Conservation Army. Within Salem's Victory Gardens, the women planted 43 acres of potatoes."

Helping Uncle Sam

THE scouts of Salem, Mass., and other towns along the New England Coast, are assisting the United States Government by making up a list of automobiles and motor boats with the names of the owners and their addresses and telephone numbers, and other information.

Another list which will be valuable to the Government is being compiled. It includes the names and locations of all public buildings and semi-public buildings which might be used as hospitals in case of war. In connection with this the names, addresses and telephone numbers of all physicians are given.

From *Boy's Life*, July 15, 1916, the magazine of the Boy Scouts of America (founded in 1910).

Coupons to ration sugar were issued by the Grocers War Service Committee of Salem, Beverly, Peabody, Danvers, Marblehead, Topsfield, Hamilton, Wenham, and Middleton.

Salem's young people have a long history of contributing to war efforts.

Salem Evening News, July 11, 1918: Derby School students "led the way in out of door war work, for they are much interested in gardening and every child in the school is helping cultivate some Castle Hill garden." Some of the boys raised pigs. The children earned their Junior Red Cross memberships as well by collecting or helping to make clothing and recruiting adults into Red Cross membership.

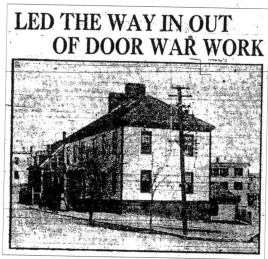

LED THE WAY IN OUT OF DOOR WAR WORK

Liberty Bond Drives

Town House Square, 1917.

In his article "Saved by the Bell," written for *Smithsonian* magazine, Stephen Fried explains that, "Just weeks after joining World War I in April 1917, the United States was in deep trouble—financial trouble ... The Treasury Department had undertaken the largest war-bond drive in history ... but it was still coming up short." On June 14—Flag Day—the Committee on Public Information, needing "some kind of national loyalty miracle," rang the (cracked) Liberty Bell in Philadelphia as a kind of summons.

The committee instructed that bells be rung all over the country to invoke the spirit of liberty this icon of the Revolutionary War represented. And then the Liberty Bell went on a cross-country tour, making 275 stops and attracting thousands in between official destinations. The Liberty Bell became "the dominant symbol of the war effort," writes Fried.

Flag Display Is General Throughout The City Today

April Momentous Month in American History; Display of Old Glory Indicates Public Confidence in Outcome of Difficulties; 2000 Shown Here.

POST 34, G. A. R. FLIES MAMMOTH FLAG.

The April 2, 1917 edition of the *Salem Evening News* notes that the GAR on St. Peter Street, along with dozens of other businesses and homes throughout Salem, proudly flew "Old Glory" to indicate "public confidence in the outcome of present difficulties" (see pp. 322-24 on the GAR). The *News* pointed out that April in America could very well be called the "War Month." The Revolutionary War, Mexican War, Civil War, and Spanish-American War all started in April.

Baby Whippet Tank Visited Salem Today in Loan Drive

Will Stir Up Interest in Loan Here Until Saturday; U. S. S. Kentucky Jackies May Parade; Bonds Sell Well

Although Salem was the first among the cities and towns of the state to obtain her quota of $2,393,000, yet her loan campaign is not at an end. Until the $4,500,000,000 asked by Secretary Glass is secured the Victory loan work must go on.

Salem may have gone over the top, and the state and New England may do so in the next two weeks or more, yet other sections may fall down. Then again, some of the larger subscribers may not be allowed as much of the loan as they have asked for, which would make Salem fall short.

For these reasons alone the Salem campaign must proceed. There is another reason, however, why the campaign is not at an end and that is that until 10 per cent. of the population of this city has subscribed for Victory bonds Salem cannot secure her honor flag.

While some profess to believe that the "edge" has been taken off the local campaign because of the first day attainment of the quota, it appears that the very fact such large blocks of the bonds were taken by the banks has stimulated persons who desire to invest in the bonds to buy earlier than usual.

Business at the banks has been increasing daily. Victory cottage is doing nicely all around. Yesterday's large subscription was for $20,000 by the Holyoke Insurance Co. Some other large ones are rumored in the offing. The factory and shop campaign is now on, the first day producing $6500 in three shops. At the Helburn Leather Co. 48 subscribed for $2700 of bonds, at the Cass & Daley shop 62 for $3450 and four of the working force at Deery Bros. decided to invest in $350 worth of bonds. Today the speakers and solicitors will visit other shops.

One of the baby war tanks

Arrived in Salem Today

and will remain here until Saturday, when it will go to Peabody. Salem is the first place in Essex county to be visited by a tank. The tank is scheduled to parade for three hours this afternoon, accompanied by speakers and possibly the Boy Scout band. Walter W. Annable, Salem's only war tank man, will be with the machine.

After a stop in Town House square, the tank will at 2 o'clock commence a trip about the city along the following general route: Essex street, Summer, Chestnut, Flint, Federal, North, Bridge, Washington, Church, Brown, around the Common, Hawthorne place, Congress, Harbor, around Lafayette park and back down Washington street to Town House square.

The U. S. Kentucky is slated to drop anchor in Salem harbor Saturday afternoon and stay over until Monday afternoon. The loan committee is making arrangements for a reception to the officers of the battleship and possible entertainment for the jackies, with a parade of the boys and their band. If it can be arranged with the captain of the Kentucky, Salemites may be privileged to visit the warship, which will be anchored out in the harbor off the Willows pier. This will be the first time in some years since a war vessel of Uncle Sam has come to Salem for a visit, and her coming will without doubt be of much interest to a large number of Salemites.

Superintendent William P. Meehan of the Metropolitan Life Ins. Co., Salem office, this morning reported to the committee that the Metropolitan company had subscribed for a large block of bonds, $15,000 of which will be credited to the City of Salem. This is the first of the corporations with headquarters outside of Salem to give credit to this city.

To help raise enthusiasm (and money) for the war, a "baby war tank" visited Salem on April 24, 1919, accompanied by Walter W. Annable, Salem's "only war tank man." While Salem's leading businesses had contributed substantially to the national bond drive, Salem would not receive her "honor flag" unless 10% of the City's population had subscribed. Meanwhile, at Salem Willows Pier, the USS *Kentucky* was tied up for the next few days to generate support.

WAR ACTIVITIES IN SALEM
Local Headquarters

FOOD ADMINISTRATION
JAMES C. POOR, Essex County Food Director. Court House
Federal St., Salem
ARTHUR H. PHIPPEN, Salem Food Director. City Hall, Salem

FUEL BOARD
ALVAH P. THOMPSON, Chairman. Salem Chamber of
Commerce

LEGAL ADVISORY BOARD
ROBERT W. HILL, Chairman. Masonic Temple
CHARLES A. SALISBURY, Probate Officer. Superior Court
WILLIAM H. HART, Probate Officer. District Court

LIBERTY LOAN COMMITTEE
HENRY M. BATCHELDER, Chairman. Merchants National
Bank
EDMUND G. SULLIVAN, Secretary. Salem Chamber of Com-
merce

PUBLIC SAFETY COMMITTEE
ARTHUR H. PHIPPEN, Chairman. City Hall, Salem

PUBLIC SERVICE
GEORGE W. PITMAN, Chairman. Salem Chamber of Commerce

AMERICAN RED CROSS
Rev. EDWARD D. JOHNSON, Chairman, Salem Chapter
ANNIE L. WARNER, Executive Secretary, Salem Chapter
Masonic Temple, Salem, Mass.

WAR CHEST
GEORGE W. HOOPER, President
D. A. DONAHUE, Treasurer   A. B. TOWERS, Clerk.
Salem Five Cents Savings Bank, Building

A page from the 1917 *Salem City Directory* showing
the organizations involved in Salem's war effort.

LEAD MILLS STORY MAY BE MORE THAN AN IDLE RUMOR

Latest Report Has It That Property Will Be Occupied Soon as Branch of American Steam Gauge & Valve Co. of Boston, Which Is Deluged With War Orders; Good Deal of Secrecy About Operations Going on Within Walls of Old Plant.

That the American Steam Gauge and Valve Mfg. Co. of Boston is to use the old Chadwick lead mills in South Salem, as a branch of their Boston and Lowell plants, is the latest report on the mill story. This company is said to have been deluged with war orders from the Allies of late and it is reported that they are to locate here. This gives additional credence to the rumor of a fortnight ago that English war materials would be manufactured there. An effort was made today to get in touch with the general manager of the Boston company, but he could not be located.

For the last month a small army of mechanics, including carpenters, painters, and also junkies have been busy about the place. The work has reached a degree where the two top floors have been cleaned of all the machinery used seven years ago for the manufacture of lead and that large floor space now awaits the installation of machinery for some other purpose. Those who claim to be on the inside say that English supplies will be the product turned out.

So far as can be determined no new machinery has yet been moved into the old lead mills. Much of the old machinery used for making lead has been removed to the main plant at Roxbury of the Chadwick Boston Lead Co. Other machinery and the lead beds in the sheds adjoining the main structures are said to be available for the manufacture of war munitions.

Little has been done on the exterior of the mills. Everything has been repaired and strengthened, although a new coat of paint is not seen on the outside. This may be one of the details in the general scheme of secrecy that is surrounding the repairs and alterations at the mills.

American Steam & Gauge of Boston expanded its operation to Salem to take advantage of available facilities and talent.

As a leading industrial center, many of Salem's manufacturing companies were tapped to support the war effort. These are just a few examples from stories in the *Salem Evening News*.

Forest River Lead Mills To Be Occupied By A Dry Color Manufacturing Concern

FOREST RIVER LEAD MILLS PLAN T.

Located in South Salem, the company manufactured ammunition.

Written on the back of this photograph are the words "Hayden at Hygrade, Salem, Mass. 1916." Hygrade, at 76 Lafayette Street and later part of Sylvania, manufactured radio tubes.

LOCAL CONCERN GETS CONTRACT FOR AIRPLANES

Pitman & Brown to Make Wooden Parts for 60 Machines for Burgess Co.; Work Has Already Started.

Pitman & Brown of Bridge street, this city, have contracted with the Burgess Co., of Marblehead, to make the wooden parts of 60 naval flying machines, the work to be done at once. The machines are modelled along the lines of those turned out by the Curtis people of New York, adapted for naval use, and the metal parts and engines will be made according to the Burgess plans. The local company has started on the work this week, and has put in special equipment to handle the work, although, as yet, no larger force of men is necessary. Charles W. Brown when seen yesterday, was enthusiastic about the work and he is delighted that his firm is able to help the government in any way possible.

By July of 1918, according to Frances Robotti, Salem "had fulfilled her Liberty Loan quota of $3,190,000 and her contribution of manpower [stood at] 1,641. Luckily, fundraising for "The War to End All Wars" would soon to be over.

The war actually ended fairly quickly once America became involved, although not soon enough for many of Salem's sons and their families. Many of those who weren't killed overseas died at home from disease.

On November 11, 1918, writes Robotti: "News of the signing of the Armistice between the Allies and Imperial Germany [at 11:00 a.m.] comes over the Associated Press wire direct from Washington to the *Salem Evening News* at 3:10 a.m. At 3:12 a.m. seven blasts of the fire alarm announce to the populace that the war is at an end. Mayor Dennis J. Sullivan issues a proclamation calling for a great victory parade on a day to be announced by Governor McCall"—Tuesday, November 12.

John Dionne of Salem, Nelson Dionne's uncle, served in the U. S. Navy. He was one of the lucky ones who came home.

President Wilson declared that the first Armistice Day Parade would take place on Nov. 11, 1919. Salem's included a procession through Town House Square. Today, Armistice Day is Veterans Day—always on 11-11, with silence at 11:00 a.m.

Pages from a tribute booklet to French Canadian men from Salem who died: T. Sgt. Arthur Morin, Pfc. Albert Madore, Pfc. Henry Jodoin, BMI Jean Delisle, Sgt. Edgar Richard, and Pfc. Roger Vaillancourt. *Courtesy of D. Michel Michaud.*

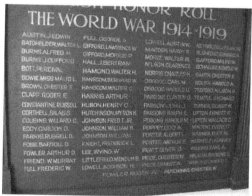

Places of worship throughout Salem installed plaques to honor their war dead. This one is from the meeting house of the First Universalist Society in Salem on Rust Street.

This memorial in the small park at Jefferson Avenue and Lawrence Street honors the men of Salem's French-Canadian neighborhood who died in World War I. It was dedicated on Veterans Day, 1986, replacing an earlier version.

The 50th Anniversary World War II
Commemorative Covers
GERMAN SUBMARINES MINE WATERS NEAR BOSTON HARBOR

German U-boats were devastating Allied shipping with a deadly weapon – a new type of magnetic mine. The mine was cylindrical in shape and charged with almost 700 pounds of explosives. These magnetic mines were incredibly dangerous since the existing mine sweeping equipment proved useless against them.

Small German U-boats planted the magnetic mines in Allied shipping lanes. The mines lay quietly at the bottom of channels until a passing ship detonated them. The magnetic field surrounding a ship's iron hull actually triggered the explosions. Fortunately, British ingenuity came to the aid by solving the problem of disarming the mines. Scientists were able to neutralise a ship's magnetic field by wrapping a cable around the ship's hull and periodically discharging a powerful current.

This method was put to the test when German submarines mined American waterways. Ten mines were planted by a U-boat off Boston Harbor on June 11, 1942. As a protective measure, a station was set up in Boston Harbor to check if ships required neutralising against magnetic mines. The station proved effective since none of the mines planted there ever exploded.

After rendering the mines harmless, Allied scientists raced to improve radar to detect the presence of U-boats. German submarines were operating much too freely in Allied waters. They were even surfacing at night to recharge batteries and attack convoys. New, portable radar equipment was developed by July, 1942 enabling Allied planes to identify U-boats and then promptly destroy them.

This Cover was postmarked in Boston, Massachusetts on June 11, 1992, the 50th anniversary of the day German submarines mined the waters near Boston Harbor.

The mint stamp encapsulated in this Cover was issued by the United States on April 8, 1990 to honour the three hundredth anniversary of the Massachusetts Bay Colony.

PWC 28

Danbury Mint

Above and below: Commemorative cover and insert, June 11, 1992, about the days when German U-boats were mining the waters off the coast. In Salem, that meant coastal patrols by the YD and Coast Guard Auxiliary, and a busy Coast Guard Air Station on Winter Island.

World War II was the test of fire that forged the modern Coast Guard. From the very beginning, Coast Guardsmen participated in almost every phase of the maritime war. —Adm. Paul A. Yost, U. S. Coast Guard, 1989

GERMAN SUBMARINES MINE WATERS NEAR BOSTON HARBOR
June 11, 1942 • Boston, Massachusetts

BOSTON, MA
JUN
11
1992
02205

USA 29

50th Anniversary of World War II
Commemorative Covers

★ World War II — *U. S. involved 1941-1945*

In 1939, when Hitler's army invaded parts of Europe and World War II commenced, America "was put on an emergency status in case of future U. S. involvement," aviation historian Paul S. Larcom explains. Under President Roosevelt's re-organization plan of May 9, the U. S. Coast Guard (including the Air Station on Winter Island) and Lighthouse Service would work more closely together. In June, Congress passed the Coast Guard Reserve and Auxiliary Act "to create a nonmilitary, voluntary organization of motorboat and yacht owners to stimulate efficient and safe operation of private boats on U. S. coastal waters and to assist the Coast Guard in its peacetime missions," according to Eleanor C. Bishop in *Naval History* magazine. "The response was immediate and favorable," she writes, including in Salem. One of these local volunteer yacht owners was William Shreve (see pp. 71-73).

In September 1939, Roosevelt declared a national emergency, and in 1940, invoking the Espionage Act from 1917, he instituted the Captain of the Port Program to increase port security. In Salem, that meant moving Coast Guard Air Station Commander Roy L. Raney's office to the Custom House on Derby Street. In May 1941, with Roosevelt's declaration of an Unlimited National Emergency, pilots from the Air Station began to conduct "Neutrality Patrols" off the coast in search of German U-boats—which they found (see pp. 268-75 for more on Coast Guard Air Station Salem).

Two twin-motored Douglas RD-4 "Dolphin" amphibians waiting to head out on Neutrality Patrol. *(A.P. photo via Paul S. Larcom; one of a set of pictures on the Coast Guard Neutrality Patrol released to the morning papers of Sunday, Sept. 7, 1941.)*

Port Security

Shoulder patches and pin worn by volunteer Port Security personnel. The sea horses depicted in the pin represent Poseidon, the ancient Greek God of the Sea. The sea horse was his "steed."

Civil Defense

Civil Defense Corps police badges.

Civil Defense Corps armband showing the insignia for Auxiliary Police.

On May 20, 1941 (still more than six months before the United States entered the war), President Roosevelt set up the Office of Civilian Defense (OCD) to coordinate state and federal measures to protect civilians in a war-related emergency. At this time, air raids and other attacks on populated areas in Europe generated fears that similar attacks could happen in the U. S. The OCD organized the United States Citizens Defense Corps to recruit and train volunteers to perform essential tasks. Each of the numerous categories of jobs filled by civilians had its own insignia. Enrolled and trained volunteers displayed their insignia on arm bands and on uniforms or civilian dress. The OCD also published a handbook, *The United States Citizens Defense Corps*, to explain the duties and responsibilities of various positions and who should join:

Who should join?—All able-bodied, responsible persons in the community—men and women, housewives, laborers, business and professional people—for the mutual protection of all. Boys and girls, and elderly people too, have work to do. The program is broad; the tasks are many; the time is now!

Qualifications for membership—Requires enrollment, physical and mental aptitude, recognition of obligation to study duties, take required training courses, and subsequently attend periodical group practice.

(Excerpted, with edits, from "Civilian Defense on the Home Front, 1942" by The Gilder Lehrman Institute of American History, New York.)

Civil Defense

Above: Cover of a booklet published in 1941 by the Federal Civil Defense Administration. The Office of Civil Defense (OCD) in Salem was located on Church Street. Below, and through page 51: the rest of the booklet.

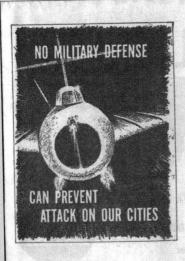

Why Is Modern Civil Defense So Necessary for U. S.?

Russia has a growing stockpile of atomic bombs, guided missiles, germ and gas warfare weapons. Russia has long-range bombers, submarines, and saboteurs to deliver these weapons. Our military and scientific leaders warn us that no military defense we have or may have can prevent an attack on us from causing widespread death and destruction.

...for the mutual protection of all

Cover of a brochure explaining the "Plan for **CON**trol of **EL**ectromagnetic **RAD**iation."

The brochure states: "the broad-casting industry and the government, working together, have devised a special system of AM (Standard) radio broadcasting to bring you official information in times of emergency ... [640 and 1240 AM] are the only dial settings where you will receive authoritative civil defense information...

CONELRAD is the only safe broadcasting system yet devised to keep you informed of important civil defense news and instructions without helping enemy bombers reach their targets."

The Air Defense Command, U. S. Air Force, was in charge of activating the CONELRAD system to warn of an attack.

Why Are Civilians the No. 1 Target In Modern War?

The strength of our Nation in wartime comes from the will of our people to defend their freedom, and from their ability to outproduce and outfight anyone who attacks us. That's why an enemy will strike first at our civilian population. Unless he can break our spirit and destroy our means of production he cannot win a war against us.

Civil Defense

Why Would an Enemy Try To Destroy Our Production Areas?

We can be beaten if our fighting men are not adequately equipped, fed, and supplied. We cannot supply the most and the best to our men in uniform if our skilled workers, our factories and farms are crippled or destroyed. In war an enemy would strike at our production centers and their workers. He will try to knock us out before war really begins.

Can Our Armed Forces Get Along Without Civilian Help?

No—as any military expert will tell you. Protection of our families, our country, and our freedom—these are the things we all fight for. The will to fight and the ability to produce are the heart of our Nation's defense. Destroy these and our fighting men are left with nothing to fight for—or to fight with.

...for the mutual protection of all

Why Is Our Will To Fight Back So Important?

Either in the foxholes or in our cities, it takes training and guts to stand up under attack—and come back fighting. That's why we civilians must have training—and the will to fight back. Strong, organized national civil defense keeps up our morale, prevents panic, and protects people and production.

Isn't It True That Our Cities Can Be Bombed?

Our Air Force generals have warned us repeatedly that even with far more radar, interceptors, antiaircraft, and other elements of air defense, seven out of every 10 enemy planes can still get through. That means that 70 out of every 100 bombers can penetrate our air defense and drop bombs on our cities anywhere in the country. We must stop them where we can. Where we cannot stop them, we must be prepared to minimize the damage they can do.

Civil Defense

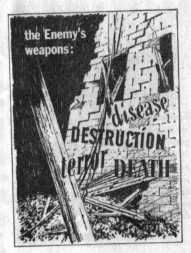

What Kind of Weapons Might Be Used Against Us?

Our Nation's scientists and security experts know that Russia now has a growing stockpile of A-bombs, guided missiles, germ and gas warfare weapons. We have seen in Europe what damage her saboteurs can do. Russia lives by propaganda and can be counted on to use all kinds of psychological warfare against us—rumor, fake radio broadcasts—anything to create fear, panic, and confusion before, during, and after an attack.

Can Civil Defense Preparedness Help Prevent War?

Our best insurance for peace is to be so strong and so well prepared that no enemy dares risk a war with us. Our military, industrial, and mutual security programs are far ahead of home-front preparedness. Inadequate civil defense increases an enemy's temptation to attack us—where it hurts the most—on the home front. YOU can help prevent that.

...for the mutual protection of all

Can We Survive a Grand-Slam Attack on Our Country?

Certainly—if we are prepared on the home front. History shows that there is a defense against every weapon ever invented. Modern civil defense is the civilian's program for protecting people, property, and production in case war comes. If the people are prepared, nothing the enemy can hit us with can knock us out.

How Can You Be a Partner In Defense?

Civil defense is common-sense protection for every civilian. It takes little time and little effort for YOU to do the two jobs that must be done: (1) Prepare your home and family against enemy attack. (2) Start training in one of the organized civil-defense services, when called upon by your local civil-defense director.

Civil Defense

TRAINED, ALERT CIVILIANS

will

- 🔺 cut our casualties in half
- 🔺 keep our production lines going
- 🔺 give our armed forces a

fighting chance

What you do in Civil Defense and <u>how</u> <u>well</u> and <u>soon</u> you do it can make a real difference in peace or war. The price you pay is the price of your freedom.

Do your part in meeting the greatest personal challenge of our time

LEARN CIVIL DEFENSE!

JOIN CIVIL DEFENSE!

LIVE CIVIL DEFENSE!

"What You Should Know About Biological Warfare.")

7. Maintain a 3-day emergency supply of food and water.

8. Get official CD identification tags for yourself and family if they are available locally. (See your local CD warden or director.)

9. Take a regular Red Cross First-Aid or Home-Nursing Course. This training will be invaluable in any emergency. (Contact your CD director or local Red Cross Chapter.)

10. Every adult American in sound health should give blood regularly. Blood is vital in any emergency in peace or war.

2. Training for Regular CD Services

Individual self-protection and family Civil Defense are the foundation of our national Civil-Defense program. The survival of your community equally depends on the organized local Civil-Defense services which are organized to furnish mutual aid and mobile support—with city aiding city, and State aiding State, wherever disaster strikes. Your second big job in Home Defense, then, is training in one of the regular Civil-Defense services—warden, fire, police, health, welfare, rescue, staff, communications, engineering, and transportation—or the Air Force Ground Observer Corps in many States. Some of the communities are now prepared to give basic and specialized training in all of these services. Call your local CD director today and volunteer for Home Defense service.

...for the mutual protection of all

Your CD Action Program

Here's what YOU can do to strengthen your family's home defenses and save lives in the event of enemy attack—an attack that may never come if you do your part NOW to make America strong:

1. Prepare your home and your family against enemy attack.

2. Begin your training in one of the active CD services when called upon by your local CD director.

1. Family Civil Defense

1. Post the CD Air-Raid Alert Card in your home and office. Carry the Alert Card in your pocket. Hold regular practice alerts at home.

2. Equip the most protected place you can find in or near your home for an air-raid shelter. Learn what steps you can take at home or work to minimize danger of injury in an atomic attack. (See CD booklets and films, "Survival Under Atomic Attack" and children's "Duck and Cover.")

3. Prepare an Emergency First-Aid Kit for your home for use in peace or war. (See leaflet, "Civil Defense Household First-Aid Kit.")

4. Practice fireproof housekeeping. Learn to fight fires in the home. (See the CD booklet and film, "Firefighting for Householders.")

5. Train your family in emergency life-saving measures. (See CD booklet, "Emergency Action To Save Lives.")

6. Learn the simple steps your family should take to protect themselves against germ and biological warfare. (See CD booklet and film,

YOUR VIGILANCE is the price of YOUR FREEDOM

ACT NOW—A TRAINED ALERT AMERICA IS A MIGHTY FORCE FOR PEACE

U. S. GOVERNMENT PRINTING OFFICE   O—16—08188—1

Civil Defense and Salem's Young People

In the interest of having young people involved in the safety of their community during war time, the Training Section of the U. S. Office of Civilian Defense, with the cooperation of the Boy Scouts of America, published this 56-page handbook for the boys and girls, young men and women, who volunteered.

These pages: Cover and interior pages of the *Handbook for Messengers.*

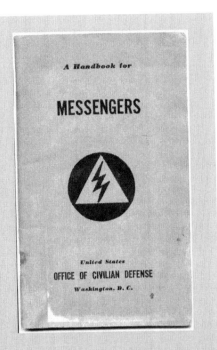

A Handbook for

MESSENGERS

United States
OFFICE OF CIVILIAN DEFENSE
Washington, D. C.

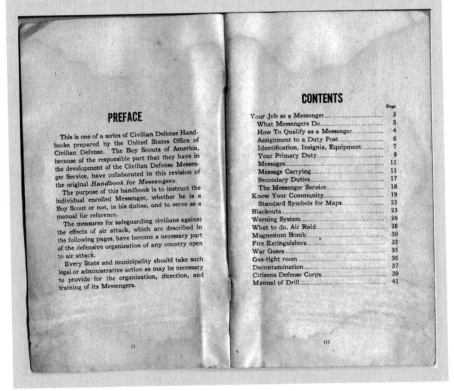

PREFACE

This is one of a series of Civilian Defense Handbooks prepared by the United States Office of Civilian Defense. The Boy Scouts of America, because of the responsible part that they have in the development of the Civilian Defense Messenger Service, have collaborated in this revision of the original *Handbook for Messengers.*

The purpose of this handbook is to instruct the individual enrolled Messenger, whether he is a Boy Scout or not, in his duties, and to serve as a manual for reference.

The measures for safeguarding civilians against the effects of air attack, which are described in the following pages, have become a necessary part of the defensive organization of any country open to air attack.

Every State and municipality should take such legal or administrative action as may be necessary to provide for the organization, direction, and training of its Messengers.

CONTENTS

	Page
Your Job as a Messenger	3
What Messengers Do	3
How To Qualify as a Messenger	4
Assignment to a Duty Post	6
Identification, Insignia, Equipment	7
Your Primary Duty	9
Messages	11
Message Carrying	11
Secondary Duties	17
The Messenger Service	18
Know Your Community	19
Standard Symbols for Maps	22
Blackouts	23
Warning System	26
What to do, Air Raid	28
Magnesium Bomb	30
Fire Extinguishers	33
War Gases	35
Gas-tight room	36
Decontamination	37
Citizens Defense Corps	39
Manual of Drill	41

II

III

THE MESSENGER BINDS
THE SERVICES TOGETHER

Administration

Every local Civilian Defense plan provides for the enrolling and training of a group of Messengers: Boy Scouts, Girl Scouts, and others, generally from groups 16 to 21 years of age. Young men and women of these ages are considered most likely to possess the necessary qualifications.

Messengers are directly under the command of the local commander of the Citizens' Defense Corps and are assigned as he, or some member of his staff that he delegates, may direct.

PERSONAL RECORD

My name is ....

Address ....

Phone* .... Age ....

In case of emergency, notify:

....

Address .... Phone* ....
*If you do not have a telephone give the phone number of someone who will call or relay a message.

Training Record: Date Completed

The Messenger's Job ....

Local Civilian Defense Organization   ....

Knowledge of Community ....

First Aid { Merit Badge ☐
{ Red Cross Certificate ☐   ....
{ ☐

Fire Defense ....

Gas Defense ....

Drill ....

Awarded Certificate No. ....

Date ....   { Junior Messenger ☐
                          { Messenger ☐

Service Record:

Duty Post ....

Hours .... from .... to ....
(Date)   (Date)

Duty Post ....

Hours .... from .... to ....
(Date)   (Date)

Duty Post ....

Hours .... from .... to ....
(Date)   (Date)

Civilian Defense Council.

1

BLACKOUTS

Blackouts are ordered only on the authority of the War Department. A blackout may be ordered during any period when hostile forces are believed to be in the vicinity, whether or not enemy airplanes have been sighted.

"Blacking Out" a city means that light sources must be so hidden or dimmed that an enemy bomber will have difficulty in finding the target and lack aiming points such as main street intersections. Following are the general plans used.

Street Lights. These are fitted with low-watt bulbs and covers that diffuse the light.

Automobiles. Headlights must be covered except for a small pair of slits and hooded.

Traffic Lights. Are treated the same way as automobile headlights.

Buildings. Windows and doors must be covered with opaque materials. Paint on the glass, heavy curtains, light "baffles" or screens are some of the ways. No cracks of light must show.

Aids to Seeing. Since people have to move about during a blackout, the lack of light may be somewhat offset and safety promoted by—

23

1. Painting curbs, trees, poles and hydrants with white paint. There is a luminous paint, also, that gives off a faint blue light quite visible in total darkness.

2. Painting signs of luminous paint or making them of fluorescent material on which shines ultra-violet or "black" light or installing dimly lighted signs with horizontal screens to diffuse the light.

3. Painting white fenders and stripes around automobiles.

Members of the Citizens' Defense Corps who have outside duties during a blackout can be identified more easily if they wear a white cap or white-painted helmet; also a white belt fitted with crossed straps over the shoulders.

24

Auxiliary Police and the Salem Police Department

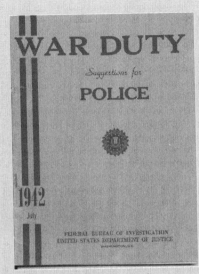

Cover of the FBI's manual, with excerpts below.

During World War II, Salem had "approximately 200 guys" serving as Auxiliary Police officers to supplement Salem's regular police force," Nelson Dionne recalls. In July 1942, J. Edgar Hoover, Director of the Federal Bureau of Investigation (FBI), issued a manual to all U.S. police departments titled *War Duty Suggestions for Police.*

1) Auxiliary Police constitute one of six services for the protection of communities from air attack. These six services consist of 15 groups, and are intended to supplement the regular services of the city to deal with the unusual hazard of air raids.

2) As such, the Auxiliary Police, when trained, qualified and sworn, become members of the U. S. Citizens Defense Corps, and are entitled to the privileges and responsibilities of that organization. The **U. S. Citizens Defense Corps** evidences their membership by an armband, and an identification certificate.

3) When sworn and accepted, they also become members of the Police Department of their city, under local rules.

4) The Chain of Command is as follows: The Commander of the U. S. Citizens Defense Corps takes command upon the receipt of an air raid alarm. He has a headquarters and staff—the Control Center and Staff Corps—to enable him to learn the

need and to make and carry out decisions. When Auxiliary Police are needed, the Commander makes known his needs to the Police Chief (or his representative) at the Control Center. The Police Chief (or his representative) dispatches his units in accordance with the need.

5) At times other than in air raids, the Auxiliary Police are available for assignment by the Chief of Police according to the rules made locally. Auxiliary Police have important duties in blackouts and at other times not in air raids, and their authority and their availability will be according to local ordinances and regulations.

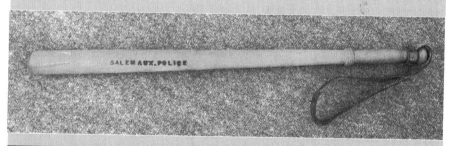

This 27" wooden night stick with leather strap was used by a member of the Salem Auxiliary Police.

Auxiliary Police, when trained, qualified and sworn, become members of the U. S. Citizens Defense Corps.

Shoulder patch worn by a member of the civilian auxiliary of the U. S. Armed Services. *From the estate of Capt. Gideon Pelletier.*

Civil Defense Corps arm band showing the insignia for Auxiliary Fire.

Salem Auxiliary Fire Department badges.

Members of the Salem Auxiliary Fire Department in front of Engine 5, Loring Avenue and Broadway, 1942. *Courtesy of Thomas Brophy.*

New York Bureau official photo caption: "Defense Corps Answers Roll Call—Boston, Mass.—140 Members of the Massachusetts Women's Defense Corps line up for roll call prior to eating a roadside meal under field conditions during a 100-mile overnight convoy trip. Col. Natalie Hays Hammond, Gloucester, Mass., is in charge of operations." (9/17/41)

Massachusetts Women's Defense Corps

In his history of the Massachusetts Women's Defense Corps (MWDC), Ronald J. McBrien explains:

The Massachusetts Women's Defense Corps was organized and served the Commonwealth during the World War II years. It was dedicated to providing war-related emergency services throughout the state ... The origin of the MWDC can be traced back to the Gloucester Civic Patrol founded by Natalie Hays Hammond and several other prominent women in August 1940. By May 1941, Governor Saltonstall authorized the formation of the Massachusetts Women's Defense Corps under the Massachusetts Committee on Public Safety.

New York Bureau official photo caption: "Nuts, Bolts and Defense—
Boston, Mass.—Capt. Betty Hall, left, of Lexington, Mass., and Miss Janet
Moore, both of the Massachusetts Women's Defense Corps., attack an
ailing motor encountered on a convoy trip. Both are well acquainted
with the innards of a motor, necessary knowledge for defense work. Miss
Moore is director of the convoy." (9/17/41)

*The MWDC was organized regionally, similar to that of the Civilian
Defense and the Massachusetts State Guard. The MWDC School in
Boston operated on private funds and trained over thirty thousand
women in emergency services. Seven thousand of these became
uniformed members of MWDC.*

*Within its nine regions, the MWDC consisted of over one hundred
and fifteen headquarters, companies, and detachments. Func-
tionally, it was organized to provide assistance in five service areas;
these included Medical, Transportation, Communications, Canteen,
and Air Raid Protection/Warden Services. The Air Raid Protection
Service was later discontinued and replaced with the Fire Fighting
Service.*

In 1944, the MWDC was transferred to the Military Division of the Commonwealth under the control of The Adjutant General. It worked closely with the Massachusetts State Guard, the U. S. Army, various state agencies, and local communities in which its units were located. Members received neither pay nor benefits for their contributions. In fact, they paid for their uniforms and equipment, supported their headquarters, and provided their private cars and rationed gasoline for military duties.

In December 1944, the MWDC's name was modified to reflect the changing war situation. It officially became the Massachusetts Women's Corps. In February 1946, several regional organizations were consolidated and those remaining were restructured into battalion organizations. The Massachusetts Women's Corps was inactivated in September 1946 with a final review by Governor Maurice Tobin.

The 4th Battalion, Massachusetts Women's Defense Corps, had its headquarters in the Salem Armory (SCD) under the command of Lieut. Col. Carolyn F. Standley of Beverly.

The Salem women who served in this battalion included 1st Lieut. Sarah S. Ballou, Sgt. Anna G. Averill, Sgt. Katherine I. Dee, Sgt. Margery L. Hoyt, Cpl. Jane E. Noszka, and Laura M. Smith.

Many thanks to Brig. Gen. Leonid Kondratiuk, Director, Massachusetts National Guard Museum and Archives, Office of The Adjutant General, for this information.

Lapel pin with the insignia of the Massachusetts Women's Defense Corps. "ARP" stands for Air Raid Protection.

Japan attacked Pearl Harbor, Hawaii, on December 7, 1941 (land acquired by the U. S. as a result of the Spanish-American War). The country was at war—again!

A draft board was activated in Salem, meeting at the Post Office on Margin Street, to accept or reject draftees. Some of the Salem men who enlisted became part of the Yankee Division, the unit that was formed and had so distinguished itself during World War I.

Among the Salem women to volunteer for overseas duty, Catharine Larkin, an officer in the U. S. Army Nurses Corps, died in an air crash over India at age twenty-nine (see p. 82). Another Salem woman, Lillian Aronson, joined the Women's Army Corps (WAC) in 1943 at the age of twenty-six. This was the year that President Roosevelt signed legislation allowing women to join the military. Aronson provided high-level staff support at Camp Patrick Henry (Virg.), Camp Stoneman (Ca.), and Fort Lee (Virg.). *At the publication of this book, Lillian Aronson had just turned 101!*

At home, women learned how to use ration books and wartime currency. They planted victory gardens, raised money, wrote letters, volunteered for the Red Cross, worked at local factories, and in every way "kept the home fires burning." At the Coast Guard Station, female personnel ("SPARS") arrived to relieve the men for wartime fighting.

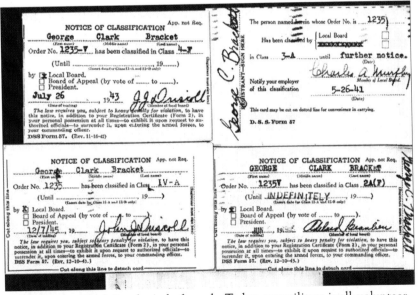

George Clark Bracket's draft cards. Today, our military is all-volunteer.

Published in Salem
For Salem, Peabody, Marblehead,
Essex, Manchester, Rowley, Boxford

-18-'41 P/

PRICE TWO CENT

Salem Breaks Record by Sending 167 Into Service As Crowd Bids Farewell

SALEM'S DRAFTEES BOARD THE TRAIN FOR BOSTON
Just a Part of the Crowd Bidding the 167 Local Young Men Farewell As They Entered Special Cars Which Wer to Take Them Into the Army For a Year or More of Training

At the Salem Train Depot, residents bid "farewell" to 167 men who were on their way to training state-side and then active duty overseas.

Dog tags belonging to Eugene Caron, a Salem native and uncle of Nelson Dionne. Caron served as a fire fighter in the Air Force as part of a specialized crash crew.

969242 **CD**

UNITED STATES OF AMERICA
OFFICE OF PRICE ADMINISTRATION

WAR RATION BOOK FOUR

Issued to *Lena Lebel*
(Print first, middle, and last names)

Complete address *43 Boston St.*

Salem Mass.

READ BEFORE SIGNING

In accepting this book, I recognize that it remains the property of the United States Government. I will use it only in the manner and for the purposes authorized by the Office of Price Administration.

Void if Altered ....
(signature)

It is a criminal offense to violate rationing regulations.

OPA Form R-145   16—35570-1

War ration book belonging to Lena Lebel of 43 Boston Street.

1945 ... 1946

JULY	OCTOBER	JANUARY	APRIL
AUGUST	NOVEMBER	FEBRUARY	MAY
SEPTEMBER	DECEMBER	MARCH	JUNE

UNITED STATES RATION BOOKS

"YOU SERVE WHEN YOU SAVE"

The Salem Co-Operative Bank

71 Washington St.   Salem, Massachusetts

Save with us - Build with us — Over Fifty Years Of Service

Cover of a war ration book courtesy of The Salem Co-operative Bank (now, Salem Five). Unlike in wartime today, during World War II everyone made sacrifices to support our military. Everyone was affected and involved.

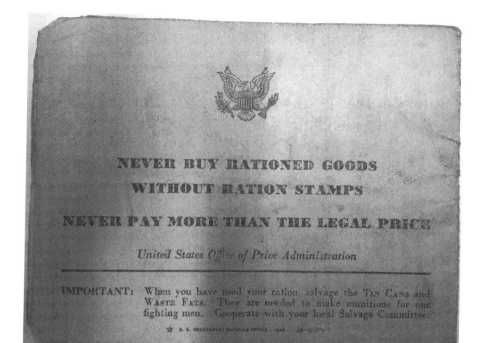

Above: Ration stamps book cover; below: ration stamps.

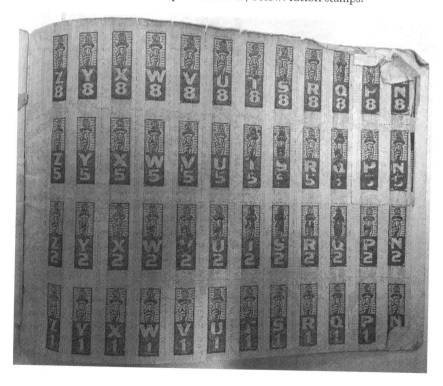

Page 1

Consumer Instruction Sheet

WHY CANNED FRUITS, VEGETABLES, AND SOUPS ARE RATIONED

Every week we are sending shiploads of canned goods to feed our fighting men and our fighting allies in Africa, Britain, and the Pacific islands. We must see that they get all the food they need.

We at home will share all that is left. Point Rationing will be used to guarantee you and everyone a fair share of America's supply of canned and processed fruits and vegetables, soups and juices.

HOW they are rationed

1. Every eligible man, woman, child, and baby in the United States is being given War Ration Book Two. (This book will not be used for sugar or coffee.)

RATION BOOKS FOR ALL

2. The BLUE stamps are for any kind of
   Canned or Bottled Fruits and Vegetables
   Canned or Bottled Juices and Soups
   Frozen Fruits and Vegetables
   Dried Fruits

   (The red stamps will be used later for meat.)

3. The stamps in this book are POINT stamps. The NUMBER on each stamp shows you how many POINTS that stamp is worth.

NUMBER SHOWS POINTS

4. The LETTERS show you WHEN to use the stamps. The year will be divided into rationing periods. You can use all BLUE stamps marked A, B, and C in the *first* rationing period. A, B, and C stamps cannot be used after the first rationing period ends.

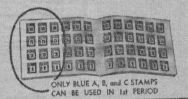

ONLY BLUE A, B, and C STAMPS CAN BE USED IN 1st PERIOD

5. You must use the BLUE stamps when you buy ANY KIND of the rationed processed foods. See the official list, showing every kind of rationed processed food, at your grocers. Different kinds of these foods will take different numbers of points. For example, a can of beans may take a different number of points from a can of peas.

RATIONED FOODS

JARS — DRIED — FROZEN — BOTTLED — CANNED

| Fruits Vegetables Soups Juices | Fruits | Fruits Vegetables | Juices Soups Cocoa Clift Sauce | Fruits Vegetables Soups Juices Baby Foods |

(See Complete Official List at Your Grocer)

6. Of course, the more of anything you buy the more points it will take. For example, a large can of peas takes more points than a small can.

7. The Government will set the points for each kind and size and send out an Official Table of Point Values which your grocer must put up where you can see it. The Government will keep careful watch of the supply of these processed foods and make changes in point values from time to time, probably not oftener than once a month. The Government will announce these changes when it makes them and they will be put up in the stores.

8. The number of points for each kind of processed food will be THE SAME in ALL STORES and in all parts of the country.

OFFICIAL POINT LIST

WATCH THE OFFICIAL TABLE OF POINT VALUES

Turn this sheet over and see how to use your Book.

Above and opposite: Consumer instructions on the use of ration stamps as determined by the Office of Price Administration in Washington, D. C. These instructions applied to the first period of food rationing. The thinking at the time was that "the boys" overseas needed to be fed, and so did every American. Everyone needed to ration for the benefit of all.

Page 2

Use Your OLD Ration Book for SUGAR and COFFEE

HOW TO USE YOUR NEW RATION BOOK

TO BUY CANNED OR BOTTLED FRUITS, VEGETABLES, SOUPS, AND JUICES; FROZEN FRUITS AND VEGETABLES; DRIED FRUITS

1. The Government has set the day when this rationing will start. On or after that day, take your War Ration Book Two with you when you go to buy any kind of these processed foods.

14 POINTS

YOU GIVE MANY POINTS FOR SCARCE FOODS

8 POINTS

YOU GIVE LESS POINTS FOR FOODS THAT ARE NOT SO SCARCE

2. Before you buy, find out how many points to give for the kind of processed foods you want. *Prices do not set the points.* The Government will set different points for each kind and size no matter what the price. Your grocer will put up the official list of points where you can see it. It will also be in the newspapers. *The points will not change just because the prices do.*

3. When you buy, take the right amount of blue stamps out of the book. Do this in front of your grocer or delivery man and hand them to him. The grocer *must* collect a ration stamp, or stamps, for all the rationed processed foods he sells. Every rationed processed food will take points as well as money.

SHOW YOUR BOOK PLEASE

4. Do not use more stamps than you need to make up the right amount. For example, if the food you buy calls for 13 points it is better to tear out an 8-point and a 5-point stamp than two 5-point stamps and a 2- and a 1-point stamp. Save your smaller point stamps for low-point foods. You can take the stamps from *more than one* book belonging to your household if you need to.

$8 \rightarrow$ [8]

$5 \rightarrow$ [5]

13 Points

5. Every person in your household, including children of any age, has a total of 48 points to use for all these processed foods for one ration period. This means that you may use ALL the blue stamps marked A, B, and C from all the books during the first period. You may use as many of the blue A, B, and C stamps as you wish at one time. *When they are used up you will not be able to buy any more of these processed foods till the next stamps are good.* The Government will announce the date when the next stamps are good.

USE THE BLUE STAMPS WITH A, B, C ON THEM

6. Use your household's points carefully so that you will not run out of stamps. And buy with care to make your points come out even, because the grocer will not be able to give you change in stamps. Use high-point stamps first, if you can.

IMPORTANT

You may use ALL the books of the household to buy processed foods for the household. Anyone you wish can take the ration books to the store to do the buying for you or your household.

A FAIR SHARE FOR ALL

We cannot afford to waste food or give some people more than their fair share. . . . That is why canned fruits and vegetables are rationed and that is why meat is going to be rationed. Rationing of some foods is the best and fairest way to be sure that every American gets enough to eat.

BE SURE TO READ OTHER SIDE

U. S. Office of Price Administration
Washington, D. C.   January 1943

Cardboard "coins," worth one cent, were also used. Blue coins (left) and blue stamps could only be used for canned, bottled, frozen, or dried fruits and vegetables, soups, juices, and processed foods. Red stamps and coins were used for meats. There were additional allowances for coffee and tea.

Matchbook cover issued by the Pequot Mills, one of Salem's largest employers at the time.

Special air mail (or "V-mail," for "Victory") to and from home was a lifeline.

A soldier's mail home to Salem, showing the stamp of approval from the Censors.

Official holiday card from 1944 from the Ordinance Section, Third U. S. Army. *Courtesy of Jerome Curley.*

Wartime matchbook cover from Stromberg's Restaurant of Salem.

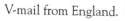

V-mail from England.

Salem Teachers College* and the CDC

At the outset of World War II, Dr. Edna McGlynn began corresponding with the students and alumni who left home to serve in the military. The Collegiate Defense Committee (CDC), with McGlynn as faculty adviser, was formed to write letters and send care packages to Salemites serving at home and abroad (below). McGlynn and the CDC corresponded with over one hundred students and alumni; they also maintained current mailing lists of those in the service and prepared and distributed *The Salem Newsletter* in which Dr. McGlynn edited summaries of news from the letters she received.

A native of Beverly, Mass., Edna McGlynn earned her bachelor's and master's degrees from Boston University and two doctorates (Boston College, medieval history, and Georgetown University, American diplomatic history). She joined the Teachers College faculty in 1936 as a professor of history and government.

* Later, Salem State University. Captions from www.salemstate.edu.

October 21, 1944:
ASR Designation

A High Honor for Coast Guard Air Station Salem

★ **Coast Guard Air Station Salem** ★
is officially designated the first U. S. Air-Sea Rescue Station on the Eastern Seaboard under the command of the Northern Group, Eastern Sea Frontier.

Coast Guard historian Malcolm F. Willoughby explains what the ASR designation meant: "Maximum coordination of all rescue efforts of the Army, Navy, and Coast Guard was the responsibility of each regional Air-Sea Rescue Task Unit, headed by the Commander of the Coast Guard Station ... Thus, all services, operating under a unified command, coordinated their activities. The Air Station later established temporary detachments at Brunswick, Maine, and Quonset Point, Rhode Island, in cooperation with the Naval Air Stations at those points. Air Station Salem now covered the entire New England coastline, from the Canadian boundary to Long Island Sound."

Air-Sea Rescue Consolidated PBY-5A amphibian in 1945. PBYs were first used at Salem in the Fall of 1944. Fort Pickering Light is on the left, painted red prior to its 1980s restoration. *Courtesy Paul S. Larcom.*

Certificate of Enrollment into the Coast Guard Temporary Reserve for Nelson L. Dionne Sr., dated 1943. During the war, Dionne was employed by Sylvania as an electronic technician.

William H. Shreve and the Fred J. Dion Yacht Yard   **Exclusive!**
23 Glendale Street (South Salem Harbor)

As Malcolm F. Willoughby wrote in his book *The U. S. Coast Guard in World War II*:

One of the earliest vital requirements was for men and craft to perform patrol for rescue work, and to track submarines and reduce their effectiveness against our coastal merchant shipping ... While there was some Coastal Picket activity on the Pacific coast, most activity was off the Atlantic shores. The Navy, short of small craft, called upon the Coast Guard to procure urgently needed motor and sailing yachts and other vessels suitable for offshore duty...

In order to be most effective in offshore areas, the Coastal Picket fleet, mostly sailing yachts with a scattering of motor cruisers, cooperated closely with naval vessels and airplanes, particularly in rescue work.

Of the many sailing yachts used by the Coast Guard at this time, one was the *Flying Cloud III* (USCG 2516) captained by William H. Shreve, USCG of Chestnut Street. Shreve was assigned to Picket Patrol in the Isles of Shoals, New Hampshire, but in the Summer of 1943, with *Flying Cloud* in need of repair, he sailed her to the Fred J. Dion Yacht Yard on the south side of Salem Harbor—a fixture in Salem since 1914 that still is today.

William H. Shreve on board the *Flying Cloud III* in 1943.

Left: Aerial view of Coast Guard Air Station Salem in 1942.

Shreve (left) at the Isles of Shoals Station.

Above and below: *Flying Cloud III* on the ways at the Fred J. Dion Yacht Yard, June 1943.

The Navy, short of small craft, called upon the Coast Guard to procure urgently needed motor and sailing yachts and other vessels suitable for offshore duty...
—Malcolm F. Willoughby

Our thanks to Racket Shreve, William Shreve's son, for sharing these family photos.

Flying Cloud III on the ways and under full sail.

Article from the *Salem Evening News*, November 25, 1944.

Even Salem's school children, members of "proud young America," helped raise money for the war effort.

—Salem Evening News

Sheridan School Pupils Show Patriotism by Buying Jeep for Army With Stamps; All Rewarded With Rides

Salem Evening News, June 5, 1945: These students, in grades 1-4, raised $1,202 in stamps and bonds to pay for an Army jeep. In return, the Army sent the school a replica of the jeep. Earlier, in 1944, the students raised $1,950 for an ambulance. Both vehicles carried the name of their school—Sheridan School, named for the Civil War hero Phil H. Sheridan (see pp. 115-17).

To support the war effort, the government took control of various manufacturing plants throughout the country, including leather tanneries in Salem and Peabody in 1943. Labor disputes ensued as a result. The "Salem-Peabody Leather Manufacturing Case" did not go well for the government, and it changed its take-over methods once the dispute was resolved.

In his book *Industrialists in Olive Drab: The Emergency Operation of Private Industries During World War II,* John H. Ohly writes:

Thirteen companies, all located in the neighboring communities of Salem, Peabody, and Danvers, Massachusetts, were involved in the takeover. They were part of the Massachusetts Leather Manufacturers Association, a group of some manufacturing establishments engaged in the initial processing of leather.

Even though all of them were involved in the same labor dispute, the decision to seize the plants of only thirteen was completely arbitrary—the result of the existence of strikes at these properties when the executive order was drafted.

At any other time the list would have been quite different, and it was thought impossible to solve the problems of any single plant or group of plants without dealing with the whole group.

The plants were tanneries rather than producers of finished consumer leather products, and this fact made evaluating their importance to the war program difficult. Initially, it was believed their production was crucial to quartermaster inventories (that is, Mukluks, helmet headbands and chin straps, military gloves, heel pads for coats and gloves, and artic felt shoes), even though the War Department had no direct contracts.

This view changed as alternate sources of supply were discovered, but at a point too late to affect seizure.

In the final analysis War Department interest in these facilities proved inconsequential because alternate sources were available and because the majority of production was for nonessential civilian purposes. At least one of these plants produced nothing for the armed forces, and only three produced more than 10 percent for war uses.

The lack of war interest was so obvious that once the facts became known the customary public posting of the executive order was omitted for fear that its recitations about vital war production would make the government appear ludicrous.

From Wide World Photos, Boston Bureau: "For release Sunday, Sept. 13, 1942, and thereafter. FOR MARCHING FEET. Salem, Mass.—George F. Clements, who has been working on shoes for 56 years, looks over the shoes as they go through the lasting room. The Army brogans are mounted on the wooden last to give them their shape. Mr. Clements helped turn out footwear for the Army in World War I."

Shelby Shoe Company, 51 Canal Street.

Factory workers at the Shelby Shoe Company. Above: These stitchers are sewing the upper parts of the shoe together. The pieces of leather, having been cut to shape and size, are sent to them from the cutting room (below).

Sylvania's "E" Award

In 1944, Sylvania Electronic Products Inc. received an Army-Navy "E" award for excellence in the production of war material. This tiny lapel pin in red, white, blue, and gold, was given to Sylvania personnel.

Below: Myra Manning of the Chicago Civic Opera Company singing at the award presentation ceremony in the Salem Armory.

Cover and pages from *The Sylvania Beam*, the company's magazine.

ID button for an employee of Surrette Batteries.

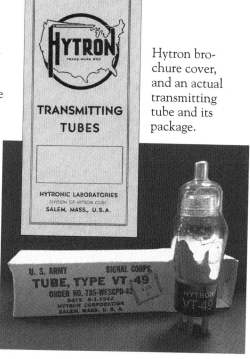

Hytron brochure cover, and an actual transmitting tube and its package.

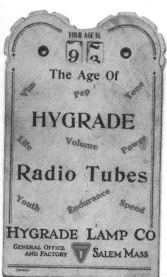

Left and below: Promotional materials for Hygrade before and after the company merged with Sylvania.

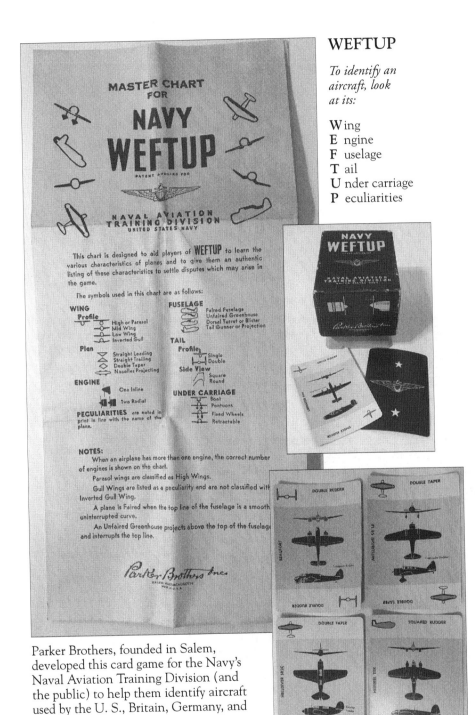

WEFTUP

To identify an aircraft, look at its:

W ing
E ngine
F uselage
T ail
U nder carriage
P eculiarities

Parker Brothers, founded in Salem, developed this card game for the Navy's Naval Aviation Training Division (and the public) to help them identify aircraft used by the U. S., Britain, Germany, and Japan.

Germany surrendered to the Allied Forces on May 8, 1945 (V-E Day) and Japan surrendered on August 15 (V-J Day). Salem's Thaddeus Buczko, then a nineteen-year-old sailor, was serving on board the destroyer USS *Bearss* when the "last shot" of the war was fired by the light cruiser USS *Concord*. Both ships were part of Task Force 92, comprised of one destroyer and three light cruisers stationed in the North Pacific. The *Bearss* was then tasked with transporting Japanese officers to the formal signing ceremony between Japan and the United States on September 2, 1945. Buczko recalls, "I was top side when [they] came on board, manning the search lights." Decades later, Buczko read an article about the "last shot" and learned that the story was flawed. The USS *Concord* set off another charge in error—and *that* was the last shot. Buczko pointed out the irony of the *Concord* firing the last shot of *that* war while its namesake is considered by some the site of the *"first shot" of the Revolutionary War.*

Salem held a Victory Parade through its principal streets, and prepared to welcome home its surviving men and women—and build memorials in honor of those who had made the ultimate sacrifice.

Victory Parade! Coast Guard personnel march down Hawthorne Boulevard past the Hawthorne Hotel.

U. S. Navy official photograph. Caption: "27 May 1946. PRESENTED SON'S MEDAL—Alfred J. Levesque, 78 Palmer St., Salem, accepted the posthumous award of a Bronze Star Medal from Capt. C. H. Pike, USN, acting chief of staff, First Naval District, in the name of his late son, Raymond August Levesque, electrician's second class USN. Levesque was cited by the Secretary of the Navy James Forrestal for his heroic service aboard the submarine USS *AMBERJACK* during its first patrol against the Japanese shipping in the Solomon Island area from September 5 to October 30, 1942."

In 1954, the developers of a new neighborhood at Salem Willows named one of the streets after 1st Lieut. Catherine Marie Larkin, USA NC, a native of Salem who "left the safety and comfort of her happy home during World War II and offered her services to ease the pain of wounded American soldiers on the battlefield," according to the *Salem Evening News*, continuing, during a flight "from one battle sector to another, the plane crashed to the ground and Nurse Larkin lost her life." Catherine Larkin was "the only Salem nurse to give her life in the last war." City Council president Louis A. Swiniuch declared at the dedication of the street sign bearing her name, "I can think of no more appropriate way to honor her memory than by placing her name at the entrance of the street where her war buddies have brought their families to live ... We are seeing to it that the next generation, too, will know of the fine girl, from a fine Salem family, who gave up her life trying to save life for others."

Larkin grew up on Boston Street. Her father ran Larkin's Market, and her two brothers served in the war. Larkin attended the Essex Agricultural School's Nursing School before enlisting. After her death, her father displayed a gold star flag in the window of his store. Today, along with Larkin Lane bearing her name, "Essex Aggie" has a cottage named in her honor. *(From salemwomenshistory.com.)*

How Salem Lost its WWII Bomber Memorial

"Shortly after the war," according to the *Salem Evening News* of December 20, 1947, "it was learned that the government would dispose of airplane equipment to cities and towns requesting same to be used for educational work and memorials." Salem residents felt that obtaining a bomber for both purposes, in conjunction with the schools, would be an ideal tribute to WWII service members and their families.

At the same time City officials learned of a "Salem boy," 1st Lieut. John ("Jack") Joseph Lee of 75 Ocean Avenue, who was a "flying fortress pilot" with the Army Air Corps. Lee had flown a B-17 bomber named "Miss X" on 50 missions over Germany as part of the 603rd Squadron, 398th Bomb Group, 8th Air Force, stationed in England.* Lee and Miss X were tasked with destroying German munitions plants, factories, and bridges.

Knowing a good idea when he heard one, Mayor Edward A. Coffey appointed a "Bomber Committee" to purchase the plane, find a location for it, and raise the funds to make it happen. Thanks to the committee, the City of Salem purchased Miss X from the Army Air Corps in 1945 for $350, and had her flown to the Beverly Airport until a location in Salem could be secured.**

Salem Common was the first suggestion for the memorial, but area residents objected and threatened a lawsuit against the City Council. Mack Park, at the corner of Tremont and Mason Streets, looked like a "go" until the Parks Department said No. They also said No to Forest River Park as Miss X's final home would require a substantial foundation and security.

Meanwhile, in Beverly, Miss X had been repeatedly vandalized. Radio equipment was stolen, and windows were smashed. But Cdr. John R. Henthorn of the U. S. Coast Guard Air Base in Salem reassured Salem officials that a crew of his men could easily "put the plane in shape" and that the Coast Guard base would contribute supplies and equipment as needed. "Eventually Salem may still have its bomber memorial to the veterans of World War Two," wrote the *Salem Evening News* of April 20, 1946.

And so, after months of negotiations about a site and Beverly's request to have the plane removed, Miss X, without her wings, made her way from Beverly to Salem on July 26, 1947. She was parked in Block House Square at the corner of Fort Avenue and Almshouse Road (near the dump) until a decision about her official location was made. Police managed enthusiastic onlookers and traffic along the way, while a telephone line crew moved overhead wires to accommodate Miss X on her journey.

But no decision came, and Miss X was desecrated again by vandals and souvenir-seekers. According to the *Salem Evening News*, "Vandalism reduced the shining aircraft to a mass of metal with its equipment being shattered, the tail assembly being torn apart, as well as the 'blisters' on the nose and turrets." Veterans groups protested her deplorable condition, not seeing a possible future. Finally, sadly, in December 1947 Miss X was sold as scrap for $200 to Greenberg's Auto Wrecking Company in Ipswich, who presumably did "something" with her remains.

Many years later, Jack Lee, now a member of the 398th Bomber Memorial Group, wrote to the editor of the *Salem Evening News* about the story of Miss X. He hoped to find details about her final days in Salem from the newspaper's archives. Lee had already spoken with the current owners of the wrecking company in Ipswich, but they had never heard of the earlier owner or of Miss X.

Lee's other clue had come from his parents in Salem who had written to him in 1947 that Miss X had been demolished and "shoved into a nearby dump." Could that be the dump at Fort Avenue in Salem? In 1991, members of the 398th Memorial Committee (friends of Jack Lee's) visited the site to investigate —to no avail.

And so the search for identifiable remains of Miss X, who should have been Salem's WWII Memorial "Fort" continues. And that's a shame, especially when you read how Jack Lee described her:

In her heyday, she was admired by many and feared by more … In her prime, she shared exciting and memorable times with the men in her life. If you were with her, you indeed had good luck.

She was beautiful. As graceful as a ballerina, as tough as a fullback, and had the instincts of a survivor.

In her waning days she was stripped and beaten. She had won all previous battles in life, but in the end she succumbed to malicious, uncaring vandals and vagrants.

*This number varies among sources.
**During the war, the Beverly Airport was used by Coast Guard Air Station Salem.

A REAL BOMBER-SHELL

This B-17 bomber Miss X, complete with her name and a buxom beauty wearing a bathing suit and boots painted on the cockpit, once graced Salem Willows as a 'Flying Fortress' memorial. After vandals had desecrated the craft, Miss X was eventually carted to the junk pile in 1947.

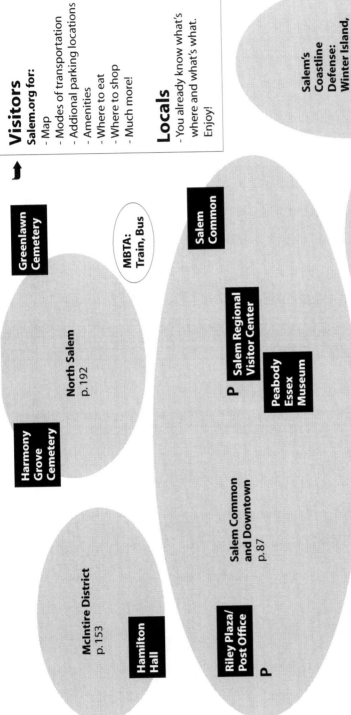

Visitors

Salem.org for:

- Map
- Modes of transportation
- Addional parking locations
- Amenities
- Where to eat
- Where to shop
- Much more!

Locals

- You already know what's where and what's what. Enjoy!

Greenlawn Cemetery

MBTA: Train, Bus

Salem Common

North Salem
p. 192

Harmony Grove Cemetery

P Salem Regional Visitor Center

Peabody Essex Museum

Waterfront and Derby Street
p.214

P

Salem Maritime National Historic Site

Salem's Coastline Defense: Winter Island, Juniper Point, Salem Neck
p.245

McIntire District
p. 153

Hamilton Hall

Salem Common and Downtown
p.87

Riley Plaza/ Post Office

P

Relational Map

Trail locations in relation to each other and to key landmarks. Visit Destination Salem (salem.org) or the Salem Regional Visitor Center for a real map!

★ Sites to Visit by Neighborhood ★

~ Salem Common and Downtown ~

Postcard of the Memorial to the 23rd Regiment, 1906. The boulder, weighing over forty tons, "was moved from its previous resting place" at the Salem Willows, according to a public notice in the *Salem Evening News* of September 27, 1905.

START: Memorial to the 23rd Regiment

Merritt Square (Intersection of Winter Street and Washington Square)
Dedicated on September 28, 1905, forty years after the end of the Civil War, the inscription on the monument reads: "To commemorate the faithful service of the 23rd Massachusetts Volunteer Infantry Regiment, in the Civil War which preserved the Union and abolished slavery." Companies A and F of the 23rd (from Salem) fought at Roanoke Island, New Berne, Kinston, Whitehall, Goldsboro, Wilcox Bridge, Wrenns Mills, Heckmans Farm, Arrowfield Church, Drewrys Bluff, Cold Harbor, and Petersberg (old spellings). The site chosen for the monument, Merritt Square, is named for Lieut. Col. Henry Merritt of Salem, a young Civil War hero who was killed in 1862 (see pp. 122-24). To learn more about Salem military units, see pp. 291-317. Civil War memorials are also located in Greenlawn Cemetery (pp. 204-6) and Harmony Grove Cemetery (pp. 210-13).

Over the decades, Salem residents "improved" the monument site (at the head of Winter Street, shown in the background) with plantings and a pair of cannon. It is presumed that the cannon succumbed to World War II metal drives.

➡ *Facing Winter Street, look straight ahead and slightly to your left to see a magnificent brick mansion (or, cross the street for a closer look—but please be courteous as the house is privately owned).*

Home of Justice Joseph Story
26 Winter Street

Joseph Story, attorney and jurist, was the youngest member ever appointed to the United States Supreme Court. He is perhaps best known for his ruling in the "Amistad Case" (1839), when he found in favor of the enslaved people who committed mutiny to secure their freedom. For this reason, Story's home is part of the National Park Service's Underground Railroad trail. During World War II, the U. S. Navy named a liberty ship for him. These were mass-produced cargo ships.

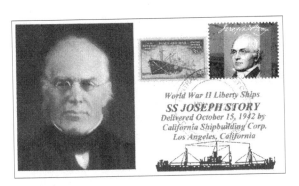

World War II Liberty Ships
SS JOSEPH STORY
Delivered October 15, 1942 by California Shipbuilding Corp. Los Angeles, California

➡ *Cross the street into Salem Common. Turn right, and follow the pathway.*

Washington Arch

Salem Common at Washington Square South

The new and first American president, George Washington, visited Salem during his tour of the New England states in 1789 where he was enthusiastically welcomed by Salem citizens. According to the Salem Common Neighborhood Association (SCNA):

In 1805, the City of Salem decided to construct a tribute to President and Commander-in-Chief George Washington. This included two arches East and West and two turnstiles North and South. Samuel McIntire, Salem's genius woodcarver and self-taught architect, was commissioned to design and construct four gateways for the sides of the common. The main gateway was designated the "Washington Arch" and was located on the westerly side of the Common at the head of Brown Street.

McIntire based his design for the arch on early engravings of ancient Rome where they were used in welcoming processions. The wood-framed structure

"Western view of Washington Square" from a wood-cut engraving for John Warner Barber's *Historical Collections of Massachusetts* (1839). The arch in the engraving is shown at the intersection of Washington Square and Brown Street. It was removed in 1850 when a cast iron fence was installed along the perimeter of the Common. The eagle was moved to the pediment of City Hall. The medallion of George Washington is in the collection of the Peabody Essex Museum.

featured ornate carvings including an oval portrait of Washington flanked by swags of drapery. It was then affixed with a gilded wooden eagle to symbolize our newly formed United States of America.

When Salem Common was remodeled in 1850, the arches were removed. But with the approach of the American Bicentennial, Salem's Bicentennial Commission "commissioned to have the arch reconstructed and designated it the 'McIntire Washington Arch.' The 'new' Arch was constructed of metal and wood and located at the corner of Washington Square South, facing where The Tavern at the Hawthorne Hotel is now," according to the SCNA. It was formally dedicated on July 4, 1976.

In the 1980s, the Arch was moved to its present location, where it hasn't always weathered northeastern storms well. The most recent restoration effort started in 2013, thanks to the combined efforts of community groups, local businesses, and the Boy Scouts. *To follow the project, visit the Salem Common Neighborhood Association's website (salemcommon.org).*

President Washington in Salem: Sites to Visit

- Assembly Hall (pp. 171-72)
- Joshua Ward House (p. 132)
- Salem Regional Visitor Center and Armory Park
  (see pp. 296-308 to learn more about the Salem Cadets, Washington's escort, also known as the Second Corps of Cadets)

No particular circumstance of the day seems to have pleased more than the plain and hearty manner in which Mr. Northey, the Chairman of the Selectmen, received the President. This gentleman is of the Society of Friends; and when the President was presented to the Selectmen, Mr. Northey took him by the hand, being covered, and said, "Friend Washington, we are glad to see thee, and in behalf of the inhabitants bid thee a hearty welcome to Salem!"
—*Salem Mercury*, November 3, 1789

President Washington in Salem: An Account

Excerpt from the *Salem Mercury*, November 3, 1789:

We recollect no event that has ever taken place in this country, which has had so universal an effect in calling forth those finer feelings of the heart, which constitute the most pleasing part of human nature, as the present Tour of the PRESIDENT of the United States. To behold the man, whom Heaven has been pleased to make the instrument, both in a civil and military capacity, of our political salvation—the man, who, to the qualities of a great Soldier and Statesman joins every amiable virtue and accomplishment which can adorn a private station—in short, to see GENERAL WASHINGTON, appeared to be the last, the fondest wish of every man, woman and child; and the gratification of that wish inspires but one uniform sentiment—from every mouth we hear the same expressions, of his virtues, his benignity, his kind and paternal care of the Great Family over which he presides…

At one o'clock, the inhabitants assembled in Court Street, and formed a Procession, under the directions of the Marshals for the day; and, preceded by a Band of Music, were conducted to the west end of the Main Street.

The Military were formed in Federal Street, under the command of Brig. General Fisk—Capt. Brown's Horse on the right; then the Salem Cadets, Capt. Saunders; Salem Artillery, Capt. Lieutenant Hovey; 1st Regiment, Col. Abbott; 5th Regiment, Col. Breed.

The President's arrival at the bounds of Salem (where he was received by the Committee of Arrangement) was announced by a federal discharge from the Fort, and another from the Artillery [i]n Federal Street. Here he quitted his carriage, and mounted a beautiful white horse. On his nearer approach, the bells began and continued ringing for 15 minutes. The Committee conducted him to the line of troops, who saluted him as he passed; and

92 — Salem Serves

when he came on the left of the line, the firings of the artillery and musketry took place.

From Federal Street he proceeded to the Main Street, where the escort coming to open order, he passed through the avenue, and was received by the Selectmen, at the head of the PROCESSION, which then moved on in the following order:

Salem Cadets.
Music.
Selectmen.
Sherrif of Essex County,
   on horseback.
Marshal of Massachusetts
   District, on horseback.
THE PRESIDENT, on horseback,
   attended by Major Jackson,
   his Secretary.
Overseers of the Poor.
Town-Treasurer and Town-Clerk.
School Committee.
Magistrates and Lawyers.
Clergy.
Physicians.
Merchants and Traders.
Marine Society.
Masters of Vessels.
Revenue Officers.
Continental and
   Militia Officers.
Strangers.
Mechanicks.
Seamen.
Laborers.
The several Schoolmasters,
   each at the head of his own
   scholars.

Salem Cadet (detail). Washington "passed some very flattering compliments on the Cadets (which is undoubtedly the best disciplined light corps in the United States) who acted as his escort, and were therefore more immediately under his observation." —Salem Gazette

The front of the Procession having reached the Court-house, the President was conducted by the Selectmen and Committees into the balcony, where he paid his respects to the innumerable crowd who pressed to see him—immediately the bells rang with their acclamations—he was then saluted with an Ode, adapted to the occasion, by a select choir of singers in a temporary gallery, covered with rich Persian carpets, and hung with damask curtains. After which, he received the affectionate address of the Town, to which he returned a kind and elegant answer. The Cadets then escorted him to his residence in WASHINGTON STREET; after which, they fired a salute, and, having received the thanks of the President by his Secretary, for their services, were dismissed.

At dark, the Court-house was beautifully illuminated, and made a most elegant appearance. The disposition of the lights did credit to the person who superintended this business.

Illustration from a *Massachusetts Magazine* of 1794 showing the Court House, ca. 1765. President Washington addressed Salem citizens from this balcony. They had renamed the street "Washington Street" in his honor. Today, this site is above the train depot. Note the ship in the background (far right), when the North River was much wider and deeper.

In the evening there was a brilliant Assembly at Concert Hall [at the old Market and Fish Streets; the streets and the building no longer exist], which the President honored with his presence. As he came from his door to the carriage, 13 beautiful rockets appeared at once in the air, and 13 others when he alighted at the door of the Hall—these had a most pleasing effect. When he retired from the company, which was at an early hour, the same compliment was again paid him.

The President appeared to be perfectly satisfied with every thing which took place. He declared to those who attended him, that he wanted words to express his gratitude for the attentions he had received. He was particularly gratified by the military exhibition—spoke handsomely of the appearance of the Militia, and of their firings—of the Artillery, whose conduct was highly applauded—and passed some very flattering compliments on the Cadets (which is undoubtedly the best disciplined light corps in the United States) who acted as his escort, and were therefore more immediately under his observation. He was highly delighted with the company at the Hall in the evening— the numbers and brilliancy of the Ladies far exceeded his expectation.

To the Committee of Arrangements, and to the gentlemen who acted as Marshals, the town is under great obligations, for that decency with which every thing was conducted, and that no unfortunate accident happened to mar the joy of the day.

Friday morning, about 9 o'clock, the President set off on his journey eastward, escorted by Capt. Osgood's and Capt. Brown's Horse, and accompanied by many respectable gentlemen. To gratify the people, he rode out of town on horseback. Essex Bridge was beautifully dressed with the flags of different nations; and the cavalcade passed it free of toll.

"...to see GENERAL WASHINGTON, appeared to be the last, the fondest wish of every man, woman and child."

Above, left: First Muster challenge coin commissioned by the Second Corps of Cadets Veterans Association (see p. 329). Challenge coins are a long-time military tradition and a high honor to receive. They indicate your privileged membership in, and respect of, what is represented on the coin. You must carry the coin with you at all times (or be no more than four steps away from it) as you may be challenged to produce it by another member. If you fail, you'll be buying the next round of drinks! Above, right: *The First Muster* by Don Troiani (detail).

Training Field, and the First Muster Marker

Salem Common Flag Pole

When colonists settled in Naumkeag (later, Salem) in 1626, this land was quite marshy. It was used for various public purposes, including grazing for animals and as a training field for Salem's militia. According to historian James Duncan Phillips, the first training day was held on "Ye Training Field" led by Capt. John Endecott when he drilled a squad of early settlers. Each had "a flint lock musket he had brought from England, mixed his own gun power, molded his own bullets, and made his own powder horn." In 1636, as threats from the French and Native Americans persisted and with the growth of the colony's population, the Massachusetts General Court established a new volunteer militia organization comprised of three regiments: East, North, and South. The East Regiment, centered in Salem, first mustered (drilled) in the early spring of 1637 on the Common. For this reason, in 2013, President Barrack Obama signed a bill designating Salem, Massachusetts, as the *Birthplace of the U. S. National Guard.*

In 2001, the Salem Rotary Club funded the "First Muster Marker" to commemorate the 1637 event. The marker features a replica of the painting by Don Troiani that depicts what might have taken place.

The original wooden Salem Common Bandstand (rear, center) was erected in 1926 and named for Jean M. Missud. Today's newer, concrete bandstand and the surrounding field are used for the annual mid-April "First Muster" event put on by the Massachusetts Army National Guard, the Second Corps of Cadets Veterans Association (see p. 329), and the Peabody Essex Museum (p. 114).

Jean M. Missud Bandstand

Center of Salem Common

The bandstand is named for the renowned band leader Jean Marie Missud (1852-1941), a native of Nice, France, and "a musician of high rank" who organized the civilian Salem Cadet Band in the spring of 1878. The Band, enlisted by the Second Corps of Cadets to serve as their official band, "attained high rank" under Missud's direction, according to Salem historians Charles S. Osgood and Henry M. Batchelder in *Historical Sketch of Salem, 1626-1879*.

"For over sixty years," writes National Park Service historian Emily A. Murphy in *Merchants, Clerks, Citizens, and Soldiers: The Second Corps of Cadets in Salem, Massachusetts*, "Missud wrote music and directed the Cadet Band in concerts, parades, and just about every other type of social gathering in and around Salem. The band also traveled, playing in London, England, for Queen Victoria in 1896, and in Washington, D. C., for the inaugurations of Presidents Taft and Wilson" (see pp. 101-4 for more on Missud).

Military Bands and Band Music in Salem

The Salem Cadet Band, led by Jean M. Missud, 1912.

Instrumental music in Salem, military or otherwise, took quite a while to become acceptable. As Thomas Carroll notes in his 1900 paper for the Essex Institute, *Bands and Band Music in Salem*: "Instrumental music, even as an accompaniment to the most orthodox tunes, was looked upon with disfavor and only tolerated at first after a period of doubt and misgiving."

It wasn't until 1743 that an organ first appeared in Salem— for (the Anglican) St. Peter's Church. It was replaced in 1754 with a newer model. In 1800, a Salem merchant imported an organ from London on one of his ships but, Carroll explains, "musical instruments were seldom offered for sale before the Revolution, and instrumental concerts were a rarity up to that time."

In 1783, Salem residents heard the Massachusetts Band give a concert "for the benefit of the poor," Carroll writes. Sixteen years later, in 1799, "several young men of Salem formed a band and were much noticed for their skillful performance." But a military band didn't take shape for another few years—not until 1805/6 with the formation of the Brigade Band, under the auspices of the Salem Light Infantry. According to Thomas Carroll, "It was the first military band in Essex County and, excepting for Boston, the first in Massachusetts." The band's first leader was Thomas Honeycomb. He was succeeded by Francis Boardman.

Even though the famous Salem Cadet Band wasn't formed until 1877, Carroll quotes this notice from the October 12, 1813 edition of the *Salem Gazette*: "The subscribers to the Cadet Band (so called) are requested to meet at Stetson's hotel this evening at 6 ½ o'clock, for important business." Carroll concludes, "There must have been a band attached to the [Second Corps of] Cadets quite early in their history."

A new Brigade Band comprised of temperance men formed in 1835, and the Salem Brass Band started up in 1837 under the direction of Francis W. Morse, a master of the E-flat bugle. The *Salem Gazette* of May 7, 1839 states:

The Salem Brass Band is now full and effective, and provided with fine instruments, music and uniforms. The members have been at great expense to furnish themselves, and have devoted much time to practice. Mr. Morse, leader, executes in first rate style on the E-flat bugle, and we think will become a distinguished performer. We hope the band will be patronized by this city and neighboring towns and that the committee on the celebration of the 4th of July will engage it for that occasion.

The band was attached to the Salem Light Infantry for many years. Their repertoire included the "Salem Light Infantry Quick Step," which concluded an 1846 concert at Salem's Mechanic Hall (see p. 125 and p. 314).

Morse was succeeded by another talented bugler, Jerome H. Smith, described by Thomas Carroll as "not only a solo performer who had already won distinction, but a diligent student in his profession, of pleasing address, [and] with a dedicated talent for organization."

Francis W. Morse (left) and Jerome H. Smith from a page in
Bands and Band Music in Salem by Thomas Carroll (1900).

In 1855, as Smith's health declined, he asked his band members
to elect a young musician from Ireland, Patrick Sarsfield
Gilmore, to his position. Gilmore had been leading the Brigade
Band of Boston, but he accepted Salem's invitation. Despite
prejudice against the Irish at the time, Gilmore eventually
earned a world-wide reputation as "versatile to an unusual
degree," Carroll writes. "He could play on many instruments,
and on all of them with excellence." Gilmore became known
as the "Father of the American Band."

In the 1850s, Gilmore's band participated in the annual
brigade muster on Winter Island along with cavalry, artillery,
and infantry units from Salem and the surrounding area. Of
Gilmore, Thomas Carroll writes, *"No bandmaster received more
loyal support than Gilmore did from his men and no man ever
strove more ardently to make every individual play a unit in one
grand harmonious whole."*

Another band joining the troops on Winter Island was the
Bay State Band, the successor of Felton's Brass Band formed

Patrick S. Gilmore

by G. W. Felt in 1852. In 1856, they led "Butler's Brigade" in the procession. Other leaders of that band included Isaac W. Wales, D. W. Boardman, and B. N. Marks. Thomas Carroll reports that, "the band had a fair share of popularity and success," but Gilmore's Salem Brass Band overshadowed them and the Bay State Band eventually disbanded.

In 1857, Gilmore's band marched in President James Buchanan's inaugural parade. The New England Guards, a militia unit from Boston, planned to participate in the festivities and wanted "the best music to be had," writes Carroll. He continues: "The leading musical organizations in the country were present on that occasion, but none attracted such attention as the band from Salem. The Washington papers spoke in the warmest terms of the excellence of their playing, as well as the gentlemanly demeanor of the men." From then on, the Salem Brass Band was in demand. With his reputation at its pique, Patrick Gilmore decided to move to Boston where "a wider field would be open to him."

Louis Kehrhahn succeeded Gilmore, but he eventually moved to Boston as well. In 1861, when the Civil War broke out, Kehrhahn returned to Salem to raise a military band for the Navy out of his former band members. The band, still known as "Gilmore's Band," served on the flagship *Minnesota*, the Navy's finest frigate, coming under attack at Hampton Roads. The band then enlisted in the 24th Massachusetts Regiment. They served at "the front in the North Carolina campaign," Carroll explains, continuing, "old soldiers tell of the beautiful music when the camp was quiet in the evening." When a general order from Washington, D. C., dissolved regimental bands, Salem musicians returned home. John Parsons assumed leadership of the Salem Band, and quickly reinstated its reputation.

In 1870, young Jean M. Missud joined the band, and in 1877 he was chosen by Col. Samuel A. Dalton (see pp. 190-91) to lead the new (civilian) Salem Cadet Band. Thomas Carroll writes:

It should be borne in mind that not all the members of the band were, at enrollment, consummate musicians; that, while the material was of the best, it required training and molding; that, unlike such organizations as the Symphony Orchestra, whose members have no avocation but music, the greater part of those who compose the Cadet Band are employed in some other calling. That it has become one of the foremost military bands in America, speaks volumes for the efficacy of the leader and the men whom he has trained.

Salem Cadet Band, 1880s

Newspaper clipping of the band performing in Philadelphia in 1905.

That it has become one of the foremost military bands in America, speaks volumes for the efficacy of the leader and the men whom he has trained. —Thomas Carroll

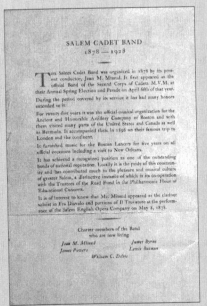

Program for the Testimonial Concert in honor of Jean M. Missud, hosted at the Salem Armory in 1928 by past and present members of the Salem Cadet Band.

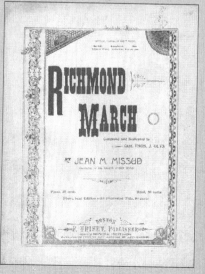

Front and back covers of Missud's march titled "London." Above, right: Salem Cadet Band pin.

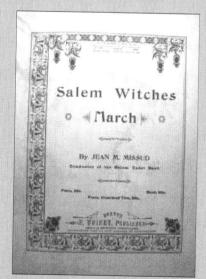

Above and right: Sheet music, written and published in Salem by Missud.

Missud composed dozens of pieces for the Cadets, including "Salem Witches March," and he also encouraged other composers. For example, Frederick Ellsworth Bigelow's march titled "Our Director" was published by Missud and premiered by the Salem Cadet Band.

Frederick E. Bigelow

Bigelow, a native of Ashland, Massachusetts, and a pharmacist by training, had organized the Ashland Brass Band in 1892. Between studying and playing, Bigelow composed marches. He dedicated "Our Director" to the director of the band, Joseph Morrisette. Several years later, when Bigelow submitted his piece to Jean Missud, "a well known publisher of band music," according to *Jacobs' Band Monthly*, "who immediately saw the possibilities in the march and published it," the tune was a hit! "Harvard Boys" (students) adapted it with their own "cheer song" lyrics, and it morphed into "The Battle Song of Liberty" in 1917.

Bigelow wrote an average of one march a year for Missud's band, but only one more was published: "The NC-4." As this new march grew in popularity, *Jacobs' Band Monthly* observed that "it gives probable signs of achieving the same broad success as his first one."

The tradition of band music continues today with the Salem Community Concert Band, which performs at the Salem Willows every summer. One of those concerts features military music.

The Salem High School Band plays rousing marches, and the Salem Philharmonic Orchestra concludes each concert with a march.

As for military bands, Salem can point to the acclaimed 215th Army Band of the Massachusetts National Guard, first organized in 1847 in the Massachusetts Volunteer Militia as the Band of the 5th Regiment of Artillery, 1st Brigade, 1st Division. As the "Birthplace of the U.S. National Guard," Salem can claim some musical heritage as well!

Sheet music for the "Salem Independent Cadet Quick Step."

The Italian Band

Salem's love of band music grew dramatically after the "Italian Band," recently discharged from the USS *Constitution*, performed on December 14, 1838, at Lyceum Hall. The band's leader, Manuel Emilio, a native of Malaga, Spain, and his close friend and protégé, Manuel Francisco Ciriaco Fenollosa of the Kingdom of Sardinia (at the time, Nice, where he was born, was part of the Spanish Empire), were brilliant, multi-faceted musicians. Salem embraced these talented men, and they chose to make Salem their home.

Emilio's son, Luis Fenollosa Emilio (his father had married Manuel Fenollosa's sister), became a Captain of the 54th Massachusetts Volunteer Infantry Regiment, the famous unit of African American soldiers and white officers formed by Governor John A. Andrew in 1863 (see p. 211).

Continue along the pathway.

Liberty Tree
Salem Common
In 1768, Salem residents Thomas Row and Robert Wood were captured and brought to the Liberty Tree located somewhere on Salem Common. There, they were brutally tarred and feathered for giving information to the British about an American ship attempting to evade payment of duties.

World War I Film Site
Salem Common
In 1918, the Salem Rotary Club arranged for a "motion picture camera" to film the "relatives and sweethearts of young men of Salem and vicinity now serving with the 102nd field artillery" overseas. Roughly 2,500 people showed up on the Common, including two new mothers who were showing their babies to their fathers for the first time. The film would be "exhibited to the young heroes in the Y.M.C.A. huts just behind the first line trenches."

➡ *Continue along the pathway to the war memorial on your left.*

MOTION PICTURE FILM FOR 102D ARTILLERY

Relatives of Salem Men to Be in It

1918

They Will Walk Before Camera on Salem Common Tomorrow

SALEM, June 22 — A motion picture film showing fathers, mothers, brothers, sisters and sweethearts of men from this district, serving on the war front in France, will be made here tomorrow and sent abroad, to be shown at Y. M. C. A. huts near which the men are located. Arrangements for the picture were made today by the Salem Rotary Club. The home folk will be shown walking about on Salem Common.

A large number of men from Salem and cities and towns near there are with an artillery command which formerly was the 2d Corps Cadets, a National Guard organization, and it is the relatives of these particularly who will be photographed.

Promotional poster, 1918.

War Memorial Honor Roll
Salem Common Entrance
This memorial honors Salem citizens who gave their lives in World War II, Korea, Vietnam, Iraq, and Afghanistan. Even though this book only describes Salem military sites and stories through World War II, Salem continues to acknowledge the sacrifices of its residents. In 2010, Salem mourned the loss of Sgt. James A. Ayube II, an Army medic serving in Afghanistan, and named a highway in his honor (see p. 346).

➡ *Exit Salem Common toward the statue of Roger Conant (who led the colonial settlers from Gloucester to Salem in 1626) and the Salem Witch Museum. Walk along Brown Street (behind Roger Conant). You will soon see the brick rear exterior of the Salem Regional Visitor Center on your left. Note the plaque in honor of the 8th Regiment, Massachusetts Volunteer Militia (see pp. 311-13). Walk around to the front of the building.*

Salem Regional Visitor Center
2 New Liberty Street
Built on the site of the old Salem Armory Drill Shed (see photo, opposite page), the Visitor Center features a wonderful exhibit on the Second Corps of Cadets including a model of the drill shed, photographs and memorabilia, early uniforms, and more. Here, you may also pick up brochures, purchase books and other Salem-themed goods, and use the rest rooms! The Visitor Center is managed by the National Park Service and the Essex National Heritage Commission.

➡ *Exit the Visitor Center into the brick walkway and small park.*

Site of the Salem Armory, and Armory Memorial Park
136 Essex Street
The Second Corps of Cadets purchased a magnificent mansion on this site from Col. Francis Peabody in 1890 to use as their head house (or headquarters). "The house had a huge Gothic-style banquet hall as well as space for offices," Emily A. Murphy explains: "After over a hundred years of renting space in other buildings, the Cadets finally had a home. In 1894, they put an addition on the back of the building—a large, open drill shed that provided them with a dry place to train."

The Joseph Peabody House, ca. 1820, was sold by his descendant, Col. Francis Peabody, to the Second Corps of Cadets in 1890 for use as an Armory "head house" (or, headquarters). The drill shed in the rear was added in 1894. Today, it serves as the Salem Regional Visitor Center.

The "new" (1908) Armory head house dominated Essex Street and downtown Salem for seventy-four years before it was destroyed by an arsonist. Today, this site is Armory Park; the entrance to the park is a replica of the Armory doorway.

The Armory was used as Relief Headquarters after the Great Salem Fire of 1914 by the Massachusetts National Guard (see pp. 188-89), the Second Corps of Cadets (see pp. 296-308), Red Cross (see pp. 163-66), and civic committees.

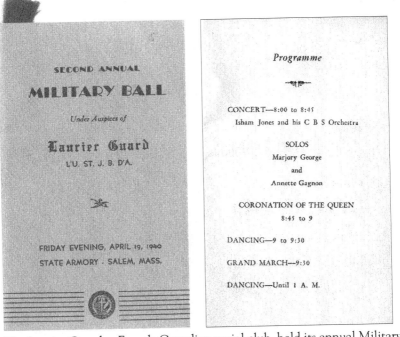

The Laurier Guard, a French-Canadian social club, held its annual Military Ball at the Armory. This program, complete with dark blue tassle, is from 1940.

Press photograph from the annual Washington's Birthday
Ball, hosted by the 102nd Field Artillery Battalion of
the Massachusetts National Guard and held at the
Salem Armory in 1959.

Farewell dinner of the 4th Battalion, Massachusetts Women's Defense Corps,
held September 5, 1946, in the Armory. In his history of the Massachusetts
Women's Defense Corps (MWDC), Ronald J. McBrien explains: "The MWDC
was organized and served the Commonwealth during the World War II years.
It was dedicated to providing war-related emergency services throughout the
state ... The MWDC was organized regionally, similar to that of the Civilian
Defense and Military Division ... The 4th Battalion of the MWDC had its
offices in the Salem Armory under the command of Col. Carolyn F. Standley
of Beverly ... The MWDC was inactivated in September 1946 with a final
review by Governor Maurice Tobin (see pp. 57-59 for more on the MWDC).

The Peabody mansion and drill shed "served as an armory from 1890 until it was razed" to make way for a much larger building, according to Salem's architectural historian Bryant Tolles. He considered the "new" Armory head house (or, headquarters), completed in 1908, to be "a fine example of turn-of-the-century, tradition-bound armory architecture." The Armory, owned by the Commonwealth of Massachusetts, was frequently referred to as the "State Armory." It was also known as the "Cadet Armory," even after the Second Corps of Cadets became the 1st Battalion, 102nd Field Artilley, Massachusetts Army National Guard.

The Armory not only served as "the local headquarters of the military," it was one of the centers of social activity in Salem. After the Great Salem Fire of 1914, the building became headquarters for aid, distribution, and information. In her book *Chronicles of Old Salem*, the historian Frances Robotti tells us:

The Cadet Armory ... of 1908 was a social as well as a military headquarters. In its halls the Cadets drilled, graduations of schools took place, orators of politics spoke, the Chamber of Commerce held its annual dinners, and Society danced at Charity Balls. In this Armory, the Salem Cadet Band, Jean Missud, leader, gave its spring concerts and [John Philip] Sousa and his band played.

In 1982, the Armory was irreparably damaged by a fire set by an arsonist. After years of lying vacant, the National Park Service transformed the 1894 drill shed into a Visitor Center for the Salem Maritime National Historic Site. It opened in 1994. The property where the head house once stood was transferred by the Commonwealth of Massachusetts to the Peabody Essex Museum (PEM). As part of a massive expansion of their campus, the PEM transformed the site into Armory Memorial Park to honor the Second Corps of Cadets and almost four centuries of military and patriotic history in Salem and Essex County (where Salem is situated). Features of Armory Park include:

- Timeline tracing the history of the citizen soldier (in the tradition of today's National Guard) and the Second Corps of Cadets;
- Replica of a Paul Revere bell;
- Replica of the 1908 Armory doorway (park entryway);

- Interpretive panels describing key events in Essex County military history;
- Brick "Walkway of Heroes" (between the Visitor Center and Armory Park) that contains lists of:
  - Officers of the 1636 East Regiment of the Mass. Militia
  - Essex County "Minutemen" who perished answering the Lexington Alarm of 1775 (including Salem's Benjamin Pierce)
  - Medal of Honor recipients from Essex County (including Salem's John Riley)
  - Military units created in Essex County
  - Twenty names submitted for special honor by the thirty-four towns in Essex County.

Salem Names on the Walkway of Heroes

COL Benjamin Gedney — *Colonial Wars*
LT Benjamin West — *Colonial Wars*
1LT Samuel Carlton — *Revolutionary War*
Jonathan Haradan (pp. 153-54) — *Revolutionary War*
COL David Mason & Hannah Mason (pp. 194-95) — *Revolutionary War*
COL Timothy Pickering (pp. 184-86) — *Revolutionary War*
CPT Luis Emilio (p. 211) — *Civil War*
PVT Edwin Hill — *Civil War*
BG Frederick W. Lander (pp. 154-55) — *Civil War*
LT James W. Nichols — *Civil War*
AG Henry Kemble Oliver (pp. 172-73) — *Civil War*
Rev. George Dudley Wildes (p. 18) — *Civil War*
PVT William H. Sanders (p. 26) — *Spanish-American War*
Ralph Cowan Browne (pp. 236-38) — *World War II*
PVTs Edward, James, John, Richard, and William Conway
  — *World War II*
SMN Norman Edwin Davies Jr. — *World War II*
CPT Lawrence A. Donlon — *World War II*
BG Albin F. Irzyk (pp. 239-43) — *World War II*
CDR J. Alexander Michaud (p. 206) — *World War II*
COL Thaddeus Buczko (p. 81) — *World War II, Korean War*

Names were chosen by Salem citizens and submitted by historian Jim McAllister.

On May 4, 2002, the Peabody Essex Museum and the Massachusetts Army National Guard (MANG) co-hosted a day-long celebration to dedicate Armory Park. Military dignitaries from Washington, D. C., attended, along with two thousand active service troops, veterans, and grateful citizens. Since the dedication, the PEM, MANG, and the Second Corps of Cadets Veterans Association hold an annual scaled-down version of the event in April called "The First Muster."

➡️ *Look across Essex Street to the entrance of the Peabody Essex Museum. You could easily spend a full day getting lost in there! For now, we suggest continuing your walking tour and making plans to return.*

Peabody Essex Museum (PEM)
East India Square
Founded in 1799, this is America's oldest, continuously running museum. While the PEM enjoys an acclaimed international reputation for its art collections, many significant, local historical works—including military—are also on display. Among these is the painting *Salem Common on Training Day* (depicting the Second Corps of Cadets) by George Ropes. The PEM's research library, the Phillips Library, houses archives of the Second Corps of Cadets and the family papers of some of the individuals featured in this book. On display at the library is Samuel McIntire's carved medallion of George Washington.

➡️ *Retrace your steps along the left side of the Visitor Center, walking toward the Gothic stone church on the corner of Brown and St. Peter Streets.*

Burying Place of Col. Stephen Abbott, and Memorial to Pvt. Benjamin Pierce
St. Peter's Church Cemetery, corner of Brown and St. Peter Street
Over the centuries, this cemetery has become smaller and smaller. But we know that somewhere beneath where you are standing lie the remains of Col. Stephen Abbott, the first commander of the Second Corps of Cadets (see p. 114). In 2002, during Armory Park Dedication Day, the Second Corps of Cadets Veterans Association held a ceremony at the church in his memory. Since then, they have continued this tradition as part of the now-annual "First Muster."

On the sidewalk across from the entrance to the church is a small memorial to Pvt. Benjamin Pierce, the only Salem man killed on April 19, 1775, during the fierce fighting at Menotomy (today, Arlington) as the British troops retreated from Concord to Boston. John Hardy Wright, a curator at the former Essex Institute and a direct descendant of Pierce, designed the bronze plaque in his ancestor's honor. It was dedicated on July 4, 1976, as part of a special service organized by Wright during the Bicentennial.

Site of Gen. Phil H. Sheridan
Post 34, Grand Army of the Republic (GAR)
17 St. Peter Street

The GAR, founded in 1866, was composed of Civil War veterans of the Union Army, Navy, Marines, and the U. S. Revenue Cutter Service (later, U. S. Coast Guard). According to the GAR's website, it "was organized into Departments at the state level and Posts at the community level. Military-style uniforms were worn by its members. There were posts in every state in the U. S., and several Posts overseas" (see pp. 322-24 for more on the GAR's history). Salem's Post, the Gen. Phil H. Sheridan Post 34, was founded on December 10, 1867, by Gen. George H. Peirson (the Post's first Commander), George A. Fisher, Capt. George M.

POST 34 G. A. R. WAS ORGANIZED IN 1867 AND HAS FINE RECORD

Memorial Day Calls Attention to Its Dwindling Ranks From High Water Membership of 1011 to But 66 Today; History and Roll

G. A. R. HEADQUARTERS, ST. PETER STREET

(Duplicate image) from the *Salem Evening News*, May 23, 1922, when the GAR was located on St. Peter Street.

Hurrah! hurrah for Sheridan!
Hurrah! hurrah for horse and man!
And when their statues are placed on high,
Under the dome of the Union sky,
The American soliders' Temple of Fame;
There with the glorious General's name,
Be it said, in letters both bold and bright,
"Here is the steed that saved the day,
By carrying Sheridan into the fight,
From Winchester, twenty miles away!

—Excerpt from "Sheridan's Ride"
by Thomas Buchanan Read

Cover of an 1889 dinner program
with a likeness of Phil Sheridan.

Convention ribbon,
1892.

Letter on Post 34
stationery. Note the
signature of J. Frank
Dalton (see p. 191).

Whipple, Capt. Robert W. Reeves, Edward H. Fletcher, John P. Tilton, Lieut. John R. Lakeman, Edward A. Phalen, and Capt. John P. Reynolds. Sheridan had visited Salem two months earlier, perhaps to visit one of his officers, Lieut. Col. George H. Woods (see p. 206). While Sheridan had no direct ties to Salem, he was a beloved hero of the Civil War. His decisive actions in the Shenendoah Valley helped bring victory to the Union forces.

Membership in Post 34, comprised solely of veterans, grew quickly to 1,011. The Post's Women's Relief Corps thrived as well. At one time, Post 34 was the second largest in Massachusetts after Lynn. By 1922, as veterans passed away, membership had dwindled to sixty-six. The GAR disbanded nationally in 1956, but the Sons of Union Veterans carried on.

Post 34 was originally located in the Bowker Block on Essex Street, moving to St. Peter Street in 1870 and the Newhall Building on Central Street in 1875. In 1884, after renovations, the Post returned to its final home on St. Peter Street.

Site of the Birthplace of Brig. Gen. John Glover

St. Peter Street

John Glover is usually associated with Marblehead, where he was raised from the age of four and built successful business and military careers. But he was born in the 1730s in a house on this street. His mother moved the family to Marblehead after the death of her husband. In Marblehead, Glover was a member of the militia long before the Revolutionary War. In 1775, he served as Lieut. Col. of the 21st Massachusetts Regiment under Col. Jeremiah Lee, taking over command of the unit on Lee's death.

Glover took part in the seige of Boston in 1775, where he established a trusting friendship with General George Washington. Washington soon chartered Glover's schooner, the *Hannah* (named for Glover's wife) to intercept British supply ships—the first of many "privateers" sent out under Washington's authority. Sailing out of Beverly, the *Hannah* was the first commissioned ship in the infant U. S. Navy. Although most Americans have never heard of John Glover (and they should!), he became a real hero of the Revolutionary War when he and his seafaring regiment daringly ferried Washington and his men across the Delaware River on Christmas Day of 1776.

Washington's Crossing Historic Park gives this account of the crossing:

In the winter of 1776, General George Washington and his ragged army had experienced only defeat and despair. The War for Independence was going badly, with failure following failure. In the preceding months, Washington's campaign in New York had not gone well; the Battle of Long Island ended in a loss when the British troops managed to out-maneuver the Continental Army. A series of defeats settled around Washington as he was forced to retreat across New Jersey to Pennsylvania on December 7 and 8.

As the harsh Pennsylvania winter set in, the morale of the American troops was at an all-time low. The soldiers were forced to deal with a lack of both food and warm clothing, while Washington watched his army shrink due to desertions and expiring enlistments. Now, more than ever, a victory was desperately needed. General Washington hatched a daring plan to cross the Delaware River under the cover of darkness, march to Trenton and attack the Hessian outposts in and around Trenton. The boats to be used for the crossing were gathered earlier in the month in compliance with Washington's orders, primarily as a defensive measure...

David McCullough, in his book *1776*, tells us that Washington's decision to move troops and equipment across a partially frozen, mile-wide river—at night—was against many odds. But he had Glover!

It was about eleven o'clock when, as if by design, the northeast wind died down. Then the wind shifted to the southwest and a small armada of boats manned by more of John Glover's Massachusetts sailors and fishermen started over the river from New York...

Glover's men proved as crucial as the change in the wind. In a feat of extraordinary seamanship, at the helm and manning oars hour after hour, they negotiated the river's swift, contrary currents in boats so loaded with troops and supplies, horses and cannon, that the water was often but inches below the gunnels—and all in pitch dark, with no running lights. Few men ever had so much riding on their skill, or were under such pressure, or performed so superbly.

➡ *Walk back to Church Street and turn right.*

Salem Fire Department Headquarters on Church Street, ca. 1910, with Engine 3, Chemical 1, and supply wagon. *Courtesy of Thomas Brophy.*

Salem Fire Department
34 Church Street
In the late nineteenth century, this was the headquarters of the Salem Fire Department. Note the tall tower in the rear for hanging fire hoses to drain. During World War II, the War Price and Rationing Board had its office here. And while fire fighters were away during the war, Salem was protected by a robust Fire Auxiliary (see p. 56).

World War II era badge.

Salem Lyceum
43 Church Street
The Salem Lyceum was established in 1830 "for the purpose of diffusing knowledge, and promoting intellectual improvement in the city of Salem," according to the 1879 *Historical Sketch of the Salem Lyceum.*

Salem's Lyceum was part of the national lyceum movement "borrowed" from England. Some of the most prominent lecturers of the day spoke at the Lyceum (which only men could join), including Ralph Waldo Emerson, Frederick Douglass, and Salem's Nathaniel Hawthorne.

As tensions between North and South accelerated in the mid-nineteenth century and the demands to abolish slavery grew louder, the Lyceum hosted speakers to address these issues. They included Caleb Foote of Salem: "The Value of the Union and Consequences of Disunion" (1832-33 season); John W. Browne: "War" (1837-38); Charles Sumner: "The Rebellion" (1861-62); Samuel Johnson of Salem: "The War and Slavery" (1862-63); Wendell Phillips: "The Present War" (1862-63); and more. After the war, Frederick Douglass spoke in Salem six times: "Equal Rights for the Freedmen" (1865); "The Assassination and Its Lessons" (1865-66); "On Some Dangers to the Republic" (1866-67); "Self Made Men" (1867-68); "William the Silent" (1868-69); and "Our Composite Nationality" (1869-70). Clara Barton, a battlefield nurse who later founded the American Red Cross (see pp. 163-66), spoke for the 1866-67 season on "Work and Incidents of Army Life."

Postcard of the Salem Lyceum as a restaurant.

➡ *Continue along Church Street to Washington Street. Cross Washington Street to Federal Street.*

Tabernacle Church
Corner of Washington and Federal Streets
This was a regular meeting place for the Salem Female Anti-Slavery Society (SFASS), the first bi-racial anti-slavery organization in the country. Its most prominent members included the women of the Remond family (Nancy [mother and daughter], Sarah, Caroline, Cecelia, Maritcha) and Laura Poor Stone, the wife of the minister of Salem's First Church. Every leading church in Salem was represented in the SFASS. After the war, the women transformed their organization into the Ladies' Fugitive or Freedmen's Aid Society.

Masonic Temple / Essex Lodge
70 Washington Street
Although the fraternal Essex Lodge was instituted in 1779 to "engage in the rich history of tradition, brotherhood, charity and community service," according to their website, this building, their magnificent new home, was completed in 1916. During World War I, the Temple served as the site of fundraising dinners, welcome-home events, and lodging for returning soldiers. The Masons also invited Salem's Red Cross Chapter to use the building for their work, one of whose

Newspaper photograph of Margaret L. Ropes.

organizers was Margaret L. (Mrs. Charles F.) Ropes (see pp. 163-66 on the Red Cross). Her obituary in the *Salem Evening News* from 1954 describes her volunteer work at the Masonic Temple:

Of her work in World War One, filling in one week an order for 1111 pairs of socks probably best expressed her capacity to organize and her ability to stimulate enthusiasm. Not only was she able to procure more knitters and increase the supply of knitting being done, but when the work was finished on Saturday of that week of sock production, Mrs. Ropes with the late Mrs. William G. Rantoul and the late Mrs. James L. Simpson met in the Masonic Temple on Sunday and packed 1111 bags for France, putting into them besides the socks, a sweater, a helmet and a sewing kit known as a "housewife."

➡ *Walk up Lynde Street.*

Site of the Home of Lieut. Col. Henry Merritt

15 Lynde Street

Although he was born in Marblehead, Henry Merritt (1819-1862) was a long-time resident of Salem, a watch maker, a member of the Mechanic Light Infantry, and part of Col. George L. Andrews' company.

Merritt enlisted in the Civil War on September 25, 1861, as a Major. Three days later, he joined the 23rd Regiment of the Massachusetts Volunteer Militia and was promoted to Lieut. Col. on October 24. On November 11, 1861, Merritt and the 23rd departed for Annapolis, Maryland, where they established Camp John A. Andrew (named for the Massachusetts Governor). They remained there until January 1862 when "it was attached to the Burnside Expedition and embarked for the coast of North Carolina. It now formed a part of Foster's Brigade, which was Burnside's Coast Division. It was present with loss at Roanoke Island, Feb. 8, and suffered a much greater loss at Newbern, March 14," according to regimental papers housed at the Civil War Archives, Acton (Massachusetts) Public Library.

One of the regiment's losses at Newbern was Lieut. Col. Henry Merritt. As Salem had just buried the young Brig. Gen. Frederick C. Lander (MHD), Merritt's death was devastating for local residents. The *Salem Gazette* of March 21, 1862, published this account:

The city is again called upon to mourn the loss of one of her most gallant sons. The field of battle and of glory, at Newbern, was also the field of death to Henry Merritt, Lieutenant-Colonel of the Twenty Third Regiment of Massachusetts Volunteers ... Colonel Merritt was about 43 years of age, and leaves a wife and three children. He has been connected with the volunteer militia of Massachusetts for more than a quarter of a century. He enlisted in the Mechanic Light Infantry, March 14, 1836, and served in that company several years as private and first sergeant ... until his promotion to the staff of General Andrews, at that time Colonel ...

He fell while bravely discharging his duty at the battle of Newbern. Following an order from Colonel Kurtz, he was getting the companies in line at the time he fell. Company A was already in place, next to the 27th, and he was engaged in bringing up the other companies when a cannon shot struck him near the hip, causing his death.

The *Salem Register* described Henry Merritt as "a man of fine personal appearance, and inestimable character. Scrupulously neat and methodical in his habits, thoughtful of the welfare of others, of pleasing address, mild disposition, and gentlemanly manners, he secured the favor and affection of his fellow soldiers, and never thought any sacrifice too great to promote their comfort. Calm and considerate, his was just the temperament to exhibit bravery without ostentation, cool and collected courage without impulsive flashes of valor."

Henry Merritt's body was sent by train from North Carolina to New York and from there to Boston, arriving on March 19. A large procession of military dignitaries, Salem City Councilors, family, and friends, accompanied the horse-drawn hearse through the streets of Boston until Merritt's body was placed on a private train, provided by Jeremiah Prescott, superintendent of the Eastern Railroad, and brought to Salem. The railroad car was draped in black; a sign at the entrance read, "Lieut. Col. Henry Merritt, We mourn his loss." The *Salem Register* detailed what happened next:

As the train entered Salem Depot, it was met by a Committee of the Common Council and a large concourse of citizens, who had gathered there to pay respect to the remains. The bell of the engine, and the bells of the churches in the city were tolled, and all together the scene was impressive and solemn, evincing the high estimation in which the deceased was held by his fellow citizens. A procession was formed and accompanied the remains to the residence of his family in Lynde Street.

From Lynde Street, Henry Merritt's family, friends, and well-wishers brought him to Harmony Grove Cemetery where he was buried (see p. 210). Following Merritt's death, the Sons of Union Veterans named a training camp for him, along with the "Merritt Triangle" at the head of

Right: Mail from the Lieut. Col. Henry Merritt Camp, 1893.

Winter Street where veterans placed a memorial to the 23rd Regiment in 1905 (photo, p. 87). Earlier, in 1886, the Lieut. Col. Henry Merritt Camp and Salem's Sons of Veterans erected a monument in Greenlawn Cemetery in honor of Merritt and the Civil War dead (photo, p. 204).

➡ *Continue along Lynde Street to Sewall Street.*

Site of Fort Naumkeag and Blockhouses
Present-day Lynde and Sewall Streets
The early colonial fort in this location, active from 1629–unknown, had eight guns to defend the fledgling community against attacks from Native Americans and the Canadian French. In those days, the fort and blockhouses would have had multiple views of an enemy approach by water. The Fort Pitt Society, owners of the Fort Pitt Blockhouse in Virginia, describe blockhouses as:

…most likely derived from the German word blochaus which means "a house which blocks a pass." Blockhouses were almost entirely an American innovation as they were mainly used on the frontier as a way to defend European settlers from Native American Indian attacks. While blockhouses were commonly stand-alone structures used by settlers for defense and/or shelter, they could also be found as part of larger fortifications. Similar to redoubts, blockhouses could take many different shapes and be constructed out of many different materials.

Another unidentified source explains that a blockhouse:

…is a small fortification, usually consisting of one or more rooms with loopholes, allowing its defenders to fire in various directions. It usually refers to an isolated fort in the form of a single building, serving as a defensive strong point against any enemy that does not possess siege equipment or, in modern times, artillery.

➡ *Turn left on Sewall Street and walk through the Sewall Street parking lot. Turn left on Essex Street.*

Site of Crombie's Tavern

Corner of Essex and Crombie Streets

In 1805, under Capt. John Saunders, the Salem Light Infantry was organized and made its first parade through Salem on July 4. The *Salem Gazette* reported that "the performance was exceedingly correct and spirited, and afforded a presage of the importance of the young corps, should that awful crisis in our country ever arrive (which heaven avert) when the peaceful citizen must repair to the field of arms and blood."

The Infantry celebrated its founding each year at Crombie's Tavern with a banquet that was "always attended by the most distinguished personages." They answered the alarm calls of 1812 and were the first volunteer company in America to provide itself with an encampment, thanks to tents captured off a British ship by a Salem privateer. During the Civil War, the Infantry became known as the Salem Zoaves (see pp. 309-10).

Site of Mechanic Hall

285 Essex Street at Crombie Street

Chas. S. Osgood and H. M. Batchelder in *Historical Sketches of Salem* wrote: "Mechanic Hall is the largest and finest in the city ... It was built in 1839 by the Mechanic Hall Corporation, and

Ticket to a Salem Light Infantry dinner held at Mechanic Hall in 1845. *Courtesy of John Hardy Wright.*

Stereo view of Mechanic Hall, ca. 1880. The building burned down in 1905.

in 1870 was enlarged and entirely remodelled. Its seating capacity is 1,093, and the stage is well adapted and furnished with good scenery for theatrical purposes. The interior of the hall is neat and beautiful, and its furnishings are in the most approved modern design. The hall has a very fine concert organ, built by J. H. Wilcox & Co., of Boston...."

Mechanic Hall was a popular event venue, including for military occasions. On November 6, 1886, it was the site of an impressive dinner following the dedication of Salem's Civil War Monument at Greenlawn Cemetery. Festivities had started that day at about 1:00 p.m. with a 500-man parade formed up on Salem Common and led by the local GAR and the Salem Cadet Band. They proceded from the Common to Greenlawn Cemetery for the dedication ceremony. At its conclusion, the crowd made its way to Mechanic Hall, where they feasted on a sumptuous dinner and enjoyed toasts and speeches. In one speech, Cdr. D. P. Purbeck of the Sons of Veterans, Lieut. Col. Henry Merritt Camp, No. 8, stated:

Of those who participated ... the lessons contained need not be urged, but upon the generation which has grown up since, they should be impressed. We were wrong in the very beginning. In 1776 good men established a government. God meant that it should be of all the people, by all the people, and for all the people, and we did not do it. We made a beginning, and a good beginning, but it was not a perfect work. For at the end of 80 years, we found ourselves with twice as many in bondage as we had numbered when we broke the British yoke, and we needed Gettysburg to complete the work of Bunker Hill. Bunker Hill was the promise; Gettysburg was the fulfillment.

Soldiers' Monument,
Greenlawn Cemetery
(see pp. 204-6).

➡ *Walk down Essex Street to Washington Street. Cross over Washington Street and turn left.*

Salem City Hall

93 Washington Street
When Salem became a city in 1836, Mayor Leverett Saltonstall and a committee began to plan a new City Hall. Designed by Richard Bond of Boston, the building opened to the public in 1838. Architectural historian Bryant F. Tolles describes it as "an outstanding example in granite of a restrained and pleasantly proportioned Greek Revival civic structure."

Salem City Hall, decorated with patriotic bunting and flags for Salem's Tercentennary Celebration in 1926. (Salem was established in 1626.)

If City Hall is open while you're walking by, step inside to see military-related items. These include portraits of President George Washington (see pp. 90-94 on his visit to Salem), the Marquis de Lafayette (see pp. 176-83 on his two visits to Salem), Gen. Henry Kemble Oliver (see pp. 172-73), and Gen. Phil H. Sheridan (see pp. 115-16). You will also see three plaques:

- A memorial to the USS *Maine* made from metal recovered from the ship, presumably by a Salem man;
- Another given by the crew of the USS *Salem* in 1909 to commemorate their visit to the City during Old Home Week (see pp. 223-29);
- A third to honor Salem veterans who served during the Persian Gulf War, dedicated on December 7, 1991, on the 50th anniversary of Pearl Harbor. *(Source: Salem.com/city-clerk.)*

➡ *Retrace your steps to the intersection of Washington and Essex Streets.*

Town House Square

Intersection of Washington and Essex Streets

Town House Square, named for the nearby Old Town Hall (or, House) was the "historic focal point for the city's economic, social, political, and religious life," according to Bryant F. Tolles. During wartime, it was the perfect location for fund drives to support war efforts and for parades when wars were over.

By July of 1918, Salem had fulfilled her Liberty Loan quota of $3,190,000 and her contribution of manpower [stood at] 1,641.

—Frances Robotti

Model "war chest" on display in Town House Square, 1918, for the country's Liberty Loan Drive. Most of the materials used appear to be wood covered with oil cloth, however, it is unclear how the lions were constructed.

Lapel pin for Salem's "war chest" fundraiser.

Rubber stamp for the campaign.

This part of Town House Square was known as "Tunnel Plaza." It was built in the 1880s by decking over roughly 40-50 feet of train tracks to create a tunnel. A group of downtown Salem merchants paid for the project to reduce the amount of smoke from the trains that permeated their businesses and offices.

Over the years, the City used this space for "all kinds of interesting things including the annual Christmas tree," according to life-long resident Nelson Dionne.

Note the Salem Train Depot in the background.

Press photo of Salem's World War I Red Cross fund drive in Town House Square, complete with thermometor and "Uncle Sam!"

Armistice Day Parade (duplicate image), held on November 11, 1919.

Two postcard views of Town House Square. Above: World War I era, when the building now owned by Rockafella's was the meeting house of the First Church in Salem; the church rented retail space on the first floor to provide income, and used the upper floors for services and offices; in 1924, when First Church merged with North Church, they sold the building to Daniel Low & Co., a popular jewelry and fine gifts store; below: looking up Washington Street toward the Tabernacle Church and the site of the current Salem Train Depot.

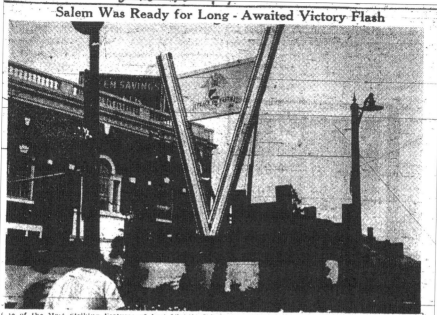

Salem Was Ready for Long - Awaited Victory Flash

One of the Most Striking Features of Last Night's Celebration Was the Dazzling "V" Sign That Blazed Above the Heads of the Thousands Who Thronged TownHouse Square. Towering Some 20 Feet Above the Tunnel, the Neon-Illuminated Shafts of Red, White, and Blue Brought Home the Inspiring Significance of Victory. The Emblem Atop the Huge "V" Bears the Legend "Peace On Earth"

Start of Celebration After Confirmation of Victory

Salem Evening News, August 15, 1945: This enormous "V" for Victory
was lit up in Town House Square once it was confirmed that
World War II had ended—and the celebrations began!

*Considering everything that happened during the war,
it's amazing how hard it is to find anything. No one
saved a damn thing.* —Nelson Dionne

➡ *Continue along Washington Street.*

Home of Joshua Ward

148 Washington Street
(The Merchant Inn)
Built between 1784 and 1788, this was the home of the wealthy ship owner Joshua Ward—and, YES!, George Washington really did sleep here! Bryant F. Tolles calls this building "Salem's oldest Federal high-style brick house, and one of the last surviving early waterfront mansions," because much of the land in this area is landfill. Where you are standing was originally part of Salem's waterfront; Ward built his mansion at the head of his wharf where he could watch his ships arrive carrying molasses

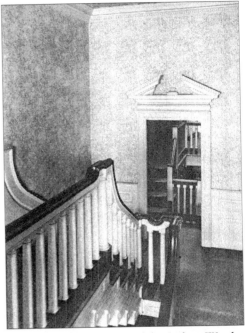

Postcard of the interior of the Joshua Ward House, ca. 1910. Note the exquisite carving created by the famous McIntire brothers of Salem.

(for rum), tea, pepper, spices, and silks from around the world.

Joshua Ward was one of the merchants in Salem who signed the "Welcome" letter to Gen. Thomas Gage when Gage assumed the (military) governorship of colonial Massachusetts in 1774. Ward and his fellow merchants hoped for many more peaceful—and highly lucrative—years of trade with England and her trading partners. Eventually, some of these men supported American independence (see "Loyalists in Salem," pp. 8-11).

Joshua Ward's son, Richard Ward, Esq., "espoused the popular cause with his father, and opposed the arbitrary measures of Parliament," Salem's Samuel Curwen wrote in his diary. Curwen continues: "He was a member of the committee of safety and protection during the entire period of the Revolution, and under the direction of Gen. Charles Lee constructed at the neck the fort bearing his name, for the defence of the harbor and town of Salem" (see pp. 281-88).

➡ *Continue along Washington Street.*

Site of the Old Salem Train Depot, and Riley Plaza

Margin, Norman, and Washington Streets

Since it opened in 1847 until its demise in 1954, the Salem Train Depot was where large crowds of Salem residents would say *Goodbye!* to loved ones heading off to war and, hopefully, *Welcome home!* to those who returned. The depot was also the site of ceremonial greetings when troops and military dignitaries visited Salem. Its impressive granite facade was designed by the famous Boston architect Gridley J. F. Bryant who was inspired by Gothic Revival architecture.

In 1854, the Salem City Guard received the Winthrop Light Guard of Boston "who were on a military excursion for drill and exercise," according a newspaper account. They were "escorted through the principal streets" of Salem, and "expressed themselves highly pleased with the courteous treatment they received" (see pp. 315-16 for more on the Salem City Guard).

The Salem City Guard escorting the Winthrop Light Guard of Boston.

On April 18, 1861, at the outbreak of the Civil War, the Salem Light Infantry marched from their Armory in the Phoenix Building (see p. 148) "to the Salem train depot, and boarded the train for Boston, to Faneuil Hall which was the gathering place for troops, and from there to the State House for orders," according to Frances Robotti in *Chronicles of Salem*. The SLI had been reassigned as the 8th Regiment and the "right flank company of skirmishes and designated as Company J." There was a huge public turnout to send them off.

Boston & Maine Railroad Depot, or, the "Old Salem Train Depot," ca. 1890.

Soldiers departed from the Depot during World Wars I and II as well. Each time, large crowds gathered to give them a proper send-off. The *Salem Evening News* of March 18, 1941, gave this account of men heading to war during World War II:

Salem sent 167 more of her most stalwart sons into the army today in answer to the nation's fifth draft call under the selective service act. It was the largest single group of draftees in history to go out of Salem. Never before, in any war, did so many leave at one time to answer the draft. They went oftener in World War days but never in such large numbers as today.

A crowd estimated as being between 1200 and 1500—relatives, friends and interested citizens, including many public officials—turned out to speed the

Salem Breaks Record by Sending 167 Into Service As Crowd Bids Farewell

SALEM'S DRAFTEES BOARD THE TRAIN FOR BOSTON
Just a Part of the Crowd Bidding the 167 Local Young Men Farewell As They Entered Special Cars Which Were to Take Them Into the Army For a Year or More of Training

Salem Evening News of March 18, 1941.

prospective soldiers on their way. Many gathered at Old Town Hall where the draftees reported to the local draft boards. Many more thronged the Salem Depot for a final farewell before the young men boarded special cars attached to the 7:29 train for Boston…

On the whole, the draftees were in good spirits. It was a gentlemanly and orderly group. Many had catches in their throats as they left. There were some tearful partings…

Mayor Edward A. Coffey, Rev. Chester G. Minton and members of the city government and school board were among those on hand. City Marshal

John C. Harkins and 20 police officers were on duty and there was a detail of 10 firemen, headed by Chief Arthur L. Flynn and Deputy Chief James P. Buckley. One of the police cruisers, equipped with a loud speaker, was on hand and played martial airs at Old Town Hall and at the depot.

A total of 81 Salem men have gone in the four previous draft quotas. Today's group raises to 248 the number who will have been inducted into the army since the first quota left on Nov. 20.

Stereo view (detail) of the Train Depot, ca. 1865. The Eastern Railroad train shed is to the right of the depot. Today, much of this land is Riley Plaza.

Riley Plaza

The site of the Salem Train Depot is named for John Phillip Riley of Salem, who served as a Landsman in the U. S. Navy during the Spanish-American War. Riley's ship, the USS *Nashville*, was tasked with interrupting underwater Spanish communication lines off the coast of Cuba as part of America's efforts to free Cuba from Spanish control. A lengthy account of his bravery appears on pages 141-42.

Riley's Medal of Honor is the only one associated with Salem. His name also appears in the "Walkway of Heroes" at Armory Memorial Park (see p. 112-14).

Salem's Medal of Honor Recipients

Excerpted, with edits, from "A Look Back at Salem's Medal of Honor Recipients" by Jerome Curley, Salem Patch, Nov. 10, 2012.

Salem is noteworthy as having had five Congressional Medals of Honor (MOH) bestowed on residents over the years since the medal was instituted in 1862. While four of the five were not accredited to Salem, these men were all born here.

Robert Buffum, Civil War (1828-1871)

The very first Medals of Honor were given to a group of Union soldiers who volunteered for a dangerous mission behind enemy lines during the Civil War. Among these men was Robert Buffum, who was born in Salem in 1828. He was the son of William and Mary (Chace) Buffum. He had enlisted in the 21st Ohio Regiment giving his home as Gilead, Ohio. He was among the group captured and held prisoner by the Confederates until they were exchanged. Robert Buffum was the third man to receive the Medal of Honor in the very first Medal of Honor ceremony.

[Buffum's life after the war took a tragic turn toward alcohol and mental illness.] In 1871, while still incarcerated [in a mental institution in upstate New York], he committed suicide and was buried in an unmarked grave on the property. It was not known that he had been a Medal of Honor recipient. After extensive research the Medal of Honor Society, which is dedicated to honoring and preserving the memory of deceased recipients, identified his resting place. In 1995, at a special ceremony with family members in attendance, a plaque was placed on his resting place. The gravesite is now maintained by volunteers. Robert Buffum's MOH is accredited to Gilead, Ohio, by virtue of his having lived there at enlistment. This raid was immortalized in the 1956 hit Disney film, *The Great Locomotive Chase* where the Robert Buffum character is featured.

Thomas Atkinson, Civil War (1824-1864)

Thomas Atkinson was born in Salem in 1824. At eighteen, he shipped out of the town as a petty officer in the U.S. Navy. He was assigned to the U.S. Frigate *Congress* which was then stationed in the Mediterranean and South America … His most memorable battle was the one for Mobile Bay, a fortified harbor. In order to enter and engage the rebel forces of gunboats and ironclads, ships had to run a gauntlet of the guns from the forts protecting the harbor. The USS *Richmond* was part of a fleet of ships under Admiral Farragut who ran the gauntlet of guns through a narrow channel that was surrounded by mines then called torpedoes.

It was in this greatest naval battle of the Civil War that Admiral Farragut made his famous declaration, "Damn the torpedoes!" as his ships were forced to sail through the minefield. Throughout this day-long battle, Yeoman Atkinson was in charge of supplying the rifle ammunition for the guns on the *Richmond*. He did so even at the height of battle when the ironclad ships as well as the forts continued to pound the *Richmond*. The citation read at the medal ceremony commended Atkinson for his coolness and energy in supplying the rifle ammunition, which was under his sole charge, in the action in Mobile Bay on 5 August 1864 … Unfortunately, little is known about Atkinson after he left the Navy. The whereabouts of his grave remains a mystery, so no suitable memorial has been established according to the Medal of Honor Society. Thomas Atkinson's Medal of Honor is accredited to Massachusetts.

[Editor's note: The Salem Veterans Council dedicated a memorial to Thomas Atkinson on Veterans Day 2015, at Greenlawn Cemetery.]

Thomas Lyons, Civil War (1838-1862)

Thomas Lyons was born in Salem in 1838. In 1862 he was a seaman in the U.S. Navy on board the USS *Pensacola*, a steamship, as it took part in the attack on Forts Jackson and

St. Phillip. Both forts were situated on the Mississippi River protecting access to the important Confederate city of New Orleans, Louisiana. In addition to the forts, there were a number of Confederate ships defending the largest city of the Confederacy. An additional defense was a large chain across the river. In order to break the chain, ships would be forced to slow down or even stop directly under the forts' powerful guns.

The Union plan of attack was to use mortar barges to bombard the forts, then steam past after the chain was broken by Union ironclad ships racing forward. This would allow the main ships to enter. The mortar barrage, while intense and sustained, did little to damage the forts' ability to defend the waters. After two days of this, Admiral Farragut (who hadn't had much faith in the mortars) ordered his ironclads to move forward and break the chain so his ships could then proceed to engage the Confederate fleet…

The USS *Pensacola*, with its 18-foot draft and top speed of 9.5 knots, was [tasked] with getting through the chain gap. Seaman Thomas Lyons was secured to the port chain holding the lead weight calling out depths as they proceeded through the narrow gap in the chain. They commenced the attack under cover of darkness at 3:00 a.m. Since they were so close to the shore they were quickly seen by the shore batteries whose personnel proceeded to rain fire down on the ships. At the same time the rebel gunboats also opened fire and attempted to ram several of the Union ships as they made for the gap. Lyons stayed on the outside of the ship even during this murderous assault and luckily didn't get hit. After battling for hours the Union forces overpowered the Confederate Navy, dealing them a fatal blow while opening access to New Orleans.

For his bravery, his citation for the Medal of Honor read that he "served as seaman on board the U.S.S. *Pensacola* in the attack on Forts Jackson and St. Philip, 24 April 1862. Carrying out his duties throughout the din and roar of the battle, Lyons never once erred in his brave performance. Lashed outside of that vessel, on the port-sheet chain, with the lead in hand to lead the ship past the forts, Lyons never flinched, although under a heavy fire from the forts and rebel gunboats." After leaving the Navy there is little known about the rest of Lyons' life. It is believed that he died in 1904, but no grave or memorial is listed for him. His Medal of Honor is accredited to Massachusetts.

Samuel Bowden, "Indian" Wars (1846-1870)

Samuel Bowden (or Boden) was born in Salem in 1846 … [and served] as a corporal in the 6th U.S. Cavalry during the [so-called] Indian wars. In 1870, in Northern Texas, there were a number of battles between U.S. soldiers and Native Americans brought on by raids on white settlements in former tribal lands.

In July 1870 a notable battle took place at Little Wichita River, Texas. In response to a raid on a mail stagecoach sixty soldiers went in pursuit of the raiders only to realize they were facing more than twice as many warriors armed with rifles. A bloody battle ensued with many casualties. The cavalry was barely able to escape … Even after the main force of the Kiowa warriors had returned to the reservation, raids continued. In response … a force of twenty-two cavalrymen … left Fort Richardson in early October in pursuit of the raiding war party. On October 5 they discovered a Kiowa war party camp at the Little Wichita River and engaged the enemy. In this fierce battle Private Samuel Bowden, along with four other men, was later honored with the Medal of Honor for "Gallantry during the pursuit and fight with Indians."

Little is known of Samuel Bowden after his time in the Cavalry. The Medal of Honor Society that seeks to keep Medal of Honor memories alive through suitable memorials has not yet been able to identify Bowden's date of death nor his burial place. Bowden is listed as a Medal of Honor recipient from Massachusetts, rather than from a specific city or town, because so little information is known.

John P. Riley, Spanish-American War (1877-1950)

Salem's most recent—and best known—recipient of the Medal of Honor was John Phillip Riley ... [who] was not born in Salem but became a long-time resident. He enlisted in the Navy from Massachusetts ... as a sailor on the USS *Nashville*, participating in a number of battles during the war. Most notable for him was the Battle of Cienfuegos, Cuba. While battles raged with Spain's fleet in Manila (Philippines), other American ships started a blockade around Cuba on April 21, 1898. They quickly captured several merchant ships. The warships USS *Marblehead* and USS *Nashville* were patrolling a large area on the southern coast, including the busy merchant port of Cienfuegos, when the first breach of the blockade took place on April 26. The Spanish liner *Montserrat* was able to unload supplies and troops in Cienfuegos. Ten days later they again breached the blockade, leaving the port for Spain.

Cienfuegos was a well-defended port with garrisons of troops, fortifications and switch-controlled floating mines in the harbor. Captain McCall of the USS *Marblehead* came up with a daring plan to isolate the port and weaken the Spanish war effort by cutting the communication cables running along the harbor floor. By May 10, he had identified how the cable had been placed and thought it was possible to use grappling hooks to raise the cable and cut it. Unfortunately, the cables ran close to shore and well within shooting range of the soldier and shore fortifications. Realizing the danger involved but feeling it was worth the risk, he and his fellow Captain Maynard from the USS *Nashville* asked for volunteers.

Twenty-six men volunteered from each ship. Forty sailors and twelve marines in all signed on for their first real action of the war. The plan was that boatloads of sailors and marines would offer covering fire while another group of sailors would use grappling hooks to pull the cable up and have it cut by the ship's blacksmith. At 5:00 a.m., the men were transported from their ships to a steam launch that brought them into the harbor. There, small boats were launched with the sailors and marines … The Spanish opened fire on the boats and men, wounding several and killing one. For almost three hours the men endured heavy seas, intense fire … and shells from the fortifications that practically lifted the boats out of the water … Eyewitnesses recounted how it was non-stop, with shells flying overhead and all around them while shooting was uninterrupted on both sides …

They succeeded in cutting the cables, then towing the cables further out to sea where more cable could be removed to hamper any repair … By the end of the action four men had been killed and seven wounded. For their courage and tenacity, all the volunteers received the Medal of Honor. Each citation read the same for the 52 men: *"On board the (U.S.S.* Nashville *or U.S.S.* Marblehead*) during the cutting of the cable leading from Cienfuegos, Cuba, 11 May 1898. Facing the heavy fire of the enemy, he set an example of extraordinary bravery and coolness throughout this action."*

John P. Riley (spelled Rilley on his medal) was one of the Navy volunteers from that action who received the Medal of Honor on May 11, 1898. After discharge from the Navy in 1899, Riley returned to Salem where he raised a family and worked for the City until his retirement in 1944. He was very active in Veterans' Affairs and a frequent participant in parades in the City and state. He proudly displayed a piece of the Cienfuegos cable in his home on Warner Street. John Riley passed away on November 16, 1950, at the age of 72. His burial was at Harmony Grove Cemetery. Riley Plaza was named in his honor in 1959.

John Riley's Medal of Honor is the only one accredited to Salem.

Postscript: John P. Riley's grandson, of the same name, died on June 20, 2019. He was a Navy veteran, and a Salem firefighter for thirty-seven years. He, too, is buried in Harmony Grove Cemetery.

Side and rear view of the new Salem Post Office under construction in 1932.

Salem Post Office and Federal Building
2 Margin Street
Built in 1932-1933, Bryant F. Tolles calls Salem's new post office "without question Salem's finest Colonial Revival-style civic structure." In 1936, Naval Communications Reserve personnel set up their offices in this federal building "to train men in communications, with a specialty in the radio branch," according to the *Salem Evening News* of December 9, 1938. The unit in Salem was the 7th Unit of the 3rd Section of the First Naval District in Boston. Lieut. Clinton R. Story of Salem was a member of the unit. The *News* continues: An "object of great import to the naval reserves is their pledge to co-operate to the fullest extent in peacetime duties with such organizations as the American Red Cross, the police and other groups especially during the time of floods and other disasters." During World War II, the building housed recruiting stations for the Army, Navy, Marines, and Coast Guard. Salem's Draft Board met there as well.

➡ *Continue along Margin Street.*

Site of the Home of Harriet M. Maxwell

12 Margin Street

As a twenty-seven-year old widow, Harriet M. Maxwell (1851-1931) emigrated to America from England in 1878. She graduated from Salem Hospital's nursing school in 1886, and went to work as a private nurse in the City where she quickly became known as "one of the best nurses in this section, whose skill has been the means of saving many a life, alleviating pain, and whose cheerfulness has transformed the sick room into a haven of rest" according to a history of Salem Hospital. After the USS *Maine* was blown up, Maxwell enlisted as an Army nurse. She was assigned to Co. I, 10th U. S. Cavalry, and stationed first at Montauk Point, Long Island, and later at Fortress Monroe, Virginia, "where she nursed back to health many of the boys who were wounded at El Caney, San Juan and Siboney," according to a story in the *Boston Globe* (11/19/1926). For her services, Harry E. Webber notes in his book *Greater Salem in the Spanish-American War*, Maxwell "won the commendation of the War Department and the personal thanks of President William McKinley."

In 1929, Maxwell "was admitted to active membership in the United Spanish War Veterans ... at a special meeting of Capt. Jacob C. R. Peabody Camp, held at the Beckford St. headquarters," as reported in the *Boston Globe* (2/25/1929). The story notes that "by her skill and personality [Maxwell] won fame. She enjoyed a long acquaintance with Ex-President Theodore Roosevelt and was personally commended for her work by Ex-President Harding. The ceremonies were the most impressive to have been conducted by the United States War Veterans in this section for some time, and were witnessed by a large audience. She is the third woman and the second Army nurse in Massachusetts to receive this distinction which, she said, was one of the pleasantest in her career."

The Harriet M. Maxwell Auxilliary No. 27, USWV did well. The January 1911 edition of *The National Guard Magazine* noted that No. 27 was "in flourishing condition" and about to hold a fair and a turkey supper "for the benefit of its treasury." That year, Maxwell was No. 27's "Conductor." Along with having Salem's USWV Auxiliary named for her, Maxwell was a charter member of the Spanish War Nurses' Association and the Army Nurses' Association. "Mother Maxwell," as she was known, spent her final years living in the "Home for Aged Women" (now, Brookhouse) on Derby Street.

Other nurses from Salem Hospital included Julia May Leach and Lillian G. Lane (see p. 150-51 on Salem Hospital).

➡ *Retrace your steps to the intersection of Essex and Washington Streets. Walk down the Pedestrian Mall to the plaque on the rear of Rockafella's.*

Site of the First Church in Salem
231 Essex Street (Daniel Low Building/Rockafella's)
As one of the only large, public structures in any given colonial town, early church buildings, called meeting houses, were used as military watch houses and places of assembly. The simple, wooden structure that was the first meeting house in Salem would have been no different.

➡ *Continue along the Pedestrian Mall. Turn right on Central Street.*

Site of Central Hall
4-4 1/2 Central Street (The Trolley Depot)
Central Hall was built in 1869 and was "well adapted for small parties and entertainment," according to *Historical Sketch of Salem* by Osgood and Batchelder. It was also one of the properties leased by Post 34 of the GAR in the 1870s. They met Tuesday evenings on this site before

Central Hall by Frank Cousins, one of Salem's most important photographers and retailers. *Courtesy of the Digital Commonwealth.*

moving to their final home at 17 St. Peter Street. The Salem Light Infantry also used the hall for meetings and events (see pp. 322-28).

Old London Coffee House

15 Central Street (Red's Sandwich Shop)

This ca. 1766 house, originally a residence (posssibly for Joseph Scott), was the meeting place of pro-independence organizers at a time of extreme distrust and tension between those who were loyal to Great Britain and those who were not. Heated discussions must have taken place near the great fireplace, especially with the growing British presence in town.

As noted in an earlier section, the military governor, General Thomas Gage, moved the General Court (government) to Salem in 1774 where he had the support of many Salem merchants. He was welcomed and feted (by some). But when Gage tried to reconvene the General Court at Salem's Court House, his secretary was refused entrance and Gage was unable to conduct business. In July, he sent two companies of the 64th Regiment of Foot to Salem to assert British power.

Color postcard (detail) of the Old London Coffee House, ca. 1970.

Ninety representatives of the earlier Massachusetts General Court met secretly in Salem on October 5, 1774, to form an Assembly. They chose John Hancock of Boston as president. On October 7, they voted to become a Provincial Congress with "sovereign powers" and quickly adjourned for meetings in Cambridge and Concord as Salem was becoming overrun with loyalists.

The eminent historian Robert S. Rantoul Jr. concluded many years later that "October 7th then was the birthday and Salem Town House the birthplace of the Commonwealth of Massachusetts."

Which planning meetings took place in the Old London Coffee House? We will never know for sure—but it's safe to say that some did!

Salem Police Station with the statue of Father Mathew, Patron Saint of Temperance, in the foreground, ca. 1920. The statue is now on Hawthorne Boulevard.

Old Salem Police Station

17 Central Street

Built in 1913, Bryant Tolles calls this structure "a good example of the Colonial Revival style in public building design ... inspired by Salem's magnificent Georgian Colonial and Federal architectural heritage." It originally housed the City Marshal (or, the Chief of Police), the Police Department, and the First District Court of Essex County.

During World War II, while police officers were serving in the military, almost three hundred Salem citizens signed up to become Auxiliary Police. "Everyone wanted to be one," according to retired Salem police officer Nelson Dionne. After the war, the Police Department displayed a temporary sign

Photo by Leland Tilford of the sign recognizing Salem Police Officers who served during World War II.

acknowledging the service of its officers. Later, during the nuclear war scares of the 1950s, this building was used as a Civil Defense shelter (see pp. 42-56 on Civil Defense).

➡ *Walk to the end of Central Street and look straight ahead to 41 Lafayette Street (the old Salem Laundry building) at the intersection of Lafayette, Central, and Front Streets.*

Phenix Hall and Central Street, showing Fr. Mathews Statue, Salem, Mass.

Color postcard of the Phoenix Building with the statue of Father Mathew in front, ca. 1905. At one time, the building housed the Salvation Army, later, the Salem Laundry.

Site of the Phoenix Building and Phoenix Hall
41 Lafayette Street
As far back as the 1860s, the Phoenix Building was used as an armory by the Salem Light Infantry, Salem Mechanic Light Infantry, and Salem City Guard. It was replaced with the current building in 1905—the first concrete building in Salem. By 1905, the Salem Light Infantry had already relocated its armory to the Franklin Building on the corner of Essex Street and Washington Square (photo, p. 152), joining the Second Corps of Cadets who were already renting space in the building for their own armory. The Salem Mechanic Light Infantry disbanded in 1889. The Salem City Guard had become part of the 40th Regiment, Massachusetts Infantry Volunteers.

➤ *From Central Street, turn left and walk up Charter Street. Continue to the Old Burying Point, or, the Charter Street Cemetery. Along the way, you will walk past 53 Charter Street, the home of the Peabody sisters—Elizabeth, Mary, and Sophia. Nathaniel Hawthorne courted Sophia here, and made the house famous as the "Grimshawe House" in two of his books. Elizabeth Peabody's account of General Lafayette's 1824 visit appears on page 182.*

Old Burying Point/Charter Street Cemetery
51 Charter Street

Started in 1637 on a point of land overlooking the South River (which, at the time, was much larger than it is now), this is Salem's oldest cemetery and the burying place of some of its earliest and most notable residents. As such, the City has a long-standing request of visitors to treat the cemetery with the respect it deserves. In 2019, as part of restoration and improvement efforts, the City Council voted to close this heavily-trafficked site for the month of October.

Most of the men buried here would have served in the colonial militia. Among the more well-known "residents" buried here are Governor Simon Bradstreet (his body was later moved), Judges John Hathorne and Bartholomew Gedney of Salem Witch Trials fame, and Samuel McIntire, the famous architect-carver whose work is referenced throughout this book.

Postcard of the "Charter Street Burial Ground," ca. 1905.

➥ *Continue along Charter Street.*

Site of the Salem Hospital

31 Charter Street

Capt. John Bertram (a ship captain, not military) purchased this three-story residential brick mansion in 1873 for the purpose of starting a hospital. The Salem Hospital, or, "City Hospital," first opened its doors in October of 1874—making it one of America's earliest hospitals. Not only did the hospital care for the "sick and disabled seamen of this port," it also provided training for surgeons. In 1879, "Miss D. Duff" founded a training school for nurses—the seventh in the country—according to a published history of Salem Hospital.

During the Spanish-American War, three nursing school graduates volunteered for service: Julia May Leach, Lillian G. Lane, and Harriet M. Maxwell (see pp. 144-45). At the same time, the facilities of the hospital "were placed at the disposal of the Commonwealth and the Massachusetts Volunteer Aid Association," according to Frances Robotti. In 1898, ten soldiers, many ill with typhoid fever contracted from the hot climate in which they served, were sent to Salem.

Color postcard of Salem Hospital, ca. 1905, showing a rare side view.

During World War I, when the American Red Cross sent out the call for over forty thousand nurses to work overseas and in this country, Salem nurses responded. They included: Marion P. Montague, U. S. Government nurse; Bessie G. Deering, Fort Devens, Massachusetts; Emma C. MacDermaid, Dansville, New York; Elizabeth M. Dickinson, Camp Dix, New Jersey; Mary C. Sherry, Dansville, New York; Gertrude L. Bastien, Camp Hancock, Augusta, Georgia.

During World War II, the hospital's Dr. Walter G. Phippen was appointed to the Commonwealth's Committee on Preparedness. He also represented the Salem area when President Roosevelt issued an executive order in 1941 creating the Procurement and Assignment Service for physicians, dentists, and veterinarians. Salem Hospital was asked to be one of ten hospitals in the state to organize an affili-ated base hospital unit with ten doctors enrolled in the Public Health Service. It would be activated only in case of need. In 1943, the hospital was approved for the newly-formed Cadet Nursing Corps.

The Great Salem Fire of 1914 damaged the hospital building severely enough that the trustees decided not to rebuild. Instead, they constructed a new, brick building on a hill just outside of town on Highland Avenue—where Salem Hospital is today.

➡ *Walk to the end of Charter Street and turn left onto Hawthorne Boulevard. Walk up Hawthorne Boulevard to the Hawthorne Hotel (and stop in for a bite to eat at The Tavern, overlooking Salem Common!).*

Site of the Franklin Building, Hawthorne Hotel, and Site of the Now & Then Clubhouse

18 Washington Square West

For many years, rooms in the Franklin Building (razed in 1924 to make room for the hotel) were used as an armory by the Second Corps of Cadets and the Salem Light Infantry. The building was owned by, and home to, the Salem Marine Society, an organization founded in 1766 "to provide relief for disabled and aged members and their families," according to their website. Some of the Society's early members were privateers during the Revolutionary War and the War of 1812, including Jonathan Haradan (see p. 153-54).

The Hawthorne Hotel opened its doors on July 23, 1925, and quickly became the go-to place for gatherings, meetings, dinners, and special events—including military. The creation of the hotel parking lot meant the demise of the Now & Then Clubhouse, another popular site for military and civic events.

— End of trail. ★

Stereo view of the Second Corps of Cadets in front of the Franklin Building, ca. 1900. The Salem Light Infantry used the building for their armory as well.

Photograph postcard of the Now & Then Clubhouse on Essex Street. The Club, organized in 1886, met "now and then" for lectures and gatherings. The building was also used for military social events. Today, this is the hotel parking lot.

★ Sites to Visit by Neighborhood ★

~ McIntire District ~

START: Salem Regional Visitor Center

2 New Liberty Street (across from the Museum Place Parking Garage and Peabody Essex Museum). Here you will see an exhibit on the Second Corps of Cadets and the Salem Armory, films and displays about Essex County, find restrooms, and a gift shop.

➥ *From the Visitor Center, walk up the Essex Street Pedestrian Mall until you reach the end, at Washington Street (about two blocks). Cross Washington Street, and continue along the left side of Essex Street.*

Site of the Home of Jonathan Haradan

299 Essex Street

Jonathan Haradan (1744-1803) first joined the Revolutionary War effort in 1778. That year, he and many other ship captains from Salem and the North Shore helped drive the British out of Newport, Rhode Island. The following spring, Haradan was given the command of the *General Pickering*, a privateer, and his career took off.

Jonathan Haradan

In their book *Maritime Salem in the Age of Sail*, the National Park Service describes Haradan as "Salem's most successful and famous privateer captain during the Revolution. [He] was celebrated for his resourcefulness, icy calmness under fire, and the absolute loyalty of those under him. He never lost a ship, and was said to have captured more than sixty vessels."

Just inside the door of the Korean restaurant on this site you will find the beautifully restored bronze plaque that used to hang on the outside of the building. The owners of Bon Chon Chicken wished to protect it from the elements for us to enjoy today and for future generations.

Early twentieth century Salem historian James Duncan Phillips describes Haradan as "one of the great characters of the Revolution, and not even John Paul Jones or John Manley had greater claim to clean, cool, courage and intrepid daring than he." When the *Pickering* and her prizes were captured in the West Indies, Haradan assumed command of the *Julius Caesar*. All told, Phillips writes, "Haradan alone is credited with capturing over one thousand guns from the enemy, and ... between two and three thousand prisoners. Few victories of the war could show such results for a captain and one hundred and fifty men" (for more on privateers, see Index).

➡ *Continue on the left side of Essex Street until you reach Summer Street/Route 114. You are now in the McIntire Historic District, named for Samuel McIntire, Salem's most famous architect-carver who resided at 31 Summer Street (the house no longer stands). His stunning late-eighteenth and early-nineteenth century work may be found throughout Salem's historic districts and at the Peabody Essex Museum. Turn left on Summer Street.*

Brig. Gen. Frederick West Lander

5 Summer Street (to the left of #7 and #9)
An engineer and surveyor before the war, Frederick West Lander (1822-1862) distinguished himself in the Civil War, first as a spy, next in the southern states as an assistant to General George B. McClellan, and then as a soldier in his own right in such battles as the Battle of Rich Mountain, Edward's Ferry (where he was wounded in the leg), Hancock, and Blooming Gap.

Lander died from his wounds in 1862. Two funerals were held for him: one in Washington, D. C., and the second in his hometown once the Eastern Railroad transported his body from Boston's North Station to Salem. The City spent $722.72 on the funeral—not an unusual sum, as Lieut. Col. Henry Merrit's funeral cost $757.20 (see pp. 122-24).

The expenses for Lander's funeral included those for telegrams ($2), printing, ($9.50), Eastern Railroad Co. fares ($9.50), carriages ($100), hack hire for the committee ($1), "Express" (.75), extra police ($39), loans of goods ($81.17), funeral charges ($10.50), decorations ($33), upholstering ($10), Army caps ($10), tolling bells ($8), hoisting flags ($2), church services ($8), Boston Brass Band music ($76), Salem Cadets' collation ($25), Salem City Guard's collation ($6), Essex

House board and collation of escort ($200), Salem Light Artillery salute ($50), cartridges ($3.88), Salem Light Infantry collation ($20), and labor ($15.62).

The funeral, like Merritt's, attracted thousands, the crowd eventually making its way to Broad Street Cemetery where Lander is buried. His wife, the English-born stage actress Jean Margaret Davenport, served as a Union Army nurse in South Carolina for two years after her husband's death.

In 1885, the GAR named its new hall in neighboring Lynn, Massachusetts, the General Frederick W. Lander Post No. 5, Grand Army of the Republic. The hall, one of many such structures across the country, was built by members of the GAR as a memorial to the Union Army veterans of the Civil War. On May 7, 1979, the building was added to the National Register of Historic Places. The hall in Lynn is now the Grand Army of the Republic Museum and is currently being restored.

➡ *Return to Essex Street and cross over to North Street/Route 114.*

Home of Nathaniel Bowditch

9 North Street (originally located around the corner at 312 Essex Street)
This was the residence of the great Salem mathematician, astronomer, and navigator Nathaniel Bowditch (1773-1838) from 1811 to 1823. Bowditch's technical book, *The New American Practical Navigator,* published in 1802, has assisted the U. S. Navy in achieving military victories in every war since the War of 1812. Referred to as "The Bowditch," the book is still used today by the Navy and Coast Guard. According to the National Park Service, Bowditch also "invented or improved many navigational instruments," some of which are on display at the Peabody Essex Museum.

After World War II, "times were tough for a lot of people," says Nelson Dionne, and the building was used to house veterans. Luckily, while the City was making plans to widen Essex Street and demolish the house, Historic Salem, Inc. (HSI) acted quickly and moved the Bowditch House to North Street. Today, it houses HSI's offices.

➡ *Walk back along North Street to The Witch House/Jonathan Corwin House and cross over Essex Street to the small pocket park with the flag pole.*

Captain William Driver Memorial Park

Corner of Essex and Summer Streets (Witch House Park)

This park was dedicated in 1968 to honor the first person to call the American flag "Old Glory." That was Salem ship captain William Driver (1803-1886), who proclaimed the name in 1831 upon receiving a ship's flag made by "Salem girls" for his birthday and first command, the *Charles Doggett*. This Memorial exists thanks to Captain Henry C. Nichols, a U. S. Navy veteran and Salem native. Wanting to involve Salem school children in fundraising for the park, Nichols, a scholar on the life of Rev. William Bentley of Salem's East Church, visited the Bentley Elementary School in 1967 to tell the students about William Driver, Old Glory, and why the American flag is so important. In a letter to the editor of the *Salem Evening News*, Nichols wrote:

> *Dr. Bentley was very patriotic and loved children ... His greatest happiness would be in the interest that the children of his school showed in patriotism and love of the American Flag. Finally, his greatest reward would have been that the children of the Bentley School contributed 100% to the Captain William Driver Fund for "Old Glory."*

On a platform in front of the Witch House/Corwin House, Charlie L'Heureux of Salem presents Jennie Volpe, the wife of Governor John A. Volpe (seated, left), with flowers at the dedication of the Driver Memorial. Assisting him is Captain Henry C. Nichols, who led the effort to create the Memorial. Nichols was also Executive Director of Salem's Boys & Girls Club for many years.

By the time the Memorial was dedicated on June 9, 1968, Captain Nichols had inspired thousands of children to donate pennies, nickels, and dimes to the Memorial Fund. According to an account in the *Salem Evening News*, "more than 10,000 public and parochial school children" participated in the ceremony to hoist a replica of Old Glory (with twenty-four stars and a ship's anchor in the blue field) and two smaller flags—the Pine Tree Flag (the 1775 symbol of the Massachusetts Militia), and a 15-star ship's flag like the one that would have been flown by the frigate USS *Essex* (see pp. 276-79).

Massachusetts Governor John A. Volpe was the keynote speaker; Salem Mayor Francis X. Collins and former Mayor Edward A. Coffey attended, along with Clifton Abbott Sibley of South Hamilton, a direct descendant of Driver.

The Memorial on Opening Day, with replicas of Old Glory, the Pine Tree Flag, and the USS *Essex's* ship's flag.

Our thanks to Ben Arlander, Captain Nichols' great, great grandson, for sharing these family photographs.

Before making his address, Gov. Volpe presented Capt. Nichols with a citation of gratitude from the Commonwealth of Massachusetts.

A Flag, a Feud, and an Abundance of Falsehoods: The True Story of "Old Glory"

In 1831, a group of "Salem girls" presented twenty-one-year-old William Driver of Salem with a massive ship's flag when he assumed his first ship command: the *Charles Doggett*. Organized by Driver's mother, Ruth Metcalf Driver, the girls were proud of William Driver's rapid rise in Salem's lucrative maritime trade since he had first apprenticed as a blacksmith's assistant and cabin boy. The flag's blue field contained twenty-four stars, one for each state, and a ship's anchor in the upper left corner.

Various apocryphal (not quite historical) accounts report that Driver named his ship's flag "Old Glory" on March 17, 1831, when he first saw it unfurl against an azure blue sky and proclaimed, "Why, I'll call her 'Old Glory!'"

Similarly colorful stories have been told about the naming of Old Glory, and we may never know the truth. But we do know that the flag represented the "glory" of American enterprise, independent spirit, and freedom that our military has protected for centuries.

First day cover, December 13, 1994.

Captain Driver proudly displayed Old Glory from the *Doggett's* main mast, writing years later, "[It] has ever been my staunch companion and protection ... Savages and heathens, lowly and oppressed, hailed and welcomed it at the far end of the wide world. Then, why should it not be called Old Glory?"

William Driver now joined the ranks of the Salem ship captains who circled the globe—so many of them, in fact, that people in faraway ports believed "Salem" was a country! Driver's trading career at sea took him to India, China, New Zealand, Fiji, and Tahiti, where he rescued the mutineers of the British ship *Bounty* who were stranded there. He returned them to their native Pitcairn Island.

Driver brought so many valuable cargoes back to Salem he was able to retire to Nashville, Tennessee, in 1838. There, he married Sarah Jane Parks. His first wife, Martha Silsbee Babbage of Salem, had died the previous year.

A Union Symbol

In Nashville, Captain Driver proudly displayed Old Glory on holidays and for special occasions, including when President Lincoln was elected. But once war between North and South erupted, Driver knew he had to hide his symbol of Northern pride before Confederate troops could find and destroy it. Driver's daughters and two neighbor girls quickly sewed Old Glory into a coverlet. The Confederate troops did come looking for the flag, but they never found it!

When Nashville was liberated by Union troops in 1864, Driver quickly tore Old Glory from its hiding place and hoisted his flag above the State House to the delight of pro-Union Nashville residents.

Where is Old Glory?

That night, due to heavy winds, Driver removed his old flag and replaced it with another. And that's where the confusion began.

What people thought was Old Glory disappeared.

Did it accompany the Ohio regiment that liberated Nashville? Was it cut up into pieces for souvenirs, like other Civil War flags? All of these stories and more have been passed down through the generations.

In fact, Old Glory was safely tucked away in a trunk in Captain Driver's home. He eventually gave it to his daughter, Mary Jane, who took it with her to Utah when she married. A second Driver family flag was draped over Captain Driver's coffin when he died in 1886. A third flag, known in the family as the "Merino Flag," found its way to Salem (presumably after Driver's death) where he still had family.

And it was in Salem where Harriet Cooke, Driver's daughter by his marriage to Martha Babbage, was busy making herself into the family historian and ingratiating herself with the prestigious Essex Institute (today, the Peabody Essex Museum). She published a Driver family genealogy, in which she barely mentioned Mary Jane Driver Roland, her half-sister in Utah, at all. She also presented the Essex Institute with an old family flag—presumably the Merino Flag—and claimed it was Old Glory. Why would they doubt her? And thus ensued a family feud.

Mary Jane Driver Roland learned of her sister's activities and was furious. She secured depositions from witnesses, had photographs of the flag taken (one is in the Phillips Library of the Peabody Essex Museum), and presented the real Old Glory to the Smithsonian Institution in Washington, D.C.

Now, the arguing became institutional, as both the Essex Institute and the Smithsonian believed they had the real Old Glory. Eventually, the Essex Institute was convinced of the authenticity of the flag in Washington. They even offered to send the Smithsonian the "phony" flag in their possession!

To this day, the Peabody Essex Museum receives inquiries about Old Glory.

People are still convinced they own pieces of the flag, which they do not. The museum's card catalog reflects many such gifts. They have been updated with this new information!

Others are convinced the museum owns Old Glory intact. It does not.

The real Old Glory is proudly on display —in its faded but lovingly restored entirety—at the Smithsonian Institution in the nation's capital.

In Nashville, a special flag pole stands over Captain Driver's gravesite, even flying the colors by night under a spotlight. It is one of the only flags in the United States that is officially allowed to do so.

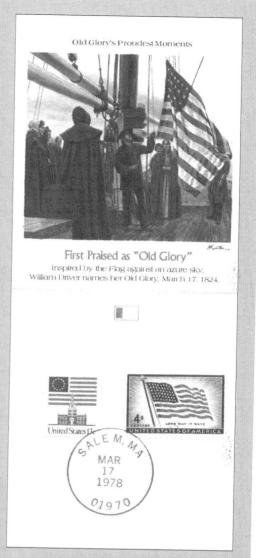

First day postcard issued March 17, 1978. The caption reads:

First praised as "Old Glory."
Inspired by the Flag against an azure sky,
William Driver names her Old Glory.
March 17, 1824.

(The date is incorrect, and the story is not documented.)

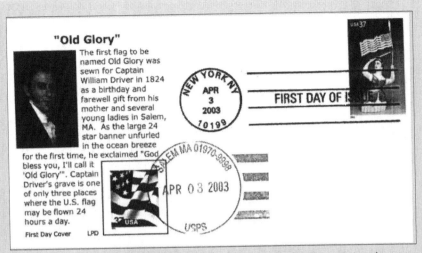

First day cover, April 3, 2003, featuring the portrait of William Driver by Charles Osgood (now owned by the Peabody Essex Museum). The caption reads: *The first flag to be named Old Glory was sewn for Captain William Driver in 1824 as a birthday and farewell gift from his mother and several young ladies in Salem, MA. As the large 24 star banner unfurled in the ocean breeze for the first time, he exclaimed "God bless you, I'll call it 'Old Glory.'"* Captain Driver's grave is one of only three places where the U. S. flag may be flown 24 hours a day.

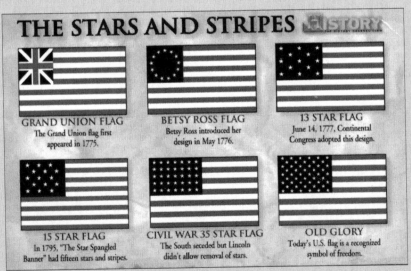

Refrigerator magnet, ca. 2000, showing the evolution of the American flag. The original Old Glory had 24 stars and a ship's anchor in the blue field.

➡ *Cross back over Essex Street to the Witch House and turn left.*

Offices of the American Red Cross
314 Essex Street

The Salem chapter of the American Red Cross began using this house for its offices in 1947, moving from 10 Rust Street. Women, men, church committees, and other groups enthusiastically donated money and volunteered their time to assist with providing clothing, bandages, and other essentials to the troops and their struggling families during the two World Wars.

The American Red Cross was founded in 1881 by Clara Barton (1821-1912), who had served as a nurse during the Civil War and as the head of the Office of Missing Soldiers in Washington, D. C. afterward. While traveling in Europe for her health, Barton learned about the Red Cross in Switzerland. She was drawn to the idea of forming national organizations to provide relief in times of war *and* peace on a voluntary and neutral basis.

Clara Barton had family ties to Salem. The Bartons date back to Samuel Barton (1664-1732), a witness for John Proctor during the Salem Witch Trials of 1692. The Bartons were among the families to leave Salem Village in 1693 and settle in "Framingham plantation," Massachusetts. In 1866, after the war, Barton gave a lecture for the Salem Lyceum titled "Work and Incidents of Army Life." Barton was also a Universalist. Today, a room in the former meeting house of the Universalist Society of Salem (on Rust and Bridge Streets, now called The Bridge at 211/Murray Hall) is named for her.

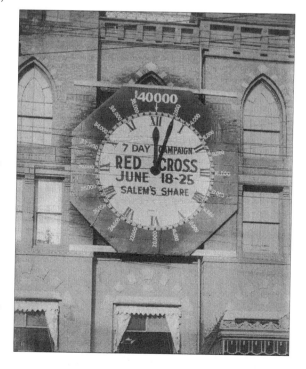

World War I-era fundraising clock mounted in Town House Square to monitor Salem's fundraising efforts for the war.

NINE ✚ THOUSAND YARDS

of material has to be cut and made up into garments and 2500 surgical dressings must be made at the Salem chapter American Red Cross before December. An army of Salem and Greater Salem women are at work upon this defense work but, despite their faithfulness and energy, a still larger number of volunteers is needed if the quota is to be filled in time.

The Salem Red Cross headquarters at 10 Rust street presents a busy and active picture every day of the week, morning and afternoon, also several evenings and there are several groups which get together in various parts of the city to work for the Red Cross. There are sewing machines and cutting machines, several of the former, which are practically in constant use daily at the Red Cross work room. Under the direction of Mrs. Josiah H. Gifford, chairman, Mrs. John S. Parker, Mrs. Alfred S. Harris, Miss Sally Todd and Mrs. Roger P. Sneedon, the committee, thousands of yards of material are cut into women's and girls' dresses and skirts, hospital pajamas, boys' shorts, convalescent robes and the many articles which go into layettes and "Toddlers packs". Volunteers, hundreds of them, are working in their spare time, many of them regular hours each week, making up the garments according to the directions of the National Red Cross.

The surgical dressings are made under the direction of Mrs. Walter G. Phippen and her committee of instructors which with Miss Mary Tay as vice chairman, and Mrs. William V. McDermott, co-chairman, includes Mrs. Channing Bacall, Mrs. Fred Cloutman, Miss Mabel Curtis, Mrs. Roger Eastman, Mrs. Thomas Fenno, Mrs. Harry P. Gifford, Mrs. John Gordon, Mrs. John C. O'Connor, Mrs. Lee Reignor and Miss Frances Wingate.

All dressings are made at the Red Cross work room and a large number of women gather there daily to sew. However the majority of the sewing, like the knitting, is done in the private homes. The knitting is another important branch of this volunteer work production and the recent annual report showed 2673 garments were knitted by Salem women last year. As for the sewing and making of surgical dressings, many more knitters are needed. Mrs. Katherine Richmond is in charge of the work shop room and one has only to visit it to become enthusiastic over the work being done and eager to join the corps of workers.

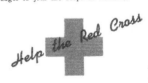

From *The North Shore On Parade*, August, 1941
(Lavendar Printing Co., Salem, Massachusetts).

Transcription of article (left):

NINE THOUSAND YARDS
of material has to be cut and made up into garments and 2500 surgical
dressings must be made at the Salem chapter American Red Cross
before December. An army of Salem and Greater Salem women are at
work upon this defense work but, despite their faithfulness and energy,
a still larger number of volunteers is needed if the quota is to be filled
in time.

The Salem Red Cross headquarters at 10 Rust Street presents a
busy and active picture every day of the week, morning and afternoon,
also several evenings and there are several groups which get together
in various parts of the city to work for the Red Cross. There are sewing
machines and cutting machines, several of the former, which are
practically in constant use daily at the Red Cross work room. Under
the direction of Mrs. Josiah H. Gifford, chairman, Mrs. John S. Parker,
Mrs. Alfred S. Harris, Miss Sally Todd and Mrs. Roger P. Sneedon, the
committee, thousands of yards of material are cut into women's and
girls' dresses and skirts, hospital pajamas, boys' shorts, convalescent
robes and the many articles which go into layettes and "Toddler packs."
Volunteers, hundreds of them, are working in their spare time, many of
them regular hours each week, making up the garments according to the
directions of the National Red Cross.

The surgical dressings are made under the direction of Mrs. Walter
G. Phippen and her committee of instructors which with Miss Mary
Tay as vice chairman, and Mrs. William V. McDermott, co-chairman,
includes Mrs. Channing Bacall, Mrs. Fred Cloutman, Miss Mabel
Curtis, Mrs. Roger Eastman, Mrs. Thomas Fenno, Mrs. Harry Gifford,
Mrs. John Gordon, Mrs. John C. O'Connor, Mrs. Lee Reignor and
Miss Frances Wingate.

All dressings are made at the Red Cross work room and a large
number of women gather there daily to sew. However the majority of
the sewing, like the knitting, is done in private homes. The knitting is
another important branch of this volunteer work production and the
recent annual report showed 2,673 garments were knitted by Salem
women last year. As for the sewing and making of surgical dressings,
many more knitters are needed. Mrs. Katherine Richmond is in charge
of the work shop room and one has only to visit it to become enthusiastic over the work being done and eager to join the corps of women.

Horse-drawn float in a World War I-era fundraising parade
to support the work of Salem's Red Cross chapter.

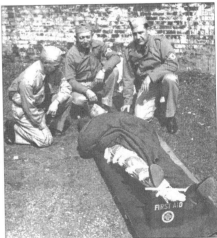

Red Cross rescue training
for Salem volunteers, ca.
1941. They are learning
how to bandage a broken
leg and safely transport a
patient using Army-like
equipment.

The First Church in Salem, Unitarian Universalist
316 Essex Street

This granite building dates to 1836, when it was dedicated as the second meeting house of Salem's North Church. The congregation's first meeting house, which had been condemned as unsafe, was located nearby at the corner of North and Lynde Streets. It was from the earlier wooden meeting house that Rev. Thomas Barnard Jr. received word that British troops were marching to Salem on Sunday, February 26, 1775. He left his pulpit to meet them at the North Bridge, and played a pivotal role in convincing British Col. Alexander Leslie to retreat from Salem in peace (see pp. 192-201 on "Leslie's Retreat"). Today, First Church's meeting house (North Church merged with First Church in 1924 and they chose this building as their home) displays a model of Leslie's Retreat, a portrait of Rev. Barnard, and a painting of the first North Church meeting house.

Among the list of veterans and chaplains associated with this church are Henry Kemble Oliver, at one time The Adjutant General of Massachusetts, who was the organist here for many years (see pp. 172-73) and the Rev. Edmund B. Willson, a chaplain for the 24th Regiment, Massachusetts Infantry, during the Civil War. Willson was just one of many clergymen from Salem who served in this capacity.

Home of Judge Nathaniel Ropes
318 Essex Street (today, owned by the Peabody Essex Museum)

The early 1770s were tense times in Salem. Many wealthy merchants and other prominent citizens had no interest in severing ties with Great Britain. As calls for independence grew stronger, suspicion toward loyalists intensified—including toward judges. If they were being paid by the Crown, how could they be objective? As historian James Duncan Phillips explains, "the province got fearfully worked up ... and threatened to impeach them if they accepted emolument from any source except the colony. Nathaniel Ropes (1726-1774) of Salem was among those who gave the necessary assurances that they would not accept such salaries."

But by 1773, with the passage of the Tea Act in London and the dumping of tea in Boston Harbor, an air of "lawlessness" took hold, including in Salem. Phillips continues: "Judge Nathaniel Ropes of the

Postcard of "The Judge's Chamber" in the "Ropes Memorial," as it was called before the Ropes family donated the house to the Essex Institute and it became known as "The Ropes Mansion." This is the room where Judge Ropes died after being terrorized by an angry mob of anti-loyalists.

An air of "lawlessness" took hold including in Salem ...
In March, 1774, [Judge Ropes] was lying desperately ill of
smallpox in his house ... Disorderly crowds gathered around
the house, breaking windows and threatening to drag him out.

—James Duncan Phillips

Supreme Court ... had disclaimed any intention of accepting any part of his salary from the Crown, but the unpopularity which attached to the Crown officer generally had not been tempered toward him thereby. In March 1774, he was lying desperately ill of smallpox in his house ... Disorderly crowds gathered around the house, breaking windows and threatening to drag him out. He had already resigned his office, but it was among such scenes that the poor man died. Before the excitement he seems to have been esteemed an honorable man, and he deserved better treatment" (see pp. 8-11 for more on loyalists, and p. 107 for the site of Salem's Liberty Tree, where "patriots" tarred and feathered suspicious Salem residents).

➡ *Continue along Essex Street.*

Home of Frank Balch, and American Legion, Post 23

329 Essex Street

Frank Balch (1881-1937) invented a machine in 1916 called the Balch Roentgen Scopic Screen that "reduced the time required for taking an X-ray picture from 20 seconds to 1/5 of a second," according to his obituary. His invention was used in Army and Navy hospitals during World War I to treat the wounded. In 1922, he filed for a patent on his work to further improve "Flourescent Screens and Methods of Making Same," and another in 1925 for further improvements to flourescent screens. These inventions intensified the clarity of x-ray images. Balch died before World War II, not knowing how many more lives he saved. He also left behind his work of science fiction, titled *A Submarine Tour* (1905).

American Legion, Post 23 purchased Frank Balch's home in 1921 for their headquarters. According to American Legion literature, the organization "was chartered by Congress in 1919 as a patriotic veterans organization. Focusing on service to veterans, service members and

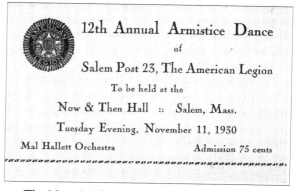

12th Annual Armistice Dance
of
Salem Post 23, The American Legion
To be held at the
Now & Then Hall :: Salem, Mass.
Tuesday Evening, November 11, 1930
Mal Hallett Orchestra   Admission 75 cents

The Now & Then Hall, where this dance took place, was located on Essex Street, where the Hawthorne Hotel parking lot is today (see p. 152).

communities, the Legion evolved from a group of war-weary veterans of World War I into one of the most influential nonprofit groups in the United States." That same year, 1919, the Legion became the chartering agency for the Boy Scouts of America.

Among their achievements over the years: creating the U. S. Veterans Bureau (today, the Veterans Administration, or VA) and the GI Bill (including a second one post-9/11); providing funds to help create the American Heart Association, National Association for Mental Health, American Legion Child Welfare Foundation, and National Emergency Fund; making the largest donation ($1 million) to the Vietnam Veterans Memorial in Washington, D. C.; and sponsoring studies on the effects of Agent Orange, a harmful chemical used during Vietnam. In 1989, The Legion succeeded in raising the VA to Cabinet-level status in the federal government. They have led the charge to account for all POWs and those missing in action.

➡ *Continue along Essex Street and turn right on Beckford Street.*

Headquarters of American Veterans, Post 53
13 Beckford Street (a former Salem Fire Station)
Salem's Post 53 of the "AMVETS" started up in 1948 with the founding of the national organization. After World War II, it was volunteer veterans who first began helping their fellow veterans obtain the benefits promised them by the federal government. As the number of returning veterans swelled into the millions, it was evident that some sort of nationally organized assistance for them would be needed. The older, established national groups wouldn't do; the leaders

of this new generation of veterans wanted their own organization. With that in mind, eighteen of them, representing nine veterans clubs, met in Kansas City, Missouri, and founded The American Veterans of World War II on Dec. 10, 1944. Less than three years later, on July 23, 1947, President Harry S. Truman signed Public Law 216, making AMVETS the first World War II organization to be chartered by Congress.

13 Beckford Street in 1881, when it was still being used as the Salem Fire Department's William Penn Hose Co. #3. *Courtesy of Thomas Brophy.*

➥ *Continue along Beckford Street to Federal Street. Turn left on Federal.*

Postcard of the front hall of the Assembly House, ca. 1900. This was one of many such items made by Daniel Low & Co., which is considered the first business in Salem to create souvenirs about local history for tourists.

Cotting-Smith Assembly House

138 Federal Street (today, owned by the Peabody Essex Museum)
Salem federalists built this Federal-style building in 1782 for social occasions and cultural events. The Marquis de Lafayette, the French Revolutionary War hero, enjoyed a festive dinner at the Hall in 1784 (see pp. 176-83), and President George Washington attended a ball here on Thursday, October 29, 1789, as part of his triumphant tour of the New England States (see pp. 90-94). After Washington's departure from Salem, the *Salem Mercury* published this account of his visit:

In the evening there was a brilliant Assembly at Concert Hall, which the President honored with his presence. As he came from his door to the carriage, 13 beautiful rockets appeared at once in the air, and 13 others when he alighted at the door of the Hall—these had a most pleasing effect: When he retired from the company, which was at an early hour, the same compliment was again paid him ... He was highly delighted with the company at the [Assembly] Hall in the evening—the numbers and brilliancy of the Ladies far exceeded his expectation.

In his diary, Washington noted: "... in the evening, between 7 and 8 o'clock, went to an Assembly, where there was at least an hundred handsome and well dressed Ladies. Abt. nine I returned to my Lodgings" (see p. 132 for where he lodged).

➡ *Continue along Federal Street.*

Home of Gen. Henry Kemble Oliver

142 Federal Street
This magnificent home is one of very few designed by the great Salem architect-carver Samuel McIntire. Henry Kemble Oliver (1800-1885) lived here for many years during his remarkable career in public service. Originally from Beverly, Massachusetts, Oliver will always be associated with Salem as he served as the City's Mayor from 1877 to 1880 and was one of Salem's most prominent and active citizens. The Oliver Grammar School on Broad Street is named for him. The *Bay State Monthly* published this account of Oliver's life after his death in 1885:

On August 12, General HENRY KEMBLE OLIVER died in Salem, Mass., at the advanced age of eighty-five years. He was born in Beverly, Mass., Nov. 24, 1800, a son of Rev. Daniel Oliver and Elizabeth Kemble; was educated in the Boston Latin School, and Harvard College (for two years) and was graduated from Dartmouth College. After his graduation, he settled in Salem, and as Principal of the High and Latin Schools, and also of a private school, he was virtually at the head of the educational interests of the town for a quarter of a century.

In 1848, he moved to Lawrence, Mass., to become agent of the Atlantic Mills. While living in Lawrence, he was appointed superintendent of schools, and in recognition of his services the "Oliver Grammar School" was founded.

At an early day General Oliver became interested in military affairs as an officer of the Salem Light Infantry and in 1844 he was made Adjutant General of the Commonwealth, by Gov. Briggs, and held this office for four years. During the war he served with great satisfaction as Treasurer of the Commonwealth, and performed the most arduous duties in a very faithful and acceptable manner. From 1869 to 1873 he was chief of the Bureau of Labor Statistics, and ever after that became interested in reducing the hours of labor in factories and in the limitation of factory work by children. From 1876 to 1880 he was mayor of Salem, and displayed almost the same vivacity and energy in discharging the duties of this office, as an octogenarian, that he had shown in his youth.

He was master of the theory and history of music, a good bass singer, a good organist, and the author of several popular compositions. Of these "Federal Street" seems likely to become permanent in musical literature. In his youth he sang in the Park Street Church in Boston and for many years he led the choir of the North Church in Salem. "Oliver's Collection of Church Music" is one of the results of his labors in this direction. In conjunction with Dr. Tuckerman, he published the "National Lyre." He was a member of the old Handel and Hayden Society and the Salem Glee Club, both famous musical organizations of his early days.

In 1825 General Oliver married Sally, daughter of Captain Samuel Cook, by whom he had two sons and five daughters, as follows: Colonel S. C. Oliver, Dr. H. K. Oliver, Jr., Sarah Elizabeth, who married Mr. Bartlett of Lawrence, and who died about four years ago, Emily Kemble, who is the wife of Colonel [George L.] Andrews, U. S. A., Mary Evans Oliver, who has been the faithful attendant of the general in his declining years, and Ellen Wendell, who married Augustus Cheever of North Andover.

➡ *Turn left on Flint Street and walk to Essex Street. Cross over Essex Street and walk to the head of Chestnut Street. Walk down Chestnut Street—known as one of the most beautiful streets in America!*

Home of Caroline Louisa Huntington
35 Chestnut Street
During the Civil War, this house was a meeting place for the Salem Sanitary Society, the local chapter of President Lincoln's U. S. Sanitary Commission. The Commission, established on June 18, 1861, was a private relief organization dedicated to helping sick and wounded soldiers. Volunteers (many of them women) raised millions of dollars through Sanitary Fairs and donations to pay for war-related expenses and volunteered countless hours to run soldiers' homes, hospital ships, lodgings, and battle field kitchens; to prepare medical supplies and sew uniforms; and to serve as nurses in hospitals on or near the battlefields.

Caroline Huntington, who organized the Salem Sanitary Society, was to married to Asahel Huntington, Esq., the Clerk of Courts for Essex County.

Phillips House
34 Chestnut Street (today, owned by Historic New England)
This house was lived in by seven generations of the Phillips family before they donated it to the Society for the Preservation of New England Antiquities (today, Historic New England). The front rooms date to 1800, and in 1911 the house was substantially remodeled.

One member of the family who served in the military was young Edward W. Phillips (1842-1867), the son of Stephen Clarendon Phillips. He joined the 5th Massachusetts Infantry in 1861 at the age of nineteen, and was promoted to 1st Lieutenant the following year. Phillips served as the Commissary of Substance on board the transport ship *J. S. Green,* sailing from New York to New Orleans. In New Orleans, he was made Superintendent of the U. S. Bakery. Phillips resigned in 1863 due to poor health, and he died in Salem four years later at age twenty-five. Charles Appleton Phillips also served in the 5th Massachusetts, achieving the rank of Brevet Major.

During World War I, Anna Phillips, the wife of Stephen ("Stevie") Willard Phillips, served as treasurer for the Salem branch of the Special

Color postcard of Chestnut Street, ca. 1900.

Aid Society for American Preparedness. The organization was affiliated with the American Red Cross. In 1928, Stevie Phillips enlisted in Battery A of the 101st Field Artillery Regiment (Boston Light Artillery, Massachusetts National Guard).

➡ *Continue along Chestnut Street.*

Hamilton Hall, ca. 1890.

Hamilton Hall
9 Chestnut Street
The Marquis de Lafayette, the Revolutionary War hero who had first visited Salem in 1784, was entertained here in 1824 with a lavish meal prepared by Salem's leading caterer, John Remond (1786-1874). A native of Curacao, Remond was active in the abolition movement in the days leading up to the Civil War. His son, Charles Lenox Remond (1810-1873), and his daughter, Sarah Parker Remond (1826-1894), were much-sought-after lecturers in America and Europe, as part of William Lloyd Garrison's American Anti-Slavery Society. In 1863, with the passage of the Emancipation Proclamation, Charles Remond "joined other black abolitionist men, including Frederick Douglass, in

the recruitment of African American soldiers into the all-black Massachusetts 54th Regiment of the Union Army," according to historian Shirley Yee, writing for blackpast.org.

Sarah Parker Remond spent the war years in Europe trying to persuade Europeans to "lend their support to the North and the 'poor enslaved Blacks of the South,'" according to her biographer, Dorothy B. Porter. As an African American woman, Remond was particularly effective. Women had only recently begun to speak from the public stage, and many of her audiences, especially in Europe, had never seen an African American woman. Sarah described how enslaved families were torn apart and terrorized, and how often women and girls were impregnated by their white masters. The evils of slavery were harmful to all involved, and anyone who stood silently by—including European textile companies that imported Southern cotton—was complicit.

Marquis de Lafayette in Salem: Sites to Visit

- Assembly Hall in 1784 (see p. 171)
- Judge Joseph Story House in 1824 (see p. 88)
- Hamilton Hall in 1824 (see p. 175)

In 1876, for the centennial celebration of the Declaration of Independence, the Salem Fire Department's Lafayette Hose 5 erected twin arches at their station house (at the intersection of Washington and Lafayette Streets) with the words "Washington Lafayette Co."

Marquis de Lafayette in Salem, 1784

As the *Salem Gazette* told the story, "his arrival was announced by the ringing of bells; and he was escorted into town by the principal inhabitants, in their carriages and on horseback, amid throngs of people in the streets, who rent the air, as he passed along, with their acclamations; to which, and to the 'Transport and rude harmony' of the populace, the Marquis returned the most obliging acknowledgments."

It was November 2, 1784, and the young French hero of the American Revolution had returned to his beloved United States to "embrace their victory" over England, explains his biographer Harlow Giles Unger. The Marquis had given his fortune and his military service to the cause of liberty on American soil, once writing, "The moment I heard of America I loved her; the moment I knew she was fighting for freedom I burnt with a desire of bleeding for her; and the moment I shall be able to serve her, at any time, or in any part of the world, will be the happiest of my life" (Unger).

Salem residents had read so many accounts of the "excellent young Nobleman's" journey through the states that by the time he and his entourage rode from Boston to Salem, according to the *Salem Gazette*, "a general joy was diffused through every class of the people, and each one strove to excel in demonstrations of respect and admiration...

[He was brought first to his lodgings, "Mr. Goodale's,"] where he was "attended by a deputation of Gentlemen, with an address from the Town ... Here, also, he was met by a number of Continental Officers, who served under him in the late war. The interview was marked with those exquisite emotions which can be conceived only by such as have mingled their toils, their sufferings, and their blood, in one great cause of Virtue and Glory."

The address from the town, published in the *Salem Gazette,* read:

Sir,

The Inhabitants of Salem feel a sincere pleasure, in common with their fellow-citizens through the United States, in showing you a publick mark of their attachment. In their name, we congratulate you on your arrival at this place.

The man who could leave his country, and bid adieu to the endearments of domestick society—who could sacrifice his ease, and hazard his life, in defence of the violated rights of America, and of human nature—merits every testimony of respect, from a generous people:—and we assure you, Sir, that the memory of the Marquis de La Fayette will be dear to the Citizens of Salem, so long as virtue has a name, or sentiments of gratitude and affection animate the human heart.

Lafayette responded:

Gentlemen,

From the early period when you generously joined in the noble contest, your efforts have been so steady and liberal, that my regard for this town dates with my attachment to the American cause. Impressed by these sentiments, I cannot but be perfectly happy in this visit, and in your flattering welcome.

Be pleased, Gentlemen, to accept the thanks of a respectful, affectionate heart:—and I pray to God the two elements, upon which your exertions have been so conspicuous, may be to the town of Salem inexhaustible sources of happiness and prosperity.
—Lafayette

From his lodgings at Mr. Gooddale's, "Officers of the late Army" and leading "Gentlemen of the Town" escorted General Lafayette to "Concert-Hall" on "Back Street" (neither of which still exist) "through a surprising croud (sic.) of people, whom the warmest affection, and the most eager curiosity, had brought together," according to the *Salem Gazette* of November 2, 1784. Francis Cabot, one of the building's proprietors, had paid architect-carver Samuel McIntire £1.8 to fix "the temporary Tables in Concert Hall." Dinner was "to be on the Table at half after two o'clock in the afternoon, at the Assembly Room," and the list of invited guests included Salem's elite merchants, jurists, physicians, and clergymen including Elias Hasket Derby, George Crowninshield, Joseph Orne, Nathaniel Ropes, William Wetmore, Doctor Joseph Osgood, and the Reverend John Prince.

James Jeffrey paid Mary Chapman £4 for a cake and milk biscuits for the dinner, and £12.6 for six musicians. Francis Cabot paid Jonathan Webb £50.9 for 92 dinners, 41 bottles of wine, 16 bowls of punch, and 12 glasses of grog; for libation later in the evening, Cabot paid £6.19 for 27 bottles of wine and one bottle of "old spirits." The following toasts were offered following the meal:

1. The United States.
2. Congress.
3. His Most Christian Majesty the King of France.
4. The Queen of France.
5. Washington.
6. The Governor and Commonwealth of Massachusetts.
7. The Heroes who have bled in our cause.
8. The Friends of Virtue and Freedom, throughout the World.
9. The late Army of the United States.
10. May the Alliances which America has formed in her adversity, be ever religiously observed in her prosperity.
11. May we never withhold from Government the essential Powers of doing Good, from a jealous apprehension of their doing Evil.
12. May the future Sons of America sufficiently prize the Legacy, which we, at so great an expense, have purchased for them.

13. May America never be so insensible to Merit, as to pass it unnoticed.

Lafayette then raised his glass and toasted to "The Town of Salem—May the elements conspire to her prosperity!"

From the *Diary of William Pynchon*, 1784:

27. Wednesday. The sick folk grow better. News that M. De La Fayette is coming to Salem.

28. Thursday. Mr. Wheeler at Mr. Fisher's. Prim. Goodale hath his hands full; no rest by day or night; the Marquis is coming!

29. Friday. Cloudy morning. The Marquis De La Fayette comes to town attended by … coaches [and] other carriages, [and] young gentlemen on horseback; they alight at Mr. Goodale's and take some refreshment, and chat awhile; then the company, clergymen, including the modest Dr. W., and merchants and mechanics, walk through the streets, the rabble giving them three cheers at each corner, the co[mpany] all having their hats on except the Marquis; the co[mpany] dine at the Assembly Room, [and] Judge John Pickering reads off a speech to the Marquis; he returns it memoritet; they drank tea at S. Page's, and had a ball at the A. Room [in the] evening. Mr. and Mrs. Oliver return from the ball; the French Chevalier walks a minuet with Miss Williams; the Marquis hath a stiff knee and danceth none; the room was full of ladies and gentlemen; they break up at half past 12 o'clock.

30. Saturday. Cloudy and some wet. The Marquis and suit went out of town at 5 a. m., to dine at Portsmouth. The employment of each circle, club, and tea-table in Salem is in finding and proving and disputing as to neglects and affronts respecting the entertainments and ball for the Marquis.

From Joseph B. Felt's *Annals of Salem*:

1784, Oct. 29. On a tour to the eastward, La Fayette, with two friends, made a short tarry here. His arrival was announced by the ringing of bells. He was escorted into town by the principal inhabitants, on horseback and in carriages. Multitudes of people, as he passed, rent the air with their cheers of welcome. His magnanimity of character—then, as ever since, commanded respect and esteem. At his lodgings, he was pertinently addressed in behalf of the town, and he similarly replied. He dined at Concert Hall. In the evening he attended a ball, as requested. Such attention to the tired wayfarer, however meant for his gratification, often adds to his weariness and exhausts his comfort. Early next morning he departed with the best wishes of a grateful community.

General Lafayette in Salem, 1824

In his book, *Lafayette in America in 1824 and 1825*, Alan Hoffman explains: "On the invitation of Congress and President James Monroe, General Lafayette sailed from Le Havre, France, on the American merchant ship *Cadmus* in July 1824 for the United States of America, his adoptive country. Although he had last visited these shores in 1784 after the Treaty of Paris formally ended the American Revolution, which he had shared the glory of winning on the battlefield, this visit—40 years later—produced a fervid outpouring of affection from the American people for the last surviving Major General of their Revolution. During his 13-month "Farewell Tour," he visited all 24 states, where he was celebrated and honored on an almost daily basis. There were parades of militia and children, festivals, banquets, speeches, balls, triumphal arches built in his honor, dedications of public monuments—he helped to lay the cornerstone of the Bunker Hill Monument in Charlestown, Massachusetts, in June 1825—and held 'meet and greets' with the people who came to pay their respects to and to touch the 'Nation's Guest,' as he was commonly called during his extended visit."

Salem's Elizabeth Peabody, then living in Boston, wrote this delightful account in a letter to her friend Maria Chase, dated "Sept. 3rd [1824]":

At last I heard the sounds of "coming-coming" and the carriage appeared. It seemed to me but a second, coming down the road and I felt precisely as if I were dipped in liquid fire when La Fayette's face, glowing with delight—flashed from the carriage. I had a handkerchief [sic] in one hand and a feather fan in the other. I dropped both—sprung towards him and caught his hand (that was stretched out) with both mine and put a kiss there, which had my whole soul in it. I must have jumped three feet from the ground. He said "Thank you thank you" with such fervour of feeling I could not believe it, and raising my hand to his lips—kissed it! I feel his lips quiver upon it now.

As before, the *Salem Gazette* reported Lafayette's movements:

He arrived "about half past 12:00," when he was met by the "committee of arrangements and selectmen." The committee included "Hon. Joseph Story, Joseph Peabody, Esq., Hon. Nathaniel Silsbee, Hon. Leverett Saltonstall, Hon. Benjamin W. Crowninshield, Hon. John Pickering, Hon. Stephen White, Willard Peele, Esq., Hon. John G. King, Joseph Ropes, Esq., John Howard, Esq., Pickering Dodge, Esq." Lafayette was then "escorted in his carriage by Hon. Judge Story, President of the Day" to be "received by Col. Putnam, chairman of the selectmen." He was followed by a "huge procession of citizens in carriages" under the orders of Edward Laner, Esq., Chief Marshal—all during heavy, pouring rain.

At the South Bridge, Lafayette was joined by Capt. Pulsifer's Salem Mechanic Light Infantry, Capt. Sutton's Danvers Light Infantry, Salem Light Infantry under Lieut. Hodges (all units under the command of Capt. Cloutman of the Salem Light Infantry). On "the plain above the bridge" two hundred sailors greeted him, all wearing Lafayette ribbons on their hats. (In fact, Salem shops were well-stocked with Lafayette ribbons, banners, broadsides, and other memorabilia.)

Decorated arches lined the entire route of the increasingly massive procession, moving from Mount Pleasant, up Central Street, to the east and west gates of Washington Square. There, one thousand children stood to greet him, each one holding his likeness. The motto on their decorted arch was: "The Children welcome with joy the illustrious benefactor of their Fathers."

From there, the procession moved to the Lafayette Coffee House on Essex Street (today, Museum Place Mall) where a stage had been erected for Lafayette, his party, and town leaders. Judge Joseph Story gave the official town welcome. That afternoon a battalion of the Salem Light Infantry escorted Lafayette to Hamilton Hall where, at 3:00, he enjoyed a gala banquet attended by three hundred "gentlemen and their guests ... This spacious and elegant hall (which bears the name of the lamented friend of La Fayette) was decorated with great taste and elegance by the Ladies of Salem ... the whole effect was beyond our powers of description. The Orchestra was ornamented with wreaths and festoons of flowers and evergreens, encircling the inscriptions—'Welcome, welcome, be the brave, To the home he fought to save; 'LAFAYETTE, our friend in times which tried men's souls.'" Lafayette departed for Ipswich at about 5:30 p.m.

We traversed the whole City at a walking pace in order to pass beneath a great number of triumphal arches which were decorated with emblems and inscriptions. On one we read: "Honor to Lafayette! Honor to the one who fought and spilled his blood for the peace and happiness which we enjoy." On another: "Lafayette, friend and defender of liberty, welcome to your favorite land!" On another, finally: "At the time of our adversity, you helped us; in our prosperity, we recall your services with gratitude. —Auguste Levasseur, Lafayette's private secretary

➡ *Turn right on Hamilton Street, and walk to Broad Street. Turn right.*

Old Pickering House, Salem, Mass.

Color postcard of the "Old Pickering House," 1955, one of Salem's most popular and recognizable historic houses. It was occupied by the Pickering family for more generations than almost any other house in the country. Today, it is open to the public for tours, lectures, and rentals.

Home of Col. Timothy Pickering

18 Broad Street

Rev. George Batchelor of Salem's North Church wrote this about Timothy Pickering (1745-1829) in *History of Essex County, Massachusetts*: "Of the last century Timothy Pickering was perhaps the most distinguished man born or living in Salem after 1750. He was conspicuous for the force and dignity of his character, for his many attainments and for his notable public services ... From the time, in 1774, when the Colonial Legislature assembled in Salem and took measures to call a General Provincial Congress in Philadelphia, Pickering was at the center of events."

Timothy Pickering started his brilliant legal and military career studying law at Harvard College, graduating in 1763. He was first commissioned into the Massachusetts Militia in 1766 as Lieutenant. In just a few years, he rose to the rank of Colonel. He was admitted to the Massachusetts Bar in 1768. The following year, 1769, having strong ideas on the drilling and discipline of soldiers, Pickering published his ideas in the *Essex Gazette*. As Salem historian James Duncan Phillips explains, Pickering "evidently made a study of military science and was an intelligent, well-equipped military officer, though he did not intend to become a professional soldier." Nevertheless, he turned these articles into a book in 1775, titled *An Easy Plan of Discipline for a Militia,* that Congress ordered be used by officers of the Massachusetts Militia.

Between 1771 and 1775, Pickering held the position of Register of Deeds for Essex County, represented Salem in the Massachusetts General Court, and served as a Justice in the Essex County Court of Common Pleas. He was appointed Colonel of the 1st Essex Regiment (an Essex County militia unit) early in 1775. Pickering had barely assumed this position when British troops arrived in Salem to seize cannon and gunpowder hidden in the northern part of town. Col. Pickering and his unit were present on February 26, 1775, for the event now known as "Leslie's Retreat" (see pp. 192-201). On that tense Sunday morning, Pickering appears to have helped negotiate a peaceful end to what could have been the start of the Revolutionary War. Two months later, on April 19, the 1st Essex Regiment was too late to arrive at Menotomy (today, Arlington) to participate in the bloody battle that ensued as British soldiers retreated from Concord and Lexington to Boston. But in May, Col. Pickering "was appointed by the provincial government to command a force to be raised to defend the seacoast about Salem," according to James Duncan Phillips.

Stereo view of the Pickering House, ca. 1880.

In July, Pickering successfully inspired ninety-two "citizens, sea captains, sailors, and tradesmen" to join his regiment, with more volunteers from nearby towns, and march to where General Washington was struggling to repel the British army. In 1777, Pickering became Adjutant General of the Army. Soon after, he became Quartermaster General, "[serving] as such and as Adjutant-General, with distinction, throughout the war," Phillips writes.

After the war, in 1783, Timothy Pickering helped found the Society of the Cincinnati "to preserve the ideals and fellowship of officers of the Continental Army," according to their website. He served as Postmaster General (1791-1795) and Secretary of War (1795) under President Washington; as Secretary of State (1795-1800) under Presidents Washington and Adams; as U. S. Senator (1803-1811), and Representative from Massachusetts in the Thirteenth and Fourteenth Congresses (1813-1817). According to the Massachusetts Historical Society, where Pickering's papers reside, he spent his final years compiling information on the history of the American Revolution, the "political struggles of the Washington, Adams, Jefferson, and Madison administrations," and on the progress of American agriculture (having been the first president of the Essex Agricultural Society). Fort Pickering on Winter Island is named for him.

➡ *Cross the street to the Broad Street Cemetery.*

Broad Street Cemetery
5 Broad Street
Established in 1655, this is Salem's second oldest cemetery after the Charter Street Cemetery (1637). At one time it was called "Ye Old Common Burying Hill" for its proximity to the early town common, which was then considered "to be the land along Broad Street bordering the cemetery," according to Salem historian Jerome M. Curley. Two colonial blockhouses, or defensive forts, were located nearby, and the almshouse for the poor, states Curly, was "on the northeasterly corner of the Broad Street Cemetery, known as Pickering's Hill."

According to the Friends of Broad Street Cemetery, seventy-one Revolutionary War veterans are buried there—including Col. Timothy Pickering—along with Civil War hero Brig. Gen. Frederick W. Lander.

The National Guard and Salem Fire

On June 26, 1914, fire broke out in the Korn Leather Factory at 57 Boston Street, caused by a series of explosions from tanning chemicals. Once the fire alarm was sounded at 1:37 p.m. and Salem fire, police, and government officials understood the magnitude of the fire, they lost no time in reaching out for help. Luckily, the fire swept past the upper end of Broad Street. When the fire was stopped, over 18,000 people were made homeless and/or jobless. Included in the 1,376 buildings destroyed by the fire were those owned by the Naumkeag Mills, the city's largest employer. In particular, the fire decimated the French Canadian section of town known as "The Point." Salem called in the Massachusetts National Guard to assist with relief efforts and to prevent looting. The following account is from the *Annual Report of The Adjutant General of the Commonwealth of Massachusetts for the Year Ending December 31, 1914* by The Adjutant General (TAG) Charles H. Cole.

> *"This tour of duty ... showed to the community that in time of great calamity and distress the militia is ready and organized at a moment's notice...."* —TAG Charles H. Cole

National Guardsmen adjacent to Broad Street Cemetery.

SALEM FIRE.

On the 26th of June, 1914, fire broke out in the city of Salem, at 1:37 p.m. At 2:31 p.m. the Mayor of Salem issued a precept to the Seconds Corps Cadets and Company H, Eighth Infantry, for duty in protecting property.

The Adjutant General arrived in Salem at 3:30 p.m., and realizing the size of the conflagration, by authority of the Commander-in-Chief, at 6 o'clock ordered on duty the balance of the Eighth Infantry, Company E, Naval Brigade, Fifth Company, Coast Artillery, companies A, C, D, E, I and L, Ninth Infantry, and detachments of officers and men from the First Corps Cadets and the sanitary troops; 20,000 rations, 1,500 cots, 1,500 tents and 1,500 blankets were ordered for relief purposes. The equipment, ordered at 7 o'clock from South Framingham, was sent by trolley, and began arriving at 10 o'clock that night.

At the time the rations were ordered the wholesale offices and stores throughout the State were closed, but through the courtesy of the Commandant of the Charlestown Navy Yard, Capt. DeWitt Coffman, U.S.N., the State was able to obtain rations at once. His prompt action and cutting of red tape enabled the Commonwealth to have food enough ready for the refugees by 4 o'clock on the morning after the fire. I desire to express to Captain Coffin the appreciation and thanks of the military department for what he did in this emergency.

I also desire to express thanks and appreciation to Mr. J. B. Blood of Lynn, who delivered a truck load of food to the [Salem] armory before 12 o'clock the first night, and to the other citizens of the Commonwealth who rendered splendid assistance during this time of trouble.

Col. Frank A. Graves, commander of the Eighth Infantry, M.V.M., was assigned to command the troops; Brig. Gen. James G. White, in charge of the Commissary Department; Brig. Gen. William B.

National Guard unit on Salem Common in the aftermath of the fire.

Emery, in charge of the Quartermaster Department; and Col. Frank P. Williams, Surgeon General, was in charge of the sanitary troops, under Colonel Graves.

During June 27 no refugee suffered for want of food, and before 10 o'clock that night tents enough were put up in five concentration camps to take care of all made homeless by the fire.

The troops were on duty at Salem from June 26 to July 7, inclusive; on June 30 the refugee camps were turned over to the Salem fire relief committee; on June 29 companies A, C, D, E, I and L, Ninth Infantry, returned to their home station; on June 30 Company E, Naval Brigade, and Company M, Eighth Infantry, were relieved. The balance of the troops were kept for police purposes in the city, detachments being relieved from time to time. The last troops left Salem on July 7.

This tour of duty was, in my opinion, as efficient a tour as was ever performed by the militia of Massachusetts. It was invaluable to the stricken people of Salem, and will prove of great benefit to the militia, in that it showed to the community that in time of great calamity and distress the militia is ready and organized at a moment's notice to perform such temporary duties as may be necessary until a proper civilian body can be organized.

The plaque features depictions of a soldier and sailor. As a seafaring community, Salem has a long history of service at sea as well as on land.

World War I Honor Roll

Broad Street and Dalton Parkway

The names of two hundred and eighty-six residents from this part of Salem are listed on this handsome bronze plaque, which was "erected by the Citizens of Ward Three of Salem to commemorate the patriotic services of these men and women in the world war." The inscription at the bottom reads, "'Tis sweet and noble to serve one's country in her hour of need."

Dalton Parkway

Broad Street, at Flint and upper Essex Streets

Dalton Parkway is named for Samuel Dalton (1840-1906), the only person from Salem to serve as The Adjutant General of Massachusetts. Samuel Dalton first joined the militia upon the outbreak of the Civil War as a member of the Second Corps of Cadets. But as the Cadets were not available for federal service, he joined and "recruited more than 100 men from Salem and surrounding towns, including his uncle, Eleazer Moses Dalton, for the 1st Massachusetts Heavy Artillery," according to his descendant and author Dorothy V. Malcolm. It was Samuel who found his uncle's body in 1864, after the Battle of Jerusalem Plank Road, Virginia. During the war, Samuel Dalton was promoted from Sergeant to 2nd Lieutenant in 1862. Just a few months

Samuel Dalton (in front), The Adjutant General of Massachusetts, in 1883. Appointed by Governor Benjamin Butler, Dalton served in this capacity from 1883 to 1905—the only Salem native to do so. A colorized version of this photograph appears on the front cover to show the handsome uniforms of the Second Corps of Cadets.

later, he rose to 1st Lieutenant. Samuel's brother, Col. Joseph Franklin Dalton (ca. 1842-1914, known as "J. Frank Dalton"), also fought and survived. After the war, both men at one time commanded the Second Corps of Cadets. In 1883, Governor Benjamin Butler appointed Samuel Dalton as The Adjutant General of Massachusetts—the highest ranking military officer in the state. Dalton retired in 1905, the same year Dalton Parkway was dedicated in his honor.

Col. J. Frank Dalton's son, Col. Arthur Treadwell Dalton (1877-1954), continued the family's military service by joining the Second Corps of Cadets in 1898 at age eighteen. Then, as a Private in the 1st Massachusetts Heavy Artillery, he served in the Spanish-American War, then fought in the Phillippine Insurrection, and wrote a compelling account of his time in the Phillippines for the Essex Institute. In his essay, Dalton described himself as "the only professional army man from Salem." The complete list of military Daltons is long, starting with Revolutionary War days. This inspires many Salem citizens to consider Dalton Parkway a memorial to them all.

— End of trail. ★

WAR IS TEMPORARILY AVERTED — BRITISH REPELLED AT SALEM — February 26, 1775

Receiving word from an informant in February, 1775, that the Patriots had eight new cannon hidden in an old barn near the Salem landing, General Gage immediately made plans for a secret expedition to locate the hidden artillery. On Sunday, February 26, the Redcoats, commanded by Colonel Alexander Leslie, sailed from Castle William, Boston, and arrived at Marblehead around noon. The soldiers were kept below decks until 2 PM when the townspeople were to be in their meetinghouse. But as the soldiers emerged to start the 5-mile march to Salem, the Marbleheaders sent Patriot Major John Pedrick to spread the alarm.

Pedrick arrived in Salem in time to have the cannon moved across the drawbridge to Danvers. Barely had the cannon been taken over with the drawbridge raised when Leslie and his troops arrived. Leslie ordered the drawbridge to be lowered and threatened to fire upon the Patriots if his order was not obeyed. But the Patriots stood firm and Leslie hesitated to initiate aggressive action. A local minister, Reverend Barnard, convinced both sides to compromise. Leslie agreed to advance only a token 30 rods if he were allowed to cross — this would technically carry out the orders from Gage. The Patriots were happy with the arrangement because the artillery was safely hidden 45 rods from the bridge. The hesitation of the Redcoats to confront the Patriots averted war for nearly two more months.

COVER CACHET: REDCOATS TURNED BACK AT SALEM, MASSACHUSETTS

Above: Bicentennial cover and insert issued February 26, 1975—exactly 200 years after "Leslie's Retreat" took place.

Salem replaced the eighteenth century "Leslie's Retreat" draw bridge a few times over the years. This photo, taken ca. 1890 by Frank Cousins, shows the North Bridge before it was rebuilt as an overpass.

★ Sites to Visit by Neighborhood ★

~ North Salem ~

START: Site of the North Church Meeting House

Corner of North and Lynde Streets (Wesley Methodist Church parking lot)
The minister of Salem's North Church, Rev. Thomas Barnard Jr., played a pivotal role in the events of February 26, 1775, now known as "Leslie's Retreat" or, the "Gunpowder Raid."

➡ *Continue on North Street, heading away from downtown. Cross over the bridge, find a place to sit, and imagine what happened here in 1775!*

Site of "Leslie's Retreat"

North Street Bridge, North Street/Route 114

Stereo view. In 1876, during the nation's Centennial Anniversary, Salem erected this arch on North Street in remembrance of Leslie's Retreat. It was placed at the bottom of the bridge heading away from town.

In the days leading up to the American Revolution, Salem was a hotbed of both patriotic and loyalist sentiment. Spies were everywhere. Secret meetings were taking place. Cannon and gunpowder were being collected and stored. What happened in Salem on the cold morning of Sunday, February 26, 1775, is considered by some historians to be the real start of the American Revolution. Why?

First, the account of what happened as told by the renowned Salem historian James Duncan Phillips in his 1937 book, *Salem in the Eighteenth Century:*

Col. David Mason (1726-1795)

Few people in Salem really thought war was coming, but they had seen British troops quartered amongst them, and they resented it. Force could only be resisted by force, and steps in that direction began in October, 1774...

During the winter of 1774–75, there was much activity among the patriots in assembling military supplies. Among others so employed was Colonel David Mason of Salem. He was born in Boston in 1726 and had seen service in several of the Indian and French wars ... As an agent of the Massachusetts Military Committee he had gone, in the autumn of 1774, to the Simsbury Iron Works in Connecticut to contract for cannon balls, and later he tried to get out of Boston some brass cannon which belonged to his former artillery company, and was probably successful. Later, he purchased some iron cannon from Captain Derby and employed Captain Foster, whose shop was in North Salem, to make the carriages while his wife and daughters sewed up the flannel cartridges.

By the last of February, many of these gun carriages were completed. One of the workmen was supposed to have been a traitor and gone to Boston on Saturday afternoon, February 25, to inform General Gage what was going on; but it seems more likely that word was sent by some of the more important Salem tories.

The fact that, when Colonel Leslie approached through the South Field, a white flag was seen displayed on the roof of Colonel Sargent's house on Essex Street seems to indicate that he knew of Leslie's coming in advance, and bears out this theory. Perhaps the workman was a spy for Sargent.

On Sunday, February 26, General Gage dispatched Colonel Leslie with the Sixty-fourth Regiment of Foot from Castle William in Boston Harbor on a transport to Marblehead. It is supposed that the regiment at the Castle was sent so that the people in Boston would get no inkling of the expedition. The transport arrived in Marblehead about noon, but appeared to be manned as usual, for the soldiers were kept below decks. The number of men is variously estimated, but apparently the whole regiment ... went from the Castle, and was from two hundred and fifty up...

Col. Alexander Leslie (1731-1794)

Colonel Leslie waited till people had gathered for afternoon service; he then ordered his men to load and fix bayonets, landed them with great dispatch at Homan's Cove on the Neck, and at once marched off toward Salem. Some people had fortunately observed the landing...

Colonel Mason, with a group of young men, rushed from his house in North Street to the shop where his guns were. David Boyce and other truck-men hurried along with their teams. There was no snow on the ground and some of the guns were dragged to an adjacent woodlot near Buffum Street, and covered with leaves and the carriages hidden. Others were sent to Orne's Point and concealed there...

[In] Salem all was excitement. The bells were ringing, drums beating, and people pouring forth from the meeting-houses into the streets ... The main body [of troops] marched right up into Town House Square ... and proceeded through Lynde and North Streets to the long causeway that led to the draw-bridge. Colonel Mason, who had come down to the center of the town, rode hastily back to the bridge ahead of the troops and crossed to the north side, so the draw could not yet have been raised.

[Accounts conflict as to exactly when Col. Timothy Pickering of Salem and the militia unit he commanded, the 1st Essex, arrived, but "Minutemen" from nearby towns were also heading for Salem.]

As soon as the troops came in sight of the bridge, Colonel Mason and the men with him raised the north leaf of the draw. Although it was low tide, this left the deep channel, which was impossible to ford, in front of the column [of troops] … When Colonel Leslie reached the open draw, he was angry beyond words … he ordered the draw to be lowered at once … Captain [Jonathan] Felt had followed Leslie … and heard him say to an officer, "You must face about this company and fire upon those people." This roused the bitter resentment of Captain Felt, who became the real hero of the occasion, and called out so all could hear:

"Fire! You'd better be damned than fire! You have no right to fire without further orders! If you fire, you'll all be dead men!"

Felt was right. There was no proof that the men on the opposite wharf had raised the draw. Open rebellion had not yet appeared. Leslie had no right to fire unless in self-defense, and probably realized it and cooled off a little … Perhaps right at that point the cooler judgment of Colonel Leslie prevented the first battle of the Revolution's being fought at the North Bridge; for the people only became more excited.

[At this point, some of the men decided to scuttle (sink) the stranded small boats the British could have used to cross the river.] In spite of prods from the British bayonets, the men succeeded in finishing their work; [two of the men] dramatically opening their shirts defying the latter to stab them. One of them did prick [Joseph] Whicher enough to draw blood—the first blood shed in the Revolution…

The people were getting angry and excited, and were pressing against the line of soldiers, who shoved them back with their bayonets. There was more talk of firing on the men on the north side when the Reverend Mr. Barnard stepped forward and said:

"I desire you do not fire on those innocent people … my mission is peace, and I pray to Heaven there may be no conflict."

Above, right: "The Repulse of Leslie at the North Bridge, Sunday, February 26, 1775," from the painting by Lewis Jesse Bridgman. Published in *The Affair at the North Bridge*, Essex Institute, 1902.

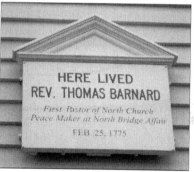

HERE LIVED
REV. THOMAS BARNARD
First Pastor of North Church
Peace Maker at North Bridge Affair
FEB. 25, 1775

Rev. Thomas Barnard Jr.
(1748-1814)

Plaque on Barnard's house, which
still stands at 393 Essex Street.

It was now nearly five o'clock, and no doubt the ardor of both sides was chilled by the intense cold of that winter afternoon. The sun was setting, and Leslie, recognizing that the dispute had been ineffective and that something must be done soon, approached Captain Felt and asked him if he had any authority to order the draw lowered ... Leslie urged his orders to cross the bridge, but pledged his word that he would march only fifty yards beyond the bridge and would return without molesting anything. Felt was reluctant; Doctor Barnard urged the people to lower the draw ... Finally Captain Felt agreed, down came the leaf of the draw, the troops marched across about as far as Mason Street, wheeled, and started back for Marblehead ... [with Leslie's] fifers playing "The World's Turned Upside Down."

And so the episode of the North Bridge passed into history. It was General Gage's first attempt to prevent the arming of the province which was definitely going on. It was likewise the first attempt of the people to obstruct and prevent the military power of Great Britain from obtaining its object. It was also the first attempt to rouse the Minutemen of a considerable portion of the country to oppose the British soldiers.

That it did not result in a bloody conflict and the wiping out of Leslie's regiment was due to Leslie's forbearance and good sense in realizing that the situation was fraught with danger. Had he fired on the people at the bridge, he would have laid a long and bloody trail to Marblehead. There were at least as many men in Salem as he had soldiers. One Danvers company was already in the town, and others were on the way and near at hand. Beverly men were coming steadily, and the companies in Marblehead could easily have cut off his retreat.

The event did not pass unnoticed in England, and was mentioned in the Gentleman's Magazine *for April, 1775. Under the date of Monday, April 17, just two days before Lexington, are these words referring to Leslie's retreat:*

"It is reported that the Americans have hoisted their standard of liberty at Salem."

If Great Britain was willing to admit before the nineteenth of April that the Revolution had begun in Salem, there seems no good reason why Americans should deny it, and perhaps our patriotic friends in Concord and Lexington might bear this in mind.

In his masterful explanation of Leslie's Retreat, *Prelude to Revolution*, published in 2013, historian Peter Charles Hoffer draws on James Duncan Phillips' telling of the story and adds an account of Leslie's Retreat presented by retired Salem ship captain Charles Moses Endicott to the Essex Institute in 1856. Endicott wrote: "Here ... we claim the first blow was struck in the war of independence by open resistance to both the civil and military power of the mother country."

Hoffer expands Endicott's account by concluding: "No blood was shed, but a significant change had taken place. An aroused civilian force, armed and determined to protect its rights, caused a British regiment to negotiate a retreat ... Endicott was right. The Revolution began in Salem."

Why do these three credible sources believe that the American Revolution began in Salem?

Hoffer continues his thesis:

Endicott understood that a Revolution in the hearts and minds of the people required a highly visible event, a ritual of the passing of legitimate power from an imperial sovereign to a sovereign people that everyone understood. Such a passing would not involve mere theory, but practice; not words on a page or read aloud, but evidence of self-government in action. One would then say that the American Revolution took place where Americans actually saw it, in the triumph of a resolute citizenry and the acquiescence of equally visible British military authority.

Such rituals are often part of the transfer of power, whether the coronation and annointing of kings or the inauguration of presidents. Such rituals in the passing of power make it legitimate in the eyes of the people. Much as such people might say they venerate a constitution of laws, of words on parchment or in statute books, without the public spectacle the words lose their credence. No agency more clearly embodied the authority of the empire in its American provinces during the crisis period than the British Army and Royal Navy.

The Revolution began when Americans could envision the withdrawal of British armed might.

This granite marker was placed on the east side of the North Bridge in 1875 during the Centennial Celebration of Leslie's Retreat. It was moved across the road in the 1970s to make way for Salem's new train depot.

PROGRAMME.

I. VOLUNTARY.

II. PRAYER.

III. ORIGINAL ODE.

BY MISS L. L. A. VERY.

Leslie's Retreat, sounding far through the years !
  Their footsteps are marching, marching to-day ;
Gone are the trials, privations and fears
  Our ancestors bore 'neath England's proud sway.
Sown in War's furrows with blood and with tears,
The harvest of Peace we are reaping to-day.

Cho.—The first shot of Freedom to-day we repeat !
  Here's to the mem'ry of Leslie's Retreat !
    A health to the brave ones of old !

Back from our borders by land and by sea,
  Born unto freedom, we turn back the feet,
Feet of oppressors, whoe'er they may be,
  They'll march to the tune of " Leslie's Retreat !"
Back from our borders by land and by sea,
  We turn back oppressors, whoe'er they may be.

Cho.—The first shot of Freedom to-day we repeat !
  Here's to the mem'ry of Leslie's Retreat,
    A health to the brave ones of old !

Between wrong and right let us e'er draw the line,
  Though poverty 's here,—there, red coats so fine ;
When Georges send down their mandates so wise,
  Our North Bridge shall rival the famed *Bridge of Sighs*.
Cherish the names of the brave and the true,—
  Barnard, and Sprague, and Pickering, too.

Cho.—The first shot of Freedom to-day we repeat !
  Here's to the mem'ry of Leslie's Retreat !
    A health to the brave ones of old !

Salem poet, educator, and illustrator Lydia Louisa Anna Very wrote
this ode for the Centennial Celebration of Leslie's Retreat in 1875.

Americans saw or read about British defeats in Lexington, Concord, Trenton, Saratoga, and Yorktown, but, Hoffer asserts, *"these were not the first of their kind, nor were British defeats in themselves withdrawals of British claims to authority. Instead, the first incidence of the gathering of a republican citizenry asserting the right to self-government of their own land and the unforced recession of British might came in Salem, on Sunday, February 26, 1775 ... [see pp. 4-11 for more on the Revolutionary War and p.146 for the Old London Coffee House, meeting place of the patriots].*

After looking at the evidence for a long time, locating it in the larger story of colonial resistance to the Coercive Acts and the even longer story of the years after the French and Indian War, one should conclude that the gunpowder raid brought together a new world of popular politics and an old world of imperial British authority. Massachusetts men and women announced by word and demonstrated by deed that they were no longer subjects of the crown. Instead, they were citizens of a new kind of polity, one in which the people ruled themselves.

By retreating, Colonel Alexander Leslie conceded the day to that new world.

➡ *Continue along North Street. Turn right on Dearborn Street.*

Dearborn Street with its stately elms, ca. 1890.

Home of Mary R. Cate

34 Dearborn Street

Mary R. Cate, a graduate of Wellesley College (1911), was part of the First Wellesley Unit sent to France under the direction of the American Red Cross. According to Florence Converse, in her book *Wellesley College: A Chronicle of the Years 1875–1938,* we learn that the Wellesley Units were organized by the college's War Service Committee which was comprised of alumnae. "By this Committee," Converse writes, "the money was raised for all the activities sponsored by the Alumnae Association during the War; and the personnel of the Units was chosen by them. For the support of the Units and their work, Wellesley raised a sum of over $100,000. The Fund was completed in January, 1920."

In her war work overseas, Cate was joined by many other graduates of women's colleges who wanted to be of service. In a letter presented to President Woodrow Wilson by his daughter, Jenny Wilson Sayre, a student at the all-female Goucher College, eight women's colleges (in addition to Goucher: Barnard, Bryn Mawr, Mount Holyoke, Rad-cliffe, Smith, Vassar, and Wellesley) signed the following pledge:

To the President of the United States.

We the undersigned Presidents and Deans of the eight largest colleges for women in the United States, speaking for ourselves and authorized by vote to speak also for the Faculties of the Colleges which we represent, hereby respectfully offer you our loyal service.

Although we believe that the settlement of international difficulties by war is fundamentally wrong, we recognize that in a world crisis such as this it may become our highest duty to defend by force the principles upon which Christian civilization is founded.

In this emergency, Mr. President, we wish to pledge you our wholehearted support in whatever measures you may find necessary to uphold these principles.

Any service which we and (as far as we are able to speak for them) any service which the thousands of trained women whom we have sent out from our colleges may be able to render we hereby place at the disposal of our country.

Mary Cate's job title for the Red Cross was "Searcher." In that capacity, Cate visited American hospitals throughout France in search of missing soldiers. She remained in France after the war to assist with reconstruction work.

➡ *Return to North Street and turn right. Turn right on Orne Street, and proceed to the main entrance of Greenlawn Cemetery (on your left). Park on the street to walk, or drive/bicycle through Greenlawn along the roadway.*

Color postcard of Greenlawn Cemetery, ca. 1880. Packages of this and other vintage postcards of the cemetery are available from the Friends of Greenlawn. Visit their website, or find them on Facebook. All proceeds benefit their work!

Greenlawn Cemetery
57 Orne Street

This cemetery was established in 1807, when John Symonds purchased 5.5 acres in Salem's "North Fields" (as North Salem was known at the time) for a burying site. More land was added over the years, and the "Old Burying Ground of North Fields" especially benefited from the "Garden Cemetery" movement (or, the "Picturesque Tradition") of the 1830s inspired by Mount Auburn Cemetery in Cambridge, Massachusetts. Over time, with the purchasing of more land, trees, shrubs, and flowers, the cemetery was transformed into the beautiful place we (and many forms of wildlife, especially birds) enjoy today.

The City of Salem assumed management of the cemetery in 1884 under its new name, "Greenlawn Cemetery." Today, there are five designated burying areas for veterans. The graves near the flagpole and Soldiers' Monument are the most visible, but others throughout Greenlawn are marked as well. Greenlawn is where official ceremonies for Memorial Day and Wreaths Across America take place, when all veterans' graves are decorated.

Soldiers' Monument

Greenlawn Cemetery
Appleton Street entrance
Salem's Lieut. Col. Henry Merritt Camp No. 8 dedicated the Soldiers' Monument on November 5, 1886, in memory of their namesake and to honor the Civil War dead. Its inscription reads:

Erected and dedicated by
Lieut. Col. Henry Merritt
Camp No. 8. S. of V., U.S.A.,
Salem, Mass. For all he was and
all he dared, remember him today.

Postcard (detail) of the monument in 1905. Sadly, a vandal stole the original sword the soldier is holding. The Friends of Greenlawn Cemetery hope to replace it with a replica.

The occasion was marked by a 500-man parade from Salem Common to the site of the monument, led by a Grand Army of the Republic Color Guard and featuring rousing marches by the Salem Cadet Band. According to the *Salem Gazette* of November 6, 1886, the soldier on top of the monument was covered by an American flag for the ceremony which "at a given signal was unloosened and fluttered in the breeze, exposing to view the statue of a veteran, clad in a great army coat, and standing at parade rest." Salem's chapter of the Sons of Union Veterans also contributed to the creation and dedication of the Monument.

Honoring veterans is an ongoing initiative at Greenlawn Cemetery, thanks to Salem's Veterans Council and the Director of Veterans Services. For example, in 2016 Salem dedicated a new gravestone near the flagpole in honor of Navy Yeoman Thomas Atkinson, a Civil War soldier and Medal of Honor recipient who died at the Battle of Mobile Bay. The following year, a cemetery restoration company discovered Civil War era markers that were overgrown with grass. They may now be seen. We hope you will pick up a copy of the Friends of Greenlawn's self-guided walking tour booklet to learn more about some of the veterans who are buried here. To name just four:

Col. John W. Hart (1839-1912)
John Hart was not a native of Salem, but his family moved here when he was a boy. He was a member of the Salem Light Infantry before the Civil War, and enlisted in President Lincoln's Army of the Potomoc in 1861. He reenlisted for three years in the 1st Massachusetts Heavy Artillery. When Hart returned to Salem, he joined the Salem Cadets and served as the City Marshal for twenty-five years.

Capt. Charles L. Dearborn Jr. (1842-1862)
Charles Dearborn served in Company A, 32nd Regiment, Massachusetts Volunteer Militia (MVM). He was killed at the Battle of Fredericksburg, Virginia, on December 13, 1862, at age twenty. From his obituary in the *Salem Gazette* of December 19, 1862, we learn that "Capt. Dearborn fell while gallantly encouraging his company to push up promptly to a charge against the enemy … he had turned to urge the sergeants to encourage and cheer on the men [when] he was struck near the heart by a ball, and expired in about 20 minutes."

Sgt. Benjamin S. Grush (1819-1891)
According to the Friends of Greenlawn, Grush was a '49er who tried his luck in California during the Gold Rush days. He returned to Salem a few years later, and joined Company B, 40th Regiment, MVM, during the Civil War. After the war, he accepted a job laying water pipes in St. Joseph, Missouri, which inspired him to relocate to Salem and help establish the City's water service. Grush served as Salem's Water Superintendent from 1883 to 1888.

Cdr. J. Alex Michaud (1909–2003)

A more recent burial at Greenlawn was that of Cdr. J. Alex Michaud, U. S. Navy. Michaud entered the Navy after Pearl Harbor was attacked. With degrees from MIT and the General Motors Institute of Technology, he was asked to design a training program on the operation of PT boats in the South Pacific and North Atlantic Theaters. He was eventually promoted to Commander, Motor Torpedo Boat Squadrons, Philippine Sea Frontier.

After the war, Michaud worked for the State Department in the Phillippines, retiring as a full Commander. Returning to Salem, he assumed the management of the famous Michaud Bus Company with impressive results. His name is on the Walkway of Heroes at Armory Memorial Park.

➡ *Return to the entrance, and to North Street. Turn right.*

Home of Lieut. Col. George H. Woods

166 North Street/Route 114 (called "Maple Rest")

George H. Woods (1828-1884) served in the Massachusetts 57th Infantry, which "was raised in the early part of 1864 and arrived on the battlefields at the height of the last year of the Civil War," according to the Friends of Greenlawn Cemetery. The 57th was "immediately and continuously involved in battle once it arrived in the South, including at Ox Ford, Petersburg, Weldon Railroad, and Fort Stedman, suffering heavy losses along the way." Woods, an officer on Gen. Phil Sheridan's staff, survived the war but he was severely wounded. Luckily, his wife, Kate Tannatt Woods (1836-1910), was with him on the battlefield as his nurse.

Upon their return to Salem, George, an attorney, was unable to work; Kate used her writing ability to support their family. She was employed as a journalist for the *Boston Transcript, Boston Globe, Boston Herald,* and as a contributor and editor for *Harper's Bazaar* and the *Ladies Home Journal.* She was also a prolific writer of books for young people and of travelogues. George Woods died of his wounds in 1884 in Decatur, Illinois, at age fifty-six, but he and his wife are buried at Greenlawn Cemetery.

➡ *To reach the next site, from North Street/114, turn right on Liberty Hill Avenue. At Sargent Street, Liberty Hill Avenue becomes Kernwood Street. Follow Kernwood, and turn left into the Kernwood Country Club.*

KERNWOOD COUNTRY CLUB

Postcard of the Kernwood Mansion, ca. 1914, the year the club opened. Nothing remains of the building today.

Site of the Kernwood Mansion

Kernwood Avenue (Kernwood Country Club)

Col. Francis Peabody (1801-1867) built this magnificent Gothic Revival mansion in the 1840s after purchasing 166 acres of land in the part of North Salem known as "Horse Pasture Point." The son of Salem's wealthiest merchant at the time, Joseph Peabody, George served as an Artillery Commander in the Massachusetts Militia. In this role, his unit helped welcome General Lafayette to Salem in 1824. The following year, Peabody was promoted to the rank of Colonel. Salem historian Jerome Curley notes that "he helped organize the largest and last muster and sham fight exercises ever held in this area in 1826. This was the last exercise under the old Militia rules that required all males within military age be enrolled and mustered."

After this event, Peabody resigned to pursue his passion for inventing. As a young man, he had turned down a college education in favor of self-taught chemistry and mechanical engineering. He founded the Forest River Lead Company, built paper and linseed oil mills in nearby Middleton, and continued to study and experiment. Curley notes:

"He rarely pursued patents, being content to just develop the best product."

Peabody was a frequent lecturer at the Salem Lyceum, served as President of the Essex Institute (having helped found it), and was instrumental in restoring the dwindling Salem Marine Society. A student of architecture and a talented designer of buildings and landscapes, Peabody designed Kernwood Mansion himself as well as the meeting house for Salem's North Church (where he was a member). Today, the building is First Church in Salem. Francis Peabody also designed the stone archway entrance to Harmony Grove Cemetery (where he is buried, see photo, p. 210).

A few years after Francis Peabody's death in 1867, Gen. Horace Binney Sargent (1821-1908) of Quincy, Massachusetts, purchased the mansion. Sargent's long military career began shortly after graduating from Harvard Law School. He was commissioned Major in the Independent (First) Corps of Cadets, MVM, but he was soon appointed Aide-de-Camp with the rank of Lieut. Col. on the staff of Massachusetts Governor Nathaniel P. Banks. Sargent filled the same position under the next governor, John A. Andrew ("The War Governor"). As the Civil War approached, Sargent, a brilliant horseman, helped form the 1st Massachusetts Cavalry Regiment. He was commissioned into the unit as Lieut. Col., and made Colonel of the regiment in 1862.

Sargent's unit served first in South Carolina. It was transferred to the Army of the Potomoc, where the men fought at Secessionville, Culpepper Court House, Rapidan Station, and in the battles of Antietam, South Mountain, and Chancellorsville. In 1863, Sargent was promoted to Chief of the Cavalry of the Department of the Gulf on the staff of General Banks (the former Massachusetts governor), according to the Sargent family genealogy. In the spring of 1864, Sargent was wounded in the thigh and had to return home. "This ended Colonel Sargent's gallant and successful military career, and with the brevet rank of Brigadier General 'for gallantry and good conduct.'"

Returning to the Boston area, Sargent purchased Kernwood in 1870 where, according to the genealogy, he "devoted much time and attention to the interests and welfare of the discharged soldiers of the Northern Army, making public appeals and writing continually in the press in his effort to obtain government assistance for them. He served as Commandant of the Massachusetts Department of the Grand Army of the Republic from 1876 to 1878, and was the founder and first

President of the Soldiers' Home in Chelsea [Massachusetts] a position which he filled until 1884, remaining on its board until his death." The Chelsea Soldiers' Home is still in operation today. The Home's Sargent Hall is named for General Sargent, where a bronze plaque hangs in his honor. In Salem, Sargent Street is named for him. (Sargent Pond in Greenlawn Cemetery is named for arborist F. Carroll Sargent, likely a very distant cousin).

Bronze plaque at the Chelsea Soldiers' Home honoring its founder, Horace Binney Sargent.

In 2014, Massachusetts Governor Deval Patrick appointed Salem native Col. Cheryl Lussier Poppe as the Superintendent of the Chelsea Soldiers' Home. She is the first woman to hold this position. Poppe served in the Massachusetts National Guard for thirty years before retiring in 2008. She worked for the state Department of Veterans Affairs and as Acting Superintendant for the Soldiers' Home before her promotion to Superintendent. Poppe was also the first woman

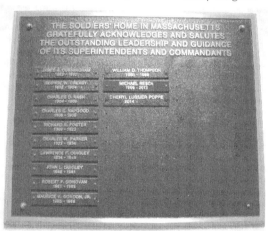

Col. Cheryl Lussier Poppe's name appears at the end of the second column of names.

member of the Second Corps of Cadets Veterans Association.

To reach the next site, *Harmony Grove Cemetery, return to North Street and turn right. At the traffic light (at King's Roast Beef), turn left on School Street. At the end of School Street, turn left on Tremont Street and proceed for a few blocks. Turn right on Grove Street.*

Stereo view of the entrance to Harmony Grove Cemetery, ca. 1895. The arch was designed by Col. Francis Peabody, who was influenced by his travels to England. Peabody also designed the meeting house of Salem's North Church in English Gothic style.

Harmony Grove Cemetery

30 Grove Street

In a booklet published by the Trustees of Harmony Grove, we learn that "the name 'Harmony Grove' was given to these grounds as far back as 1824 by several school girls in Salem, who were accustomed to coming here on May-day to gather flowers and welcome spring in all its splendor."

Over a decade later, in 1837, the wealthy inventor Col. Francis Peabody (owner of Kernwood) proposed the idea of having a "rural" cemetery in Salem. He, too, was following the growing national movement away from crowded church and urban burying grounds. Harmony Grove Cemetery was the eighth "garden cemetery" in the country. Greenlawn Cemetery, described earlier, evolved into a similar kind of burying place over time.

It took almost two years of meetings, fundraising, and land purchasing to move the project forward, but work commenced in October of 1839 using the surveying and design expertise of Alexander Wadsworth (who had done the same for Mount Auburn Cemetery in Cambridge, Massachusetts) and under the supervision of Francis Peabody himself. Among the long list of veterans buried at Harmony Grove are:

Brig. Gen. William Cogswell (1838-1895)

William Cogswell was a native of Bradford, Massachusetts, and the son of a founder of the state Republican Party. After graduating from Harvard's Dane Law School in 1860, Cogswell opened a law office in Salem. That same year, he joined the Second Corps of Cadets. In 1861, Cogswell was appointed Captain of the 2nd Massachusetts Infantry; he was promoted to Colonel in 1862. In 1864, Cogswell was bevetted Brigadier General, commanding the 3rd Brigade, 3rd Division, 20th Corps. After the war, Cogswell returned to his law practice and began an impressive political career. He served as Mayor of Salem (1868-1869, 1873-1874) State Representative (1870 -1871, 1881-1883), State Senator 1885-1886) and Member of Congress (1887-1895). Cogswell School is named for him.

Capt. Luis F. Emilio (1844-1918)

Capt. Luis F. Emilio

In 1861, sixteen-year-old Luis Fenellosa Emilio lied about his age and enlisted in Company F, 23rd Massachusetts Volunteer Infantry. He distinguished himself on the battlefield, earning the rank of Sergeant a year later. In 1863, after President Lincoln signed the Emancipation Proclamation and African American soldiers could fight for the Union, Massachusetts Governor John A. Andrew created the all-black 54th Regiment. He chose Emilio as one of the white officers. Emilio was mustered in that March as 2nd Lieutenant, and he was quickly promoted to 1st Lieutenant. In May, he was made Captain of Company E. Emilio fought with the 54th until the end of the war, mustering out in 1865 shortly before his twenty-first birthday. Years later, in 1891, Emilio published *Brave Black Regiment*, a history of the 54th Regiment (reissued in 1894). His book inspired researchers and, in 1989, an award-winning movie: *Glory*.

Hon. William Crowninshield Endicott (1826-1900)

A graduate of Harvard College and Harvard Law School, Endicott served on the Massachusetts Supreme Judicial Court from 1879 to 1882 after an unsuccessful run for Congress. He lost the race for Governor in 1884, but was appointed Secretary of War by President Grover Cleveland. Endicott is best remembered for creating a system for the promotion of officers and for the "Endicott Board," which was tasked with improving America's coastal defense during the Spanish-American War. Many of these installations were in use through World War II.

Cdr. David M. Little (1860-1923)

A native of nearby Swampscott, Massachusetts, David Mason Little served in the Spanish-American War and World War I, retiring as Commander. He served for a time as Quartermaster of the Salem Cadets, and as District Construction Officer for the Charlestown Navy Yard. David M. Little was the Mayor of Salem from 1900 to 1901. He was married to Clara Bertram Kimball, one of the philan-

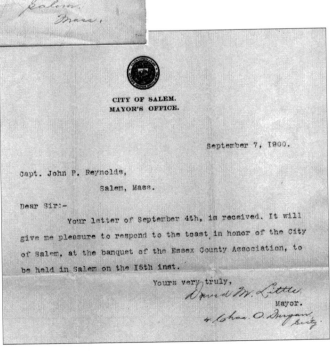

Letter and envelope from the office of Mayor David M. Little addressed to Capt. Joseph P. Reynolds of the Salem Light Infantry Veterans Association, with the date of September 7, 1900.

CITY OF SALEM.
MAYOR'S OFFICE.

September 7, 1900.

Capt. John P. Reynolds,

Salem, Mass.

Dear Sir:-

Your letter of September 4th, is received. It will give me pleasure to respond to the toast in honor of the City of Salem, at the banquet of the Essex County Association, to be held in Salem on the 15th inst.

Yours very truly,

David M. Little

Mayor.

thropist John Bertram's granddaughters. She and her more famous sister, Caroline Emmerton, volunteered for and supported the Red Cross during World War I. One of Little's ancestors was Col. David Mason of "Leslie's Retreat" fame.

Seaman Jean Missud (1852-1941)

Jean Missud enlisted in the U. S. Navy in 1869 when the USS *Sabine* was in his home port of Nice, France. When the ship returned to the Charlestown Navy Yard in 1870, Missud decided to make the United States his home, eventually, Salem. There, he founded the Salem Cadet Band (see pp. 96-7, 101-4), and was honored by having the Salem Common Bandstand named for him (see photo, p. 96).

Capt. Joseph Peabody (1757-1844)

Joseph Peabody was an officer on privateers during the Revolutionary War—a long way from his modest, uneducated farm upbringing in Middleton and Boxford (both in Massachusetts). After the war, Peabody became a wealthy merchant and ship owner—especially in the pepper trade. He was the richest man in Salem for many years after 1807. His son was Col. Francis Peabody (see pp. 207-8).

Pvt. Jesse Smith (1756-1844)

Jesse Smith was a native of Lincoln, Massachusetts, and one of the Lincoln "Minutemen" who fought in Concord on April 19, 1775. The next year, he was chosen for Gen. George Washington's First Foot Guard (or, body guards). When he retired from the Continental Army, Smith moved to Salem where he signed on with a privateer. His ship was captured by the British, and he was sent to Mill Prison in England until the end of the War of 1812. Returning to Salem, Smith became an accomplished shipmaster. When he died, Jesse Smith was the last surviving bodyguard of Gen. George Washington.

Gen. Frederick Townsend Ward (1831-1862)

As a soldier for hire, Ward fought in Mexico, Europe, and with the Texas Rangers. In 1859, he sailed to Shanghai, China, and became militarily indispensible to the Chinese government. He was shot and killed in China, and buried there. His monument in Harmony Grove is a cenotaph (see 231-33).

— End of trail. ★

COMMISSIONING DAY SPECIAL EDITION

WITCHCRAFT
PUBLISHED BY
U.S.S. SALEM

VOL. 1, NO. 1   14 MAY, 1949

THE U.S.S. SALEM (CA-139)

General Information of the U.S.S. SALEM

THE USS SALEM, one of the "heaviest" Heavy Cruisers in the world, will be commissioned on 14 May 1949 at the Boston Naval Shipyard, Boston, Massachusetts.

The SALEM is the third and last ship in the DES MOINES Class of 17,000 ton Heavy Cruisers to be commissioned. Like her sister ships, the USS DES MOINES (CA-134) AND THE USS NEWPORT NEWS (CA-148), the SALEM is equipped with new eight-inch batteries capable of firing approximately four times faster than any guns of the same or larger caliber.

Her overall length of 716 ft. and displacement of 17,000 tons make her comparable in size with some of the famous "dreadnaughts" of the first World War. Compared with the Heavy Cruisers which saw service in

World War II, the SALEM displaces almost 3500 tons more than the BALTIMORE Class Heavies, and 7000 tons more than the "Treaty" Heavies.

In efficiency and sea-worthiness, she will be unsurpassed by anything afloat.

The SALEM shares with her sister ship, the NEWPORT NEWS, the distinction of being the Navy's only completely air conditioned warships. To increase the fighting efficiency of her crew and to improve living conditions on board, virtually all her living and working compartments will be air conditioned.

Keeping pace with the latest developments in sea-air power, the SALEM will carry a helicopter rather than the catapult-type cruiser float planes used during World War

II. The helicopter will be used to assist her gun crews in laying down precise, accurate fire when engaged in shore bombardment.

The greatly increased firepower of the SALEM is perhaps her most important feature. Her new eight-inch main batteries, automatic to the gun muzzles, eject cartridge cases from the mounts. By abandoning powder bags, and devising the delicate machinery and controls to handle cartridge cases, the Navy has increased the rate of fire of the SALEM to approximately four times the rate achieved by our wartime Heavy Cruisers. The SALEM's main battery consists of nine eight-inch, 55-caliber guns, triple mounted in three turrets. (See page 8)

According to a story on the back cover of this special edition newsletter, the name of the publication, *Witchcraft*, was the result of a contest held among the ship's officers and crew. A brief history lesson on the definition of "witchcraft" and its relationship to Salem was included in the paper, without an explanation of how any of this is connected—excepting the word "craft" as another term for "boat"

★ Sites to Visit by Neighborhood ★

~ Waterfront and Derby Street ~

START:
Salem Maritime
National Historic Site
(National Park Service)
Derby Street and adjoining wharves

Postcard of the ship *Mount Vernon* owned by Elias Hasket Derby. She was built and armed for the Quasi-War with France of 1798.

Salem Harbor

Military activities in Salem Harbor over the years included ship building and repair, defense, training, and hosting visiting vessels. In Salem's earliest days, lookouts and forts guarded the harbor from invasion (see pp. 245-75). At various times, that could mean British, French, Dutch, or German vessels. As a wealthy, strategically positioned port, Salem was vulnerable to attack.

During the Revolutionary War, Salem ship captains excelled as privateers. As the Park Service explains in the book *Maritime Salem in the Age of Sail*:

When economic resistance escalated to revolution, patriot seafarers carried the battle to sea. The port took full advantage of the Continental Congress' decision to augment its tiny navy by licensing hundreds of commercial ships as privateers to harass and capture British vessels. Other vessels carried "letters-of-marque," allowing them to take prizes in the course of regular commercial voyages. Privateering, called by John Adams "a short, easy, and infallible method of humbling the British," was crucial to the American effort in the early years of the war, hurting British commerce, tying up British warships that otherwise would have blockaded American ports, and capturing supplies and arms desperately needed by the Continental Army.

➡ *Continued on page 217*

How Salem's "Sea-fencibles" Saved the USS *Constitution*

Matchbook cover from the Coast Guard's Constitution Base, Boston, ca. 1940, with an image of the USS *Constitution*.

Military historian Charles A. Benjamin writes:

During the war, in addition to the ordinary militia and the volunteer companies of the town there was a company of sea-fencibles, so-called, organized and composed entirely of masters and mates of merchantmen who were idle, to serve as artillerists or otherwise, as the coast was threatened from time to time by British men-of-war. The venerable William H. Foster ... a member of the cadet company of that day ... remembers various alarms, musterings and marches hither and thither on various occasions. When the frigate Constitution *was forced to take refuge in Marblehead harbor from a pursuing squadron of the enemy, the company of fencibles dragged their twenty-four pounders over to the shore of that town to play on the enemy in case they should follow her. The English vessels, not being acquainted with the shore and depth of the water, did not venture in, and an attack with boats upon a formidable frigate was out of the question, of course. The next day, the* Constitution *was brought around to Salem by Joseph Perkins, the harbor pilot ... and anchored under the guns of the fort* [Lee, see CD].

BAKER'S ISLAND LIGHT
Rescue of the U.S.S. "Constitution"
by Keeper Joseph Perkins in the War of 1812

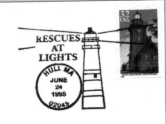

One in a series of covers sponsored by the Hull Life-saving Museum on Cape Cod, Mass., June 24, 1995.

It was a relatively easy matter to convert a merchantman to a privateer, and only a few months after the opening shots of the war, Salem's small but heavily armed schooner Dolphin *captured the port's first prize—the British trading sloop* Success. *Derby and Union Wharves became the center of privateering activity in Salem. Fishermen mounted swivel guns on their fishing smacks and went out in "wolf packs" to dog the heels of British convoys, cutting out lagging merchant vessels twice their size...*

Capt. John Carnes (1756-1796) of Salem

Postcard of Capt. John Carnes (1756-1796), one of Salem's most successful privateers.

Salem proved adept at this combination of profit and patriotism. Over the course of the Revolution, the port's 158 privateering vessels took 445 British vessels, accounting for more tonnage than any other American seaport.

While the war seriously impaired Salem's regular trade activity, many of her privateers made a fortune. The Park Service notes: "Privateering helped the port survive, in good part by providing jobs for hundreds of seamen and fishermen."

Privateering went on again in force during the War of 1812, which was not at all a popular war in Salem. Merchants had suffered economically during the Revolutionary War, and again during President Thomas Jefferson's embargo of 1807 that prohibited international trade. In Europe, England and France were in conflict again, leading the British to "impress" (kidnap) thousands of American sailors into their Navy. Today, a replica of an 1812 privateer, the Schooner *Fame*, is moored in Salem Harbor and available for public or private sails. Their website and publications are rich with information about privateers, including:

In a war against the world's most powerful navy, the mariners of Salem had few options open to them. They could carry on with business as usual, bringing back cargoes of tea, silks, and pepper from the rich East—but they ran the risk of being captured by British cruisers or privateers and losing everything. They could go privateering themselves, playing cat-and-mouse with fat British merchant ships and dangerous British men of war. Or they could 'swallow the anchor'—sit at home and watch their savings dwindle, praying for peace.

    Many Salem mariners chose privateering as being the least of the three evils—or at least the one in which they had most control over their destinies.

Charles A. Benjamin adds this about Salem privateers:

In writing of the exploits of the privateers of Salem in this war, it is difficult to know how to begin and where to end. For three years forty vessels, practically men of war, cruised from this port heavily armed, and officered, and manned by as skillful and brave navigators and seamen as were then afloat. And this does not include over one hundred letter of marque trading vessels, that kept the sea and did some fighting as well as trading.

The War of 1812 war was the last time Salem Harbor was used for specifically war-related activities. Through World War II, war efforts shifted to Winter Island (see pp. 245-75) or men (and, later, women) were sent overseas (see "Salem During Wartime").

Jonathan Haradan, Privateer

In their book *Maritime Salem in the Age of Sail,* the National Park Service describes Jonathan Haradan (1744–1803) as "Salem's most successful and famous privateer captain during the Revolution. [He] was celebrated for his resourcefulness, icy calmness under fire, and the absolute loyalty of those under him. He never lost a ship, and was said to have captured more than 60 vessels carrying perhaps 1,000 guns and 2,000 to 3,000 men."

James Duncan Phillips describes Haradan as "one of the great characters of the Revolution, and not even John Paul Jones or John Manley had greater claim to clear, cool courage and intrepid daring than he." (For more on Haradan and to visit the site of his home, see p. 153.)

Postcard of an artist's rendition of the *Quero* departing from Derby Wharf.

Derby Wharf

It was Richard Derby's ship *Quero*, captained by his brother John Derby, who carried the news of the British troops' retreat from Concord and Lexington to Boston on April 19, 1775. Specifically, he carried copies of the *Salem Gazette* and *Essex Gazette* detailing what had happened. Interestingly, among the papers Derby carried, according to Salem historian James Duncan Phillips, "there was enclosed an appeal to the inhabitants of Great Britain," signed by Joseph Warren, President *pro tem* of the Provincial Congress, and twenty affidavits, including two from British soldiers, "that the troops fired first [in Concord] and without provocation."

The news from Salem apparently "shook the throne of England," but this one last olive branch was unsuccessful. Derby returned in haste first to Cambridge to report to General George Washington, and then to Salem. According to historian Fred Gannon, "Lafayette, in Paris, learned of the news from Salem. He bought a ship, loaded it with supplies, and sailed for America. From his own purse he paid for ship and cargo. He volunteered to fight in the War for Liberty, and he fought on until the war was won at Yorktown. After the war he twice returned to Salem and each time was welcomed as a gallant soldier and a friend of America."

➡ *Continue along Derby Street.*

Central Wharf

The Naval Reserve Training Center, located here after World War II, included four war-time submarines and a mine sweeper, the USS *Ruff*. About one submarine, the USS *Shad* (SS-235), the *Salem Evening News* of September 24, 1948, published:

The sleek gray submarine Shad, Portsmouth-built veteran of 11 war patrols in both the European and Asiatic waters, yesterday arrived at the berth in Salem, from which it will continue its peacetime job of training naval reservists. With two yard tugs from the Boston naval

Matchbook covers, sponsored by Salem-based Parker Brothers, for the Naval Training Center.

USS *Shad* tied up at Central Wharf, ca. 1952.

Submarine Shad Now at Permanent Berth in Salem

USS SHAD AT HER NEW BERTH

Submarine, Which Has Been Tied Up At the New England Coal Wharf in Beverly For Several Months, Shown At Central Wharf In Salem Where She Will Be Stationed Permanently

Salem Evening News, September 24, 1948.

shipyard nudging her from her temporary berth in Beverly Harbor, the Shad, stripped of her own driving mechanism, was towed to a place that had been prepared for her at Central Wharf.

    To get to her new station, the Shad passed along the new channel that has been dredged to the Salem Naval Reserve Training Center on Central Wharf. Aboard was her crew of 20 men, under the command of Lieut. Kenneth G. Curtis of Saugus, who remarked that "Salem is the smallest city that ever got a sub." Half the crew are men whose homes are in the Greater Salem area. Soon the Shad will be open for public inspection on Saturdays, Sundays, and holidays, but first, everything has to be made ready at the Central Wharf, according to Lieut. Curtis.

First day cover, October 27, 1957.

Press photograph of the USS *Shad*'s torpedo chamber.

The sleek gray submarine Shad, Portsmouth-built veteran of 11 war patrols in both the European and Asiatic waters, yesterday arrived at the berth in Salem, from which it will continue its peacetime job of training naval reservists. —Salem Evening News

SEA DOG LEAVES — A popular maritime attraction for many years on the downtown Salem waterfront, the submarine Sea Dog vacated its berth Friday alongside the Naval Reserve Training Center near Derby Wharf. Tours of the undersea craft delighted visitors, especially children. The Sea Dog saw plenty of action in the Pacific during World War II. Tug was employed to tow the submarine on the first leg of its journey to Boston. The submarine is consigned to Tulsa, Okla., to be enshrined there as a national monument.

Newspaper clipping of the USS *Sea Dog*, part of the Naval Training Center.

Ship Visits

Navy ships have made port visits to Salem for many years, including as recently as 2002 for the Bowditch Bicentennial (see p. 234 on Nathaniel Bowditch). In 1934, to cite an example from years

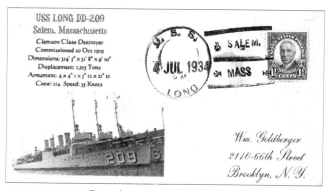

First day cover, July 2, 1934.

ago, the Clemson-class destroyer USS *Long* (DD-209) visited Salem. Launched in 1919, she was assigned to Destroyer Division 26 and patrolled the Adriatic, Meditteranean, and South China Seas until she was decommissioned in 1922. The *Long* was recommissioned in 1930, operating out of San Diego, until she was assigned to the "rotating reserve" and Destroyer Squadron 20 from 1933 to 1935. The *Long* was refitted as a mine sweeper and reclassified DMS-12 in 1940. She was sunk by a kamikaze in 1945 off the coast of Japan.

Color postcard of the first USS *Salem*, ca. 1908. (Turn the page for more about the three ships named USS *Salem*.)

The Three Ships Named USS *Salem*

Postcard of the first USS *Salem*, ca. 1907.

According to U. S. Navy records, the first USS *Salem* (CS-3/CL-3), Scout Cruiser No. 3, was a Chester-class Scout cruiser. She was the first Navy ship named for the City of Salem, Massachusetts. Her keel was laid down on August 28, 1905, by the Fore River Shipyard in Quincy, Massachusetts. She was launched on July 26, 1907, sponsored by Mrs. Lorna Pinnock (wife of the Mayor of Salem) in fine Navy tradition,* and commissioned on August 1, 1908, Commander Henry B. Wilson in command. She was one of the Navy's first turbine-engine warships.

The *Salem* was in service from 1908 to 1921. Before World War I, she was deployed off Haiti, placed on reserve in Boston and Philadelphia as a receiving ship, and assigned to the Special Service Squadron in Mexican and Dominican waters to assist in radio communication, among her other assignments.

The USS *Salem* visited her namesake City from July 26 to 31, 1909, for Old Home Week. A massive celebration took place, including an illumination of the shoreline, a military and civic parade, a reception for the officers and crew where they were presented with gifts, and a banquet at the Salem Armory.

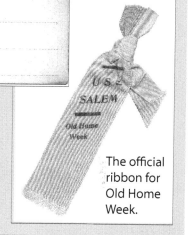

Postcard invitation to Old Home Week 1909. The "entertainment" was provided by the Salem Cadet Band. Saturday's athletic event was a baseball game between the ship's crew and the Highland Athletic Club. During her visit to Salem, the ship was commanded by Albert L. Key. Below: Two versions of the postcard invitation front.

The official ribbon for Old Home Week.

Postcard of the USS *Salem*. She was four hundred and twenty-three feet long, forty-six feet wide, and drew nineteen feet of water.

Postcard of the silver service presented to the captain and crew of the USS *Salem*, "paid for by Dime Contributions from the Citizens of Salem, Massachusetts."

During World War I, the *Salem* served as a submarine chaser across the Atlantic and off the coast of Florida. In 1930, she was sold for scrap metal.

The second USS *Salem* was built in 1916 by William Cramp and Sons in Philadelphia. A civilian ship, she was originally named the SS *Joseph R. Parrott*. The Navy acquired the ship on June 8, 1942; she was commissioned as the USS *Salem* (CM-11) on August 9, 1942. During World War II, she served as a mine layer, net layer, and cargo ship in the waters of Casablanca, Italy, Japan (where she survived frequent air attacks), and Guam. This USS *Salem* received two battle stars.

On August 15, 1945, *Salem* was renamed USS *Shawmut* to allow a new ship to bear the name of "Salem." Navy records tell the end of her story: "*Shawmut* was ... transferred to the Maritime Commission on 20 June 1946. She was sold on 7 March 1947 to the West India Fruit and Steamship Company, and served as SS *Joseph R. Parrott* under the Honduran flag until 1970."

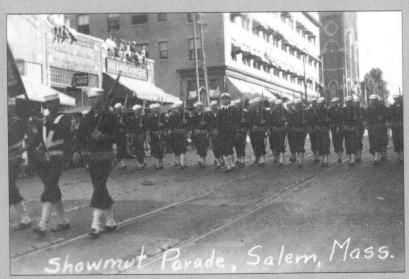

After the USS *Salem's* name was changed to the USS *Shawmut*, she visited Salem again and her crew paraded through downtown—shown here on Washington Street, ca. 1945.

The third USS *Salem* (CA-139), according to Navy records, "is one of three Des Moines-class heavy cruisers completed for the United States Navy shortly after World War II. Commissioned in 1949, she was the world's last all-gun heavy cruiser to enter service. She was decommissioned in 1959, after serving in the Atlantic and Mediterranean."

Salem's keel was laid down on July 4, 1945, by the Bethlehem Steel Company's Fore River Shipyard in Quincy, Massachusetts. She was launched on March 25, 1947, sponsored by Miss Mary G. Coffey.* She was commissioned on May 14, 1949, Captain J. C. Daniel in command. According to the Navy, "her main battery held the world's first automatic 8-inch guns and were the first 8-inch naval guns to use cased ammunition instead of shell and bag loading."

The USS *Salem* visited Salem on July 4, 1949, before beginning her career. During her years of service, she made seven deployments to the Mediterranean as flagship for the 6th fleet. She was the first American ship to arrive in the Ionian Islands (Greece) to provide relief after a devastating earthquake. A newspaper account at the time states: "Lives of refugees from the earthquake-ridden island of Greece rest today in some measure on the navigational skill of a Lock Haven navigation officer, Lieut. Cmdr. William S. Hitchens, navigation officer of the heavy cruiser, U.S.S. *Salem*."

First day cover, May 29, 1954.

Salem Mayor George Bates (far right) and city officials on board the third USS *Salem* in 1954.

In 1954, *Salem* participated in war games with the Atlantic fleet. In1955, she participated in NATO and Franco-American exercises with Under Secretary of the Navy Thomas S. Gates as an "observer." She was in the Mediterranean in October 1956, when the Suez Crisis broke out, and she represented U.S. support for Jordan in 1958 when their government was being threatened.

USS *Salem* portrayed a German battleship in the 1956 movie *The Battle of the River Plate*, and she represented the U.S. again in Monaco for the celebration of the birth of Prince Albert II, the son of Prince Rainier and former American movie star Princess Grace Kelly. *Salem* was then sent to Lebanon, as part of a show of American support in a time of crisis.

The ship was decommissioned on January 30, 1959, and sent to the Philadelphia Naval Shipyard to be stored as part of the Atlantic Reserve Fleet. She was essentially "mothballed" for thirty-five years until she was returned to Quincy, her birthplace, where she is now a museum ship as part of the U. S. Naval Shipbuilding Museum in that city. As the Museum explains:

On 14 May, 1995—46 years to the day since her original commissioning—Salem was re-commissioned—this time as a member of the Historic Naval Ships Association. She now serves her country once again with her new mission of teaching people of all generations our nation's rich history of shipbuilding and naval duty … Although Salem never fired her mighty guns in anger, her very presence served as a stimulus for peace during those troubled times that came to be called the Cold War. She served as a Lady of Diplomacy, rather than as a means of exerting brute force.

*A ship sponsor, by tradition, is a female civilian who is invited to "sponsor" a vessel, presumably to bestow good luck and divine protection over the seagoing vessel and all that sail aboard. In the United States Navy and Coast Guard, the sponsor is technically considered a permanent member of the ship's crew. She is expected to give a part of her personality to the ship, as well as advocate for its continued service and well-being.

K1USN • USS SALEM CA139
SPECIAL EVENT STATION • QUINCY, MASSACHUSETTS

Postcard of the USS *Salem* (CA-139), ca. 1995: "She served as a Lady of Diplomacy, rather than as a means of exerting brute force."

Photograph of the Custom House, ca. 1940.

Custom House

In 1940, with the prospect of war looming, President Franklin D. Roosevelt invoked the Espionage Act of 1917, expanding the U. S. Coast Guard's port security role through the Captain of the Port Program (COTP). The Commander of Coast Guard Air Station Salem, Roy L. Raney, became Salem's COTP and his office was relocated to the Custom House as it was the most important federal building in Salem (and part of the Salem Maritime National Historic Site).

An older Custom House, on Central Street, has an earlier military connection. Following the "Boston Tea Party" of 1773, the British Parliament passed the Boston Port Bill—the first of several Coercive Acts—which closed Boston Harbor to all foreign trade. In response, independence-minded officials shifted customs functions to Salem. The men involved often met at the Old London Coffee House across the street (see p. 146).

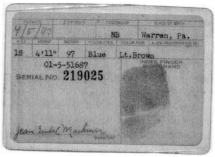

Identification cards issued by the office of the Captain of the Port were
required for anyone working, studying, or living along the coast.
This ID card belonged to Jean I. Machner, a student at Endicott Junior
College in the Pride's Crossing neighborhood of North Beverly.

During World War II, oil tankers were named for national parks
and monuments including the SS *Salem Maritime,* built in 1945
by the Kaiser Company of Portland, Oregon. Salem Maritime
—the nation's first national historic site—was established
under the Roosevelt administration in 1938.

➡ *Continue along Derby Street.*

Home of Frederick Townsend Ward

96 Derby Street (note the house plaque)

The son of a ship's captain and two seafaring families, Frederick
Townsend Ward was born in 1831 and raised in the house owned by
his grandfather, Moses Townsend. At the age of fifteen, young Frederick
went to sea on board the clipper ship *Hamilton* bound for China. A
couple of years later, he was his father's first mate on a ship heading for

San Francisco. Salem historian Jim McAllister explains, "On both of these voyages, Ward was given a position of authority over men many years older and more experienced. It was apparent the vessels' owners recognized the young man's leadership qualities."

But Frederick Townsend Ward's interests lay in a military career, not in the maritime trades. Although his father prevented him from joining the army during the Mexican War, and West Point turned him down in favor of a more politically connected applicant, Ward headed for Vermont in 1849—to what is now Norwich University, then, the American Literary, Scientific and Military Academy. "Rebellious by nature," according to Jacque Day writing for *The Norwich Record*, Ward only studied at Norwich for a brief period of time before leaving to pursue a career as a (for-hire, independent) soldier-of-fortune.

During the 1850s, Ward fought with William Walker's filibuster army in Mexico, with the French Army in the Crimean War against Russia, and with the Texas Rangers in his home country. By the time Ward returned to China in 1859, to Shanghai, he had become an impressive military leader—just when the Tai Ping rebels posed a real threat to the Manchu dynasty, or Chinese government. Jim McAllister explains that Shanghai was:

…*one of the five Chinese port cities in which Westerners were allowed to trade and live. It appeared that Shanghai would fall to the rebels. The forces of the imperial emperor had been unable to stop the Tai Pings in the past and the British, French, and American governments were committed to a policy of neutrality.*

Ward approached local Chinese government officials with an offer to raise an army and drive out the Tai Pings in return for a substantial fee. The desperate Manchu officials agreed to the arrangement, and the force that would become known as Ward's "Ever-Victorious Army" was born.

Ward's army "wore western-style uniforms, used American drill, and were equipped with British weapons," writes military historian Chris Kolakowski for *Emerging Civil War*, continuing, "after training much of the last half of 1861, in January 1862 the Ever Victorious Army went into action. The force lived up to its name, as discipline and modern weaponry proved decisive against the Taiping rebels."

Ward was wounded fifteen times, including in the face, surviving each time and earning the name "Devil Soldier" by the Tai Pings. Their rebellion was eventually crushed in 1863, but Ward didn't live to see it. He was shot on September 21, 1862, and died the next day at the age of thirty. His remains are somewhere in China, but a cenotaph in his memory stands in Harmony Grove Cemetery (see p. 213). Before his death, Ward was able to dictate a will to care for his sister, brother, and Chinese wife. Some of his personal relics and the bullet that killed him are in the collection of the Peabody Essex Museum.

Portrait of Frederick Townsend Ward from his *carte de visite* showing where he was shot in the face.

Book plate created by the Essex Institute (today, the Peabody Essex Museum) for the Frederick Townsend Ward Memorial Fund.

In China, where Ward was deeply mourned, "a temple was dedicated to him and, by imperial mandate, he was worshiped as a deity," according to the *Salem Evening News* of September 17, 1934, on the occasion of the visit to Salem of Gen. Tsai Ting Kai, "the hero of Shanghai." The thirty-year-old general had successfully put down the Japanese in 1932 and was touring the U. S. In Salem, he placed a wreath at Frederick Townsend Ward's cenotaph. Ward's accomplishments are also remembered in a Songjiang Roman Catholic Church and in the Taiping Heavenly Kingdom Historical Museum in Nanjing. American Legion China Post 1, formed in 1919, was named for him. Interestingly, some of the sons and grandsons of the Chinese soldiers who fought with Ward journeyed to America to attend Norwich University.

➡ *The trail continues on page 238.*

Three Salem Inventors Who Helped "Win the War" at Sea

Nathaniel Bowditch

One of Salem's "sons" of whom the City is most proud is Nathaniel Bowditch (1773-1838), whose groundbreaking 1802 book, *The New American Practical Navigator,* "saved countless lives and fortunes by making accurate navigational calculations accessible to the ordinary sailor," according to a Salem Maritime National Historic Site publication on Bowditch.

Bowditch's irregular education ended when he was ten, it continues, "but he was able to encourage his natural genius for astronomy, mathematics, and physics through access to books in some of the earliest libraries in America [including today's Salem Athenaeum]. He also applied his theories to experiments during his years sailing on merchant vessels."

That Bowditch was able to achieve what he did is, simply, remarkable. At the age of eight, he worked with his father in the cooperage (barrel making) business to help support the family. Two years later, after learning bookkeeping, he apprenticed in a ship chandlery shop (supply store). From there, he went to sea for several years, first as clerk and second mate on one of Elias Hasket Derby's ships. All of Bowditch's life experiences, and his self-studying, led to the publication of *The New American Practical Navigator.*

Bowditch continued his scientific inquiries after publishing *Navigator,* and he was eventually offered the position of Professor of Mathematics at Harvard College, the University of Virginia, and West Point. He also became President of the East India Marine Society in Salem, the director of insurance companies in Salem and Boston, and the founder of several "benevolent institutions."

Today, all Navy and Coast Guard vessels carry a hard copy of "The Bowditch" just in case. The next time you're on board a Navy ship or a Coast Guard cutter, ask to see their "Bowditch!"

Moses G. Farmer

Moses Gerrish Farmer (1820-1893), a native of Boscawen, New Hampshire, was a brilliant inventor who lived and experimented in Salem for twenty-four years. He lived at 11 Pearl Street.

Farmer had spent his early career teaching in Maine and New Hampshire, but he had always shown "in a variety of ways his innate ingenuity and an intense interest in mechanics and natural philosophy," according to the *Dictionary of American Biography*.

Farmer was particularly drawn to electricity and the electro-magnetic telegraph. He worked for a time as the wire examiner of the new Boston-Worcester telegraph line, and in his spare time Farmer learned telegraphy. In July 1848, he was appointed operator in the telegraph office in Salem, where he moved with his family.

During his years in Salem, Farmer continued his experiments at home. With the assistance of Dr. William F. Channing, according to the *Dictionary*, he invented "an electric-striking apparatus for a fire alarm service," which gave each fire box its own, distinct ring. If a fire alarm was pulled, fire fighters could rush to the fire station or to the fire's location (later, towns used whistle blasts). Farmer also invented a "special water motor to drive the electric dynamos." Boston implemented these inventions in 1851, hiring Moses Farmer as the system's Superintendent.

After leaving that position, Farmer continued to experiment in multiplex telegraphy, electro-typography, and tobacco-extracting. From 1858 to1859, seeing the possibility of electricity as a source of light, Farmer invented an incandescent electric lamp.

In 1859, "he used two of these lamps to light the parlor of his home for several months"—the first house in the world to be lit by electricity, predating Thomas Edison's exhibitions. Farmer then "conceived and patented what is now called the 'self-exciting' dynamo,'" using it to completely light a house in Cambridge, Massachusetts, in 1868. Moses Farmer left Salem in 1872 for Newport, Rhode Island, where he "was selected to fill the office of Electrician at the United States Torpedo Station." The *Dictionary* maintains: "He greatly advanced the art of torpedo warfare for the United States Navy."

Ralph C. Browne

The *Salem Evening News* called Ralph Cowan Browne (1880-1959) "the man who won the war." That war was World War I. Born in Salem and raised on St. Peter Street, Ralph C. Browne attended Salem public schools through high school. After graduating, like Thomas Edison, he did not attend college but instead forged a self-taught career in the new and exciting field of electricity.

In the early days of World War I, German U-boats preyed on American merchant vessels in the North Sea. As Byron Farwell explains in his book *Over There: The United States in the Great War*:

When the war began there was no way in which a submerged submarine could be sunk. Not until 1916 was the depth charge, a 300-pound drum of TNT ... invented by the Royal Navy...

Two American inventions were particularly helpful [including] the development by two Americans, Commander S. P. Fullinwider and a civilian, thirty-seven-year-old Ralph C. Browne, a roentgenologist (a kind of radiologist), of an electrical system and mechanism that made possible an improved mine. Up to this time mines were all of the 'contact type,' needing direct contact before they exploded.

What was needed was a mine with a much larger radius of danger.

The new mines, called Mark VI, loaded with three hundred pounds of TNT, were often called 'antenna mines,' for a long thin copper cable, suspended just below the surface by a small metal buoy, electronically fired the mine below." Browne's obituary in the *Institute of Electrical Engineers Magazine* states:

Mr. Browne was the inventor of the mine apparatus that was credited with turning the tide of battle in World War I and bringing the war to a halt. When Mr. Browne's invention was perfected, the United States had a device that multiplied by three the power of ➡

Photograph of Ralph C. Browne and caption from Acme Photo, New York:

Ralph C. Browne, inventor of Salem, Mass., with one of the magnetic mines he invented during the last war, a barrage of which crippled the German submarine offensive, at his home here. Browne recently described a device that will protect ships from mines of all types. It consists of a torpedo-like vessel powered by a 100-horse power electric motor. The torpedo is attached to the bow of the ship and synchronized with the ship's steering gear. A cable an eighth of a mile long powers the torpedo as it forges along ahead of the ship. From either side of the torpedo cables stretch out to paravenes and drag up any mines in the path of the ship.

the mine previously used. The theory of the mine not only increased its potential power but practically eliminated the possibility of any failure of the mine to perform its mission. Attached to the mine was a long wire antenna which would form a circuit that exploded the mine's contents when the antenna came into contact with a metal other than copper. The ocean water provided the battery liquid, and the contact with the hull of a submarine or any vessel formed a circuit which caused the explosion."

After the war, Browne moved to 123 Federal Street, later, to 17 Beckford Street, where he continued his experiments and inventions. These included a portable x-ray machine and a microphone for telephones.

If you think about it, because Salem was settled by minor nobility, talented tradesmen, craftsmen, and their families, right from the git-go there's been a little something extra about this place in terms of the talent pool.
—Nelson Dionne

Veterans of Foreign Wars / VFW, Post 1524
95 Derby Street
The Veterans of Foreign Wars was founded in 1899 after the Spanish-American War to care for veterans and their families. Their essential mission has not changed over time. Salem members of this VFW Post are "committed to helping make a difference for veterans and their families in the Salem Community," according to their website, and they do. VFW members raise funds, make visits, support Salem's Veterans Services Department, and are a visible presence on Veterans' Day, Memorial Day, and other military-related events. This VFW Hall is also a popular community gathering place for meetings, watching sports games, playing pool, and enjoying "libations" and conversation (see p. 333 for more on the VFW).

➡ *Continue along Derby Street.*

Albin Irzyk as a Tank Commander

Home of Albin F. Irzyk
6 Derby Street

Before Brig. Gen. Albin Felix Irzyk (b. 1917) passed away on September 10, 2018, at age 101, he had been the oldest living veteran of the 3rd Cavalry Regiment. His autobiography, *He Rode Up Front for Patton,* documents an extraordinary yet humble life story.

"Al" Irzyk grew up in what was then the Polish-American neighborhood of Salem, and throughout his life he remained tied to his strong Polish Catholic roots and his hometown. He graduated from Salem High School, where he excelled at sports, and received his B. A. from the University of Massachusetts and a commission as Second Lieutenant from the Reserve Officers' Training Corps (ROTC) in 1940. Irzyk joined the Horse Cavalry, but after the Japanese bombed Pearl Harbor he was trained in tank warfare. He joined the 4th Armored Division in 1942. As the twenty-seven/eight-year-old Commander of the 8th Tank Battalion, he and his men "spearheaded Gen. Patton's Third Army across much of Europe," according to the military website *Traces of War* and other sources. One of these men, Lieut. Leonard H. Kieley, a long-time Salem resident, turned 100 in 2019.

Irzyk was wounded twice during his service in Europe, for which he earned the Distinguished Service Cross for extraordinary heroism, the nation's second highest honor. According to Army records: "Albin F. Irzyk received his Distinguished Service Cross for action in Germany on 18 March 1945. After four assaulting tanks were destroyed, Colonel Irzyk immediately advanced to the head of the column and charged headlong against the opposing anti-tank guns. When his tank was destroyed he, although wounded, lead the infantry forces forward through a hail of fire to secure the town." During his years of service, Irzyk also received two Silver Star Medals, four Bronze Star Medals, two Purple Hearts, the Legion of Merit, the French Croix de Guerre, and

Congressman William H. Bates greets Brig. General Albin F. Irzyk while he was serving as Commanding General, U. S. Army Headquarters, Area Command, Saigon, from 1967 to 1968. Both men were born in Salem and attended Salem High School.

the Czechoslovakian War Cross.

In 1946, befitting his status as a war hero, a delegation of Salem City officials and police met Albin Irzyk at Boston's North Station to escort him home.

After the war, Irzyk continued his military education, including Armor School in Fort Knox, Kentucky (1947-49, 51-54; also faculty), Command and General Staff College (1950), and National War College (1958).

Irzyk served as Staff Officer to the Commander-in-Chief Pacific (Hawaii) from 1954 to 1957, then Chief Officer of International Affairs, Army General Staff, from 1958 to 1961; Regimental Commander, 14th Armored Cavalry, Fulda, Germany, from 1961 to 1962 during the Berlin Crisis/Cold War; Assistant Chief, Staff Plans, Operations and Training Headquarters, 7th United States Army, Stuttgart, Germany, also Allied Land Forces, Central Europe, Fontainebleau, France, from 1962 to 1965; Assistant Commandant, U. S. Army Armor School, Fort Knox, 1965 to 1967.

During Vietnam, Irzyk was Commanding General, U. S. Army Headquarters, Area Command, Saigon, from 1967 to 1968; and Assistant Division Commander, 4th Infantry Division, Vietnam, from 1968 to 1969. "Forces of his command defended the U. S. Embassy during the 1968 Tet offensive," writes Tom Dalton for the *Salem Evening News*. For his service in Vietnam, Irzyk received eleven Air Medals and the Distinguished Service Medal, the nation's third highest honor.

Albin Irzyk retired from the military in 1971 while serving as Commanding General of Fort Devens, Massachusetts. He turned to writing, publishing numerous articles about his wartime experiences in leading publications and his autobiography. In 1998, Irzyk returned to Salem to serve as Grand Marshal for the annual Heritage Days parade. In 2002, he was an honored guest for Armory Park Dedication Day. His name is engraved on the Park's Walkway of Heroes (see pp. 112-13).

In 2017, on the occasion of his 100th birthday, Salem Mayor Kim Driscoll sent General Irzyk a loving tribute and congratulations from the City. "He wrote an endearing and loving letter back to Mayor Driscoll and the City Council," recalls Councilor Tom Furey. "I got goose bumps reading it."

➡ *Continue along Derby Street. Turn left on Memorial Drive, just past the hydrant. Irzyk Park is on the right.*

Irzyk Park
Memorial Drive
On June 18, 1999, Salem renamed Memorial Park for "hometown hero" Brig. Gen. Albin F. Irzyk. Sitting on stage with his wife of many years, Evelyn, and Salem Mayor Stanley J. Usovicz Jr., the tank commander in Gen. Patton's Third Army "was moved almost to tears by a ceremony that paid tribute both to his Polish roots and military record," according to Tom Dalton of the *Salem Evening News*. In his remarks, the 82-year-old Irzyk noted:

I've had a long and eventful life, but this just has to be one of the most momentous and unforgettable experiences of that life ... I am deeply humbled. There is now a spot in my hometown with my name on it, today and long after I am gone.

Irzyk and City officials unveiled the plaque set into a "bunting-draped stone on a hillside ... designating the land next to the Bentley School as 'Irzyk Park,'" Tom Dalton reported. The ceremony also included music by the U. S. Air Force Band, a howitzer salute by the National Guard's 101st Field Artillery, a performance by the Polish Dancers from St. John the Baptist Parish, and Polish food.

Unfortunately, the tank was not present for the park's dedication due to "military red tape," writes Tom Dalton, but it finally arrived in Salem thanks to the efforts of Brig. Gen. William Quigley of

Marblehead and Salem Veterans Agent Jean-Guy Martineau.

The 52-ton M60-A3 tank began its journey from Fort Drum, New York (north of Syracuse) at 8:00 a.m. on Monday, February 28, 2000. Dalton describes its journey: "Once it reached the Massachusetts border, it was escorted by two State Police cruisers all the way down the Massachusetts Turnpike, up Route 128 North, over Route 114, and down Derby Street. It spent the night parked at Cat Cove. 'It was a big deal to get it here,' said the driver of the 30-wheel, tractor-trailor truck that hauled the behemoth tank and its imposing 105-millimeter gun."

The tank is larger than the one driven by Irzyk in Europe. Dalton explains, "it was built in the Cold War era to combat the Russian threat." According to Brig. Gen. Quigley, "it most likely saw action in Desert Storm."

News photos/Nancy Shackleton

From left, Ola Prochorska, 10, of Wilmington; Philip Marchwinski, 9, of Danvers; Patricia Zysk, 8, of Peabody and fellow dancers from St. John the Baptist Polish Church in Salem entertain Mayor Stan Usovicz, Brig. Gen. Albin F. Irzyk, his wife Evelyn and the audience at the dedication yesterday afternoon.

City honors hometown hero

Salem names park for retired general

By TOM DALTON
News staff

SALEM — An old soldier and war hero was honored in his hometown yesterday when the city renamed Memorial Park for retired Army Brig. Gen. Albin Irzyk.

Irzyk, a tank commander in Gen. Patton's Third Army, was moved almost to tears by a ceremony that paid tribute both to his Polish roots and military record.

"I've had a long and eventful life, but this just has to be one of the most momentous and unforgettable experiences of that life," said the 82-year-old Irzyk, whose 31-year military career spanned World War II and Vietnam.

"I'm deeply humbled," he said, his voice cracking with emotion. "There is now a spot in my hometown with my name on it, today and long after I am gone."

After Irzyk, dressed in his Army uniform, walked from the stage to a bunting-draped stone on a hillside, city officials unveiled a plaque designating the land next to the Bentley School as "Irzyk Park."

The unveiling was followed by a three-blast salute from howitzers fired by Bravo Battery of

Brig. Gen. Albin F. Irzyk addresses a dedication ceremony for the new park named in his honor.

Before its journey to Salem, the tank's motor had been removed. In Salem, a crew from Fort Devens "demilitarized" the vehicle and sealed its hatches. Finally, the tank rolled off the flatbed truck and on to its concrete platform at Irzyk Park on Tuesday, February 29, 2000. "The sighs of relief were almost audible from the crowd, shivering in a corner of the Bentley School playground," Tom Dalton observed.

Salem Evening News,
June 19, 1999.

2527 South Flagler Drive
West Palm Beach, FL 33401
31 July 2004

Dear Nelson,

Hardly a week goes by without the phone or mailman bringing me a "voice from the past." This week you were that "voice." And what a "voice!" It was incredible that I would come face to face with stories from the "Salem Evening News" that appeared over 64 years ago. As you can imagine, it was a total, stunning surprise. Unbelievable.

Now that I have them, I can only wonder and be intrigued by the research that produced them.

At any rate, I am deeply grateful to you for your great thoughtfulness in sending the copies to me, which I will greatly value. It was a most kind gift.

As you may be aware, I truly love Salem. I had a tremendous boyhood in that City. A few years back I had an aging aunt whom I visited for four days every other month for three years. While she napped, I roamed all over the city visiting all my old haunts. More recently, I try to visit it each year, and I was in Salem this past June.

Your name is a familiar one. During my youth in Salem, there were several families with your name.

I hope that you had a very rewarding career on the Salem police force. Several of the guys I played with over time became policemen or firemen.

As you might guess, while in Salem I visited the tank. It always gives me a great thrill when I see the kids climbing on it.

Once again, my warmest thanks for remembering me in such a unique way. I send my best regards.

Sincerely and gratefully,

Al

Letter from Brig. Gen. Albin F. Irzyk to Nelson Dionne,
thanking him for material he had just received.

— End of trail. ★

➡ *To reach Winter Island for the Coastline Defense Trail, reverse your direction and return to Derby Street. On your right, note the sign for Block House Square, the site of a colonial blockhouse. Veer left at the Footprint Power Station. Turn right on Winter Island Road.*

Early Merchant Marines of Salem

In his foreword to the 1943 book *Americans Who Have Contributed to the History and Traditions of the United States Merchant Marine,* Captain R. R. McNulty, D-M, USNR, and Supervisor, U. S. Merchant Marine Cadet Corps, wrote: The traditions of the United States Merchant Marine anchor on the accomplishments, past and present, of men who have given something of themselves to this silent service … [they] are remembered for their contributions to the building, expansion and prestige of our Merchant Marine. Masters, engineers, builders, owners, authors and others, they were, without exception, men of the sea."

Men associated with Salem who were among these mariners include **Captain Charles P. Low** (1824-1913), born in Salem, whose clipper ships traded in San Francisco and China; **Benjamin Carpenter** (1751-1823), a native of Rehoboth, Massachusetts, who moved to Salem as a young man and became a pioneer in the East India trade, also sailing to China and other foreign ports; **Nathaniel Bowditch** (1773-1838), mathematician, astronomer and navigator "who presented to the world the science of navigation as it is known today," to quote from the book, also noting, "the first edition of Bowditch's 'Practical Navigator' appeared in 1801. It has been translated into a dozen languages, passed through countless editions, and still remains the standard American treatise on navigation;" **Jacob Crowninshield** (1770-1808), one of four sons of the famous merchant family to command a ship by age twenty-one, who traded in the West Indies, Calcutta, and the Ile de France, famously transported, by armed ship, the first live elephant seen in America (to New York), and served in the Massachusetts Senate and U. S. Congress; and **James Devereux** of Ireland, who came to Salem as a boy "in the ship commanded by his uncle, John Murphy, master mariner and merchant," according to the book, and who opened up trade in Japan in 1799 on a voyage carefully documented by his clerk, George Cleveland.

★ Salem's Coastline Defense ★
~ Winter Island, Juniper Point, Salem Neck ~

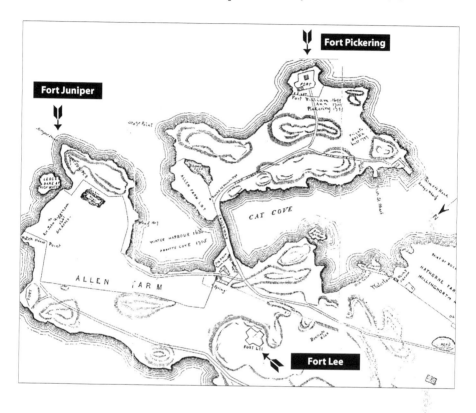

Stereo view of Winter Island from Fort Lee looking toward Marblehead, ca. 1865.

7 ➡

Entrance to Beverly Harbor.   1   2   Baker's Island Light House.   3   4   Lowell Island.   5   6   Fort Pickering.   7   Naugus Head, Marblehead.   Salem Inner Harbor.

1 Gen. Butler's Quarters
2 Third Brigade, Brig. Gen. Benj. P. Butler
   Second Battalion of Rifles, Maj. E. Moors
   Fifth Regiment, Col. C.B. Rogers
   Sixth Regiment, Col. E.F. Jones

3 Fourth Brigade, Brig. Joseph Andrews
   First Battalion of Rifles, Maj. Ben Perley Poore
   Seventh Regiment, Col. Lyman Dike
   Eighth Regiment, Col. Fred J. Coffin
4 Gen. Andrews' Quarters

5 His Excellency Hon. Nath. P. Banks & Staff
   Accompanied by Adj. Gen. E. W. Stone,
   escorted by the Waltham Dragoons,
   Capt. Wm Gibbs

6 Major General Wm. Sutton's Quarters
7 Divisionary Corps of Cadets,
   Capt. S.B. Fraser [Second Corps of
   Cadets, near flag pole]

~ Winter Island ~

Winter Island has played an essential role in Salem's coastline defense for centuries. The name "Winter Island" goes back to the seventeenth century, when English colonists discovered that Aquidneck ("the Island") was a perfect place for fishing and shipbuilding. Since the colonists moored their boats there during the winter, they changed its name to "Winter Island." The earliest known military site on the island dates to colonial days. It came to be known as Fort Pickering after the Revolutionary War. The fort was in use up to the close of the Spanish-American War, when it was no longer needed by the government.

However, the use of Winter Island for defense purposes expanded in 1935 with the establishment of U. S. Coast Guard Air Station Salem. The station played a vital role before and during World War II.

➥ *Make your way down Winter Island Road and on to the island, stopping at the security booth. Follow signs for the Winter Island Office. Fort Pickering will be on your left. Look for a dirt walkway and stone walls. You will also find interpretive signs and a spectacular view at the top!*

START: Fort Pickering
In a paper written for the Essex Institute, G. L. Streeter tells us that "as early as 1628, we find that '[early settlers] had both small and great guns, and powder and bullets for them.'" More military supplies arrived for the Salem fort in 1630 with Governor John Winthrop and his *Arbella* fleet, including "five pieces of ordinance 'for the fort' in charge of Samuel Sharpe, an experienced engineer." Streeter continues:

They soon began the erection of fortifications, and one of them was started at an early day on Winter Island. We do not know precisely when it was begun, but it was as early as 1643, at which time it was not completed nor apparently for many years afterward.

Image, left: Numerous military encampments took place on Winter Island over the years from pre-Revolitionary War times through the Spanish-American War. This lithograph shows the1858 encampment on Winter Island of the 2nd Division, Massachusetts Volunteer Militia (MVM). *(Courtesy of the Anne S. K. Brown Military Collection, Brown University).*

Salem historian Joseph B. Felt takes us back to 1643:

1643, July 26, Mr. Endicott [former Gov. John Endecott] in a letter to Mr. Winthrop [Gov. John Winthrop] mentions that work was to be done on 'our fort.' This indicates that such a fortification had been commenced on Winter Island, and was made to supply the place of Darby Fort, on Naugus's Head, Marblehead side, built there in 1629.

From G. L. Streeter we learn:

In 1644, Capt. Thomas Breadcake was permitted by the General Court to take two small guns from 'Winter Island by Salem' for his cruise against Turkish pirates.

In 1652, the General Court gave £100 towards the fort. In 1666, every male in town, above sixteen years of age, was required to take his turn in working upon it, and the town spent £320, and the next year it was ordered 'that the great guns be carried to the fort with speed.' In 1673, it was repaired, the 'great artillery got ready for use, and all else done as this juncture requires.' The juncture was apprehension of hostile movements by the Dutch.

England had declared war on Holland, and Salem feared naval attacks such as the kind inflicted by the Dutch on Virginia in 1677. The fort was repaired again in 1690 and "eleven great guns and ammunition were brought to the town," Streeter adds; in 1699, "our Fort was called Fort William in honor of the King," Felt tells us, and "in 1704, it was called Ann in honor of the Queen."

Interestingly, it was during Queen Ann's (or, Anne's) reign that England, Scotland, and Ireland were united under the 1707 Acts of Union to become Great Britain. After her death in 1714, Salem did not name the fort for the new king, George I. Instead, the fort was once again called Fort William until its final name change. In 1710 cannon from Fort Ann were loaned to "the Crown" for "an expedition against Port Royal" [Nova Scotia, Canada] according to Felt.

★ Revolutionary War – War of 1812

In January of 1775, Salem loaned three cannon to the Provincial Congress. Joseph Felt notes that on March 3, 1775, "At night, 27 pieces of cannon were removed out of this town, to be out of the way of robbers"—meaning, the British.

Only five days earlier, British troops had been dispatched to Salem in search of illegal cannon and gun powder. In the incident now known as "Leslie's Retreat," Salem men successfully negotiated a peaceful retreat with Col. Alexander Leslie, the British commanding officer (for more on Leslie's Retreat, see pp. 192-201).

During the Revolutionary War, Fort William was prepared to defend Salem and its neighbors against the greatest Navy in the world—the British Royal Navy. Gloucester, to the North, had already been attacked by British ships and successfully driven them off. Salem was spared this fate, but the fort played an essential role in protecting Salem privateers when they returned with British "prizes" (captured vessels). "Privateers" were American vessels licensed by the Continental Congress to harrass and seize British trading ships. In exchange, the privateer could make a substantial profit from the sale of the ship's goods. Many Salem privateers made a fortune (for more on the Revolutionary War, see "Salem During Wartime").

In 1794, Fort William was ceded by Salem to the United States government. Felt explains:

1794, May 25, A report is made by Bechet Rochefontaine, a Frenchman, Engineer to superintend the fortifications of New England ... It says that "the garrison of Salem is to be, in time of peace, 23 men. On account of [Fort] Juniper's Battery, it ought to be in time of war, 60 men.

In case of an attack, the militia will occupy the above fort, Juniper's Battery, and the old Fort Lee, securing the passage to the Neck. In that case, 12 or 15 hundred men may fight with great certainty of success."

In 1798, Felt continues, "The Forts [are] to be put in a state of defence and the one on Winter Island to be manned. The occasion of this, were various aggressions on our commerce by the English and French." During these days, President John Adams hoped to avoid war. While some criticized his methods, he was successful.

Finally, Felt writes, "1799, Oct. 30, Under a discharge of Artillery commanded by Captain Gould, Proclamation is made by order of Secretary of War, that Fort William be called Fort Pickering." Streeter's account reads:

...in 1799 the royal name it had borne for a hundred years was exchanged for that of Fort Pickering, in honor of the distinguished Timothy Pickering, who had been Secretary of State and War in Washington's cabinet. The day chosen for this purpose (October 30) was the sixty-fourth anniversary of the birth of President John Adams, which was everywhere celebrated with great rejoicing. The fort had just been rebuilt, under the superintendence of Jonathan Waldo, an apothecary of this place, and a capable man; and it was thought to be in some respects a model fortification, especially on account of semi-circular stone carriage-ways on which the guns were worked. On this patriotic occasion the Salem Artillery, Captain Gould, paraded in honor of the day.

Streeter then quotes an account from the local newspaper:

At 12 o'clock the company marched to an eminence near the Fort, where the superintendent of the works, agreeable to the direction of the Secretary of War, made proclamation under a federal discharge of artillery, that the Fortress of the United States, formerly called Fort William was from that day forward to bear the name of Fort Pickering. The company then repaired to Captain Felt's where they dined ... a number of toasts appropriate for the occasion were given; and they concluded the day with the decent regularity of citizen soldiers.

A few years later, in 1809, quoting a report from the Secretary of War, Felt wrote: "the fortifications of Salem had 'been repaired and a new barrack erected.' Fort Pickering thus put in order, was occupied by a company of U. S. Infantry, commanded by Captain Stephen Ranney, a distinuished officer.'" The report continues:

Our Forts are much out of order and of course need great repairs. At first, when the question came up for having them put in order, to meet a proper stage of defence for the necessities of our coast, Fort Juniper was named in common with Forts Lee and Pickering. But a result of discussing the question of repairing all three, was the selection of the last two, here named, so that the great stir, now daily manifested in a suburb of our city, is applied to the Forts, Lee and Pickering.

With regard to the genius, exhibited in the plan and execution of these two fortifications, Col. Alexander recently remarked to some of our city authorities, that there are none in all our Country, which exceed those of our forts, Lee and Pickering. While Pickering particularly commands the Marblehead side of our harbor, it assists in the defence of our whole Port, and Lee takes the lead in affording those assistances and commands the operations of Pickering and Juniper.

The work to be done, on these two forts, is principally earth works. They are expected to be done not before Winter. The area of the works at Pickering are expected to be made three times larger than they are at present...

The United States government hold themselves responsible for the expenses of the enterprise. They are willing to pay $1.25 a day for laborers. As those could not be obtained short of $1.50, the Salem government have agreed to pay $5,000 to make up the lacking 25 cents a day...

May the work progress with all due diligence and success. May it prove sufficient for all our necessities of defence and help contribute its due proportion of security to the best interests of our beloved Republic.

Postcard of Fort Pickering with its moat, bridge, and entrance, ca. 1920.

The following June, Secretary of War General Alexander Hamilton visited Salem to inspect Fort Pickering. His visit was timely as hostilities with Great Britain were growing, placing the fort in demand once again. Salem merchants, who had suffered economically under President Thomas Jefferson's 1807 embargo against foreign imports and exports, did not support another war with England. But when America declared war in 1812, Fort Pickering was needed to defend the coastline. Rev. William Bentley of Salem's East Church noted in his diary entry of August 13, 1814:

At Fort Pickering, belonging to U. S. A., is a regular body of men under Capt. Greene & Lt. Earle. The men are under good discipline, in good health & able bodied men. In front of the fort is, on the right as you stand at the Fort gate on the west side, a level ground for a parade secured by a sea wall on the North side. On the left upon the higher ground where once stood an unfinished breast work, is a garden disposed in good order.

The fort commands only on the line of the shore upon half a circle, but it is well covered by Fort Lee on the north west distant not half a mile. At the same distance nearly is the redoubt at the hospital. The men all appeared cheerful, & willing, & in all respects well disposed for their situation. Two English ships of war seen beyond the Islands, distance six miles.

★ Civil War

During the Civil War, according to the *Salem Register* of August 30, 1864, the federal government "requested the city to cede to the United States the whole of Winter Island, and this disposition of it seems to be desirable on many accounts. It might be made an important station to the country, being easy of access, easily protected, and with water communication not surpassed by any harbor on the coast." Salem complied, and Fort Pickering was "expanded and brought up to standards during the Civil War," writes Jerome Curley. G. L. Streeter adds:

The last reconstruction of this early fortification was during the war of the Rebellion, in 1863, when a conflict with England seemed likely to grow out of the Mason and Slidell affair. * *The old fort was then demolished, and new and more extensive works were constructed, with bomb-proofs, magazines, a ditch, platforms for heavy guns, and a line of earthworks in the rear* *extending across the island. When completed the fort was occupied by a garrison, consisting of the 12th unattached Company of Heavy Artillery, Capt. J[ames] M. Richardson, and the heavy guns were mounted. But, happily, the fortification was not needed during the war, and after its evacuation it began to decay, so that it is now a ruined fortress.*

In the early part of the war, barracks were built near the dwelling of the light-keeper, and companies of volunteers were quartered there previous to leaving for the front. The first company to occupy this temporary camp was the "Andrew Guard," raised and commanded by the late General Cogswell, who became so distinguished. Subsequently, troops who joined General Butler's expedition to New Orleans were collected here, and others followed. For some months the island was the scene of great Military activity and was visited by large numbers of people.

* In 1861, Jefferson Davis, President of the Confederate States, dispatched James Mason and John Slidell to Great Britain to persuade the government to grant the Confederacy full diplomatic recognition. This would be a departure from the neutral positions taken by both Britain and France. The men slipped through the Union blockade at South Carolina, but they were captured *en route* to England on board the *Trent* out of Cuba.

Two "Salem boys," ca. 1863, at the newly refurbished entrance to Fort Pickering. Part of the wall still stands today. The entire fort is currently being restored.

Civil War Service at Fort Pickering: Images from the Stearns Family Collection

Exclusive!

The photographs in this section were contributed by the great, great granddaughters of Joseph Oliver Stearns (1838-1917) of Salisbury, Massachusetts, who served in the 3rd Unattached Company, Massachusetts Infantry, Massachusetts Volunteer Militia. Stearns mustered in on May 3, 1864, and was assigned to Fort Pickering essentially for guard duty. He mustered out on August 5, 1864. Stearns was one of many "90-day men" who volunteered for the militia in response to President Lincoln's periodic calls to duty as the war dragged on.

The photographs were carefully placed in an album, each one framed by an ornate border. In the interest of showing as much of the photographs as possible, the frames have been cropped out as much as possible without losing part of the image. However, p. 261 shows one photograph as-is on the page of the album.

We are so grateful to Ruth Stearns and other descendants of Joseph O. Stearns for sharing these rare images from their ancestor's time of service at Fort Pickering.

NCOs (non-commissioned officers).

Barracks complex, looking toward Marblehead.

Another view of the barracks complex.

Images from the Stearns Family Collection

Formal group picture outside the mess hall.

Barracks and mess hall. In the foreground, a woman
appears to be picking wild flowers.

Images from the Stearns Family Collection

Mess hall and kitchen crew.

This photograph shows the moat and walls that were removed.
In the foreground appear to be stacks of firewood and a wood shed.

Images from the Stearns Family Collection

Cigarette break!

Corporals, one presumably reading his mail.

Images from the Stearns Family Collection

What is known today as Waikiki Beach, looking toward the
Naumkeag Mills. The Great Salem Fire of 1914 destroyed
the mills and the surrounding neighborhood.

Day sail off Waikiki Beach.

Images from the Stearns Family Collection

Group picnic, looking toward Marblehead.

Families could visit their loved ones at the fort from time to time. The man with the star on his hat is the local Constable, who was there to maintain order.

Images from the Stearns Family Collection

An uncropped page from the photograph album of Joseph O. Stearns.

When we consider that from the State of Massachusetts, the total number of officers and enlisted men was 111,681, from which number there were 3,358 killed, 1,926 wounded, 5,671 died of disease, and 1,843 died in rebel prisons ... it seems as if there could be hardly a family in the State that has not furnished a member to the ranks, or that has failed to contribute liberally of its substance to their support and comfort when in the field.

Massachusetts actually furnished more men to the war than were found in any one year in the State liable to military duty.

—T. J. Hutchinson and Ralph Childs in *Patriots of Salem: Roll of Honor of the Officers and Enlisted Men ... from Salem, Mass.*

★ Spanish-American War

Even though Cuba was many miles away, Salem's Mayor David P. Waters had received reports that "Spanish raiders" were "on their way to destroy Gloucester's fishing fleet and to bombard the factories from Lynn to Newburyport," according to historian Frances Robotti, continuing, "considerable nervous tension [was] felt along the whole of the Atlantic Coast of the United States as Admiral Cervera assembl[ed] the Spanish fleet at Cape Verde Islands before sailing for the west."

Fort Pickering was occupied by two companies of the 1st Massachusetts Heavy Artillery during the Spanish-American War, "serving as Infantry during that short struggle," according to an account in the *Salem Evening News* of October 5, 1925. The account continues:

The local occupancy of Fort Pickering by the First Heavies began June 5, 1898, when a detail arrived in the morning followed shortly after by Batteries C and D. Regimental headquarters were also established at the fort, Col. Charles A. Pfaff in command. Battery A was stationed at Nahant and Battery D at Plum Island. Later in the summer both of these batteries were transferred to the Fort Pickering camp, Major Perley Dyer was battalion commander of these four outfits.

Soldiers on the training field.

Layout of the Camp:

Battery C street was laid out from east and west along the northern moat, which surrounded the fort on two sides, while Battery D street extended north and south, along the other angle of the moat. Headquarters was established on the high knoll to the northeast of the camp...

Later, when Battery A came from Nahant, that outfit pitched its tents along the waterfront of the harbor at right angles with Battery D street and beyond the lightkeeper's house ... When Battery B came from Plum Island, its street was laid out to the west of the lighthouse and barn.

The Camp included a guard tent, hospital "headquarters," a rifle range, and "small guns." Massachusetts Governor Roger Wolcott visited the Camp during the summer. The men held well-attended parades. All in all, the *Salem News* concludes, "the tour of duty here was far from dull or uninteresting." The Camp only lasted at Fort Pickering from June 5 to September 13.

Onlookers, dressed for a fashionable outing, watching the soldiers train.

View of the entrance to Fort Pickering,
showing signs of wear since Civil War days.

A rare photograph of the moat at low tide.

The rehabilitated entrance, 1898.

Lightkeeper's house, built in 1871.

Above: VIP tent set up for visiting dignitaries; below: the ceremonial stage. The flag on the left belongs to the First Massachusetts Heavy Artillery; the flag on the right is the regimental color. It became the basis for the state flag in 1908.

Spanish-American War officers. After this war, Fort Pickering became inactive.

★ World War I

As early as 1901, America was suspicious of Germany. The *Salem Daily Gazette* of April 27 reported that "Kaiser William II is strengthening his navy against us. The expansion of the German navy is more in preparation for a contest with the United States than with Great Britain because the readiest causes for future naval conflicts will be found in the struggle for the partition or the exploitation of the great South American continent" (quoted in *Chronicles of Old Salem* by Frances Robotti). Any naval attack would involve Fort Pickering.

In 1917, Germany announced "a policy of unrestrained submarine warfare," according to Robotti. But Salem's forts were not activated during the World War. Instead, Fort Pickering became a place to visit and explore as it aged.

➤ *Exit Fort Pickering and walk back toward the Winter Island Office. Walk straight ahead to the massive airplane hangar.*

U. S. Coast Guard Air Station Salem in 1944. *(U.S.C.G. via Paul S. Larcom)*

The seaplanes helped turn the tide. —Alan Burke

Heading out on patrol from the hangar in early 1942 are four Vought OS2U-3 "Kingfishers," and a Grumman JRF-5 "Goose" at the far end. *(Paul S. Larcom)*

U. S. Coast Guard Air Station Salem

The U. S. Coast Guard (USCG) operated this Air Station on Winter Island from 1935 to 1970. During World War II, Salem seaplanes armed with machine guns and bombs "prowled" the Atlantic to spot German U-boats hoping to sink vessels bound for Great Britain. Decades later, on April 2, 2003, the *Salem News'* Alan Burke wrote:

It's seldom appreciated today, but the sight of burning or sinking vessels off America's coast was not unknown during the war.

At first, German U-boats were so successful in sinking vessels bound for embattled Great Britain that the survival of the island nation was in doubt ... The seaplanes helped turn the tide.

The following paragraphs on the Air Station during World War II (including the use of the Beverly Airport) are from the book *U. S. Coast Guard Air Station Salem, Massachusetts, 1935–1970*, the first title in the "Salem's Forgotten Stories" book series, of which this book is #2.

President Franklin D. Roosevelt declared an Unlimited National Emergency on 27 May 1941. At that time, the Neutrality Patrol was created "to insure the rights of American merchantmen on the high seas," according to Coast Guard historian Ed Schnepf. Another historian, Eleanor C. Bishop, wrote: "[In 1941] the Neutrality Patrol was established, putting Coast Guard personnel and facilities under tremendous pressure. To meet this crisis, Congress changed the title of the Coast Guard Reserve to Auxiliary ... thus authorizing the Coast Guard to use sailing yachts, motor cruisers, and fishing boats for neutrality enforcement and harbor duties" (see pp. 71-73).

Assuming a wartime role in November 1941, Air Station Salem was transferred to the command of the Inshore Patrol Force, First Naval District, Boston, for all operational activities. As hostilities between the U. S. and Japan raged on, patrols increased, leaves were cancelled, and the Air Station was even more tightly secured against sabotage. When Japan attacked the United States at Pearl Harbor on 7 December 1941, the U. S. entered the war.

According to the USCG Historian's Office, "with the outbreak of war on December 7, there came a gradual change in significant functions: anti-submarine warfare with its corresponding patrol and escort duties became the order of the day." In June, Air Station Salem was placed under the Northern Air Patrol of the Eastern Sea Frontier.

In the Spring of 1942, two Salem Air Station pilots were killed. On 3 April 1942, AMM2 Edward Werner and RM3 Cecil V. Bratu took off on an anti-submarine patrol and were never seen again.

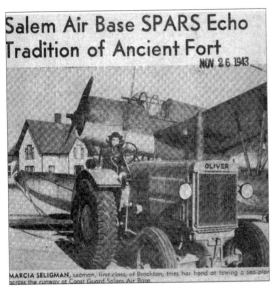

Marcia Seligman tows a seaplane across the runway. *Salem Evening News,* November 26, 1943.

On 27 July 1943, thirty-four SPARS arrived in Salem to free Coast Guard men for active duty. ("SPARS" is a contraction of *Semper Paratus,* the Coast Guard's motto, and its English translation to "Always Ready.") Their Officer in Charge, Ens. Edna Mae Lloyd of Worcester, was the first woman officer of the Coast Guard Women's Reserve to be assigned to an air station. Her principal job in Salem was "to operate a highly confidential air communications machine essential to Coast Guard patrol bomber operations." (*Salem Evening News,* November 26, 1943.)

Consolidated PBY-5A "Catalina" amphibian at Beverly Airport in 1946. With more land than on Winter Island, Salem's Air Station made liberal use of the airport during the war. (*Harland Wood, U.S.C.G., via Paul S. Larcom.*)

★ **Coast Guard Air Station Salem** ★
is officially designated the first U. S. Air-Sea Rescue Station
on the Eastern Seaboard under the command of the
Northern Group, Eastern Sea Frontier

In September 1944, Air Station Salem acquired Special Air-Sea Rescue (ASR) equipment, including "Gibson Girl" radios, flares, dye markers, emergency kits, spare life rafts, and message blocks.

"Maximum coordination of all rescue efforts of the Army, Navy, and Coast Guard was the responsibility of each regional Air-Sea Rescue Task Unit, headed by the Commander of the Coast Guard Station ... Thus, all services, operating under a unified command, coordinated their activities," writes Coast Guard historian Malcolm F. Willoughby. The Air Station later "established temporary detachments at Brunswick, Maine, and Quonset Point, Rhode Island, in cooperation with the Naval Air Stations at those points. Air Station Salem now covers the entire New England coastline, from the Canadian boundary to Long Island Sound."

Air-Sea Rescue Consolidated PBY-5A amphibian near the harbor downramp in 1945. PBYs were first used at Salem during the Fall of 1944 along with Martin PBM-3 "Flying Life Boats," replacing anti-submarine "Kingfisher" float planes and other types after the German submarine threat subsided. Fort Pickering Lighthouse is on the left, painted red prior to its 1980s restoration. *(U.S.C.G. photo via Paul S. Larcom)*

A rare 1942 photo showing a Coast Guard seaplane at the Salem Air Station armed with a 250-pound bomb. This is a Vought OS2U-3 "Kingfisher."

World War II was the test of fire that forged the modern Coast Guard. From the very beginning, Coast Guardsmen participated in almost every phase of the maritime war ... At sea, Coast Guard manned vessels and aircraft sank eleven U-boats during the Battle of the North Atlantic ... [and] our coasts needed to be patrolled ... On shore, merchant mariners needed training and certification. Coast Guard men and women performed numerous less publicized but no less vital tasks.
—Admiral Paul A. Yost, Commandant, U. S. Coast Guard, 1989

Air Station Salem matchbook cover. Pilots dropped bombs on German U-boats to "keep 'em under!"

The volunteer-run Witch City Canteen opened at the Pequot House in 1943 for "the Coast Guard boys at the Salem Base" and all visiting military personnel. *(Salem Evening News)*

Shoulder patch worn by Salem personnel once the Air Station received SRA designation.

Air Station personnel at the Hawthorne Hotel, ca. 1944.

Germany surrendered to the Allied forces on 8 May 1945. In July, officials in Washington, D. C. approved an expansion of the Salem Air Station making it "one of the largest and most important along the Atlantic seaboard," according to the *Salem Evening News.*

World War II ended in August 1945, with the surrender of Japan and the formal surrender ceremony between Japan and the United States on August 15. President Harry S. Truman declared that day V-J Day. Coastguardsmen from Air Station Salem marched in Salem's Victory Parade (see p. 81). Hundreds of Reservists and Auxiliary men and women were honored for their service at the Air Station.

In the 1950s, during the Korean Conflict, control of the Coast Guard was transferred to the Department of Transportation. This war-time change was made because unlike in earlier wars, when the Coast Guard was placed under the U. S. Navy, "Korea" had not been declared a "war." The same transfer happened in 1967 during "Vietnam." Several Salem pilots served in Vietnam.

The Coast Guard shut down Air Station Salem in 1970, and transferred its air functions to Otis Air Base on Cape Cod. They left a small crew to wrap up, but that part of Winter Island became neglected. Buildings were eventually torn down for safety reasons by the National Guard, and vandals made matters worse.

In 1972, under the leadership of Mayor Samuel Zoll, the City of Salem retrieved ownership of the land from the U. S. Government— unless Winter Island is needed again for defense purposes.

Today, very few of the original Coast Guard buildings remain. Those that still do are in various stages of disrepair. Conversations about "what to do" are ongoing, but numerous studies and reports have proposed solutions to maintain the area for public use.

The Hangar

Construction of the Coast Guard hangar commenced in 1934 in preparation for the opening of the Air Station the following year. The building was declared by the *Salem Evening News* on November 24 to be "a structure of which the people of this vicinity may well feel proud." The hangar's floor is 100 x 100 feet wide and twenty-six feet high. Its folding canopy steel door is 120 tons and runs the length of the entrance. At the time it was the only one of its kind in the U. S. that consisted of a steel frame and concrete foundation.

Two twin-motored Douglas RD-4 "Dolphin" amphibians waiting to head out for Neutrality Patrol. *(A.P. photo via Paul S. Larcom; one of a set of pictures on the Coast Guard Neutrality Patrol released to the morning papers of Sunday, Sept. 7, 1941)*

Douglas RD-4 amphibian "Dolphin" #137 inside the hangar, ca. 1935. *(Courtesy of Paul S. Larcom)*

The work was completed by Marden Construction Co. of Boston. Today, it is one of only two World War II-era hangars left in the U. S. (the other is in Florida). Discussions continue about its preservation and reuse.

➡ *Walking back toward the Winter Island Office, you will see the Coast Guard* **Motor Pool.**

➡ *Head out of the parking lot to leave Winter Island. On your right, before you exit, you will see the old* **Coast Guard Radio House,** *a small, square white building. As you follow the road, you will see the* **Enlisted Mens' Barracks** *and* **Annex** *off in the distance on your left, and the old* **Coast Guard Ammunition Bunker** *on your right—a semi-circular area with storage shelves for stocking depth charges. Pilots dropped these small bombs on German U-boats to "keep 'em under." The shelves were originally covered with sliding steel doors. The circular design "kept one discharged bomb from blowing up the place," according to Nelson Dionne.*

Above, left: Among the vehicles stored here in the Coast Guard Motor Pool were tractors, trucks, picket boats, and crash boats. Above, right: A crash boat in 1944 at Pickering Wharf.

A view of the enlisted men's barracks in 1947 with PBY-5A (ASR) "Catalina" approaching. The barracks opened in 1937. *(U.S.C.G. via Paul S. Larcom)*

Sikorsky HNS-1 Rescue Helicopter—the first type used by the Coast Guard—shown at the Salem Air Station in 1944/5 flying over the painted brick Enlisted Men's Barracks and Annex. *(U.S.C.G. via Paul S. Larcom)*

➠ *Continue along, noting Cat Cove on your left.*

Site of Revolutionary War-era Powder House
Near Cat Cove
There were a few of these round, thick-walled, domed, windowless buildings in various locations in Salem, although none are still standing. They were used to store arms, ammunition, and gunpowder. This one would have been handy for soldiers to access if they were arriving or departing by sea. (A pre-Revolutionary War powder house still stands in Marblehead, on Green Street, and another in Beverly, on Powder House Lane/Prospect Hill.)

Site of the Enos Briggs Shipyard
Cat Cove
The USS *Essex* was built at Cat Cove to defend Salem's booming maritime trade against the French Navy in the event of war (see p. 12).

Building the USS *Essex*

Postcard of the USS *Essex*.

Salem historian G. L. (Gilbert Lewis) Streeter presented a paper titled "The Story of Winter Island and Salem Neck" to the Essex Institute in Salem on March 1, 1897. He said then:

"There was never a ship in our Navy so successful before or since."

Salem residents paid for the *Essex* to be built in 1799, and donated her to the U. S. Government to protect American vessels during the "Quasi-War with France." The *Essex* later participated in the first Barbary War and the War of 1812 before she was captured by the British and sold at auction in 1837.

While the shipyard where the *Essex* was built is unmarked, the home of the master shipbuilder who constructed her, Enos Briggs, still stands overlooking the northern side of Salem Common. A historic marker about the *Essex* is located on the harbor side of Pickering Wharf.

Streeter's remarks:

The building of the Essex Frigate, on Winter Island, in the summer of the year 1799, was a naval event of unusual interest and importance at the time of its occurrence. It was when war with France seemed to be imminent and hostilities had actually taken place on the sea. The administration of President John Adams was actively engaged in forming a navy for the United States, for, up to that time, we had none of any account. "Adams said 'let there be a navy' and there was a navy," was a spirited and laconic saying in those days.

The patriotic citizens of Salem resolved to aid in this great work by building a frigate, at their own expense, and giving it to the government. Other large towns did the same. The feeling against the French ran high, especially among the Federalists, who were then in a very large majority in Salem. They abhorred the then recent French Revolution, and detested the Jacobins and their successors. The proposition to build a Frigate was adopted and carried out with great zeal and enthusiasm. In response to a patriotic appeal made for subscriptions the merchants of Salem pledged the very generous sum of $74,700, with which the building of the vessel was commenced; but the final cost, including the rigging, was over $150,000.

An appeal was made to the public for suitable timber for the ship which was "to oppose French insolence and piracy." The patriotic federalists in the country towns lost no time in hurrying forward the best sticks in their wood-lots as a contribution to the country. Danvers, Topsfield, Andover and Boxford, furnished their quotas of good white-oak trees, and so prompt was the response that in one month all the timber that was wanted was supplied.

The keel of the frigate was laid April 13, 1789, on the cove just south of the residence of the keeper of the lighthouse. The island immediately became the resort of hundreds of patriotic and curious citizens, who visited the shipyard daily. Connoisseurs pronounced a favorable opinion of the outlines of the hull as it rose upon the stocks. It is not recorded that there was even a single grumbler (strange to say) who detected errors in her build.

"Day by day the vessel grew,
With timbers fashioned strong and true, Stemson and keelson and sternson knee. Till, framed with perfect symmetry,
The skeleton ship rose up to view."

The work was pressed with great vigor and success, and it was finally announced that the frigate would be launched on Sept. 30, at which time all those who were "curiously disposed" were invited to attend "and join in the Federal Salute."

During the closing week the island was thronged with eager spectators of the scene of which they were so proud. When the day arrived a vast number of people assembled on the hills and the rocks around the cove, and as the frigate slid into the water "with the most easy and graceful motion," as an eye witness related, she was greeted "with the acclamations of thousands of spectators." At the same time the battery on the hill near by [Fort Lee] thundered forth the Federal salute, which was returned by an armed vessel in the harbor. It was a great and joyous exhibition of patriotic and popular enthusiasm.

All the sails and spars for this frigate were made in Salem, and she proved to be a splendid piece of naval architecture. She was soon equipped with men and guns and put in commission, and as she sailed out of the harbor on Dec. 22, with flowing sheets and a favoring gale, she fired a parting salute which was returned from the great guns of Fort William [Pickering].

It was the fortune of the Essex never to fight the French—as the troubles with that power were shortly settled. But in the War of 1812 with Great Britain, the Essex Frigate gained a renown which has given her an illustrious record in the history of the American Navy.

She proved to be a very staunch and able vessel and the fastest ship in the United States navy. She was the first naval vessel of our country to pass around the Cape of Good Hope and of Cape Horn. She took the first naval prize in 1812—the English ship Alert, of twenty guns and ninety-eight men, which she captured in a short and sharp engagement of only eight minutes. Subsequently she took a larger number of prizes than any other American ship.

Her heroic commander, Capt. David Porter, of imperishable fame, was finally vanquished, and was compelled to surrender the Essex to two English frigates of superior size, after a desperate and frightful conflict of two hours and a quarter off Valparaiso. The loss of the Essex, in this sanguinary combat, was fifty-eight men killed, and sixty-six wounded, a total of one hundred and twenty-four, or nearly half of all who were on board.

Up to this time not a dollar had been drawn from the government to meet the expenses of the frigate. She had captured from the enemy all needed supplies, and even money for payment of the men. There was never a ship in our navy so successful before or since.

Commodore Porter said it cost the British government near six millions of dollars to possess the Essex. After her capture she was added to the British navy in which she remained until she was sold at auction in 1837.

The Essex is also distinguished because of the great names she bore upon her rolls. Among those who served on board the ship in their younger days were Commodores [Edward] Preble, [James] Barron, [William] Bainbridge, [Stephen] Decatur, [Charles] Stewart, and Admirals [David] Porter and [David] Farragut—a galaxy of naval heroes.

Non sibi sed patriae (Not for self but country) is an often-used Navy motto. In 2017, the Navy adopted "Forged by the Sea" for its recruiting campaign.

~ Juniper Point and Salem Neck ~

➡ *After you leave Winter Island, turn right on Fort Avenue toward the Salem Willows. If you were to turn right on Columbus Avenue, and right again on Bay View Avenue until it becomes High Avenue, this is probably where the Revolutionary War fort called Fort Juniper was located (so named for the abundance of juniper bushes that grew there). Nothing of it remains today except the name of the neighborhood: Juniper Point.*

★ Fort Juniper
Juniper Point at Bayview and High Avenues
We know from the report of the Secretary of War in 1809 that Fort Juniper was abandonned after the Revolutionary War:

Our Forts are much out of order and of course need great repairs. At first, when the question came up for having them put in order, to meet a proper stage of defence for the necessities of our coast, Fort Juniper was named in common with Forts Lee and Pickering. But a result of discussing the question of repairing all three, was the selection of the last two, here named, so that the great stir ... is applied to the Forts, Lee and Pickering.

➡ *Return to Fort Avenue and follow the road around to the left. You are on Salem Neck, which is a large peninsula of land stretching from the power station to Juniper Point. On top of the hill is Fort Lee. There is a path to the top, but Fort Lee is quite overgrown and sorely needs to be restored. At this time, it is also not a safe area.*

The grove of tall red oak trees on the east side of the hill was planted on Arbor Day (the last Friday in April) of 1922. Originally, the Salem Park Commission planted fifty-nine trees to honor the fifty-nine Salem men who were killed during World War I. "Several hundred persons" were present for the dedication of Oak Grove, according to the Salem Evening News *of April 30: "The gathering included a goodly number of gold star mothers and fathers and members of the families of the deceased heroes, park commissioners, Mayor Denis J. Sullivan, city council members, G.A.R. post and J. C. R. Peabody Camp, U. S. W. V. representatives. American Legion post officers and members, and a goodly gathering of Salemites interested in seeing the honor done the late war heroes."* (See pp. 330-31 for more on the Peabody Camp.)

Salem Willows, Mass. Old Fort Lee.

A 1975 postcard of Fort Lee, which was restored during the nation's Bicentennial and updated with a walking trail, signs, and cannon. Today this area is completely overgrown, but many Salem residents hope to restore the fort to what you see here—with replica cannon!

★ Fort Lee

Salem Neck

An earthwork and gun platform were installed on this site ca. 1690. The Salem military historian Charles A. Benjamin described later improvements: "The work on the hill on the neck to the North of Winter Island, is the successor of a breastwork existing on that spot at a very early day, that has from time to time been restored."

The fort was "enlarged and modernized" in 1742 during conflicts and possible war with the French. But in 1775, the newly-named Fort Lee was built, according to Benjamin, "to command Salem harbor, and a company of men, under Captain John Symonds and Lieutenant Benjamin Ropes, Jr. stationed as its garrison." In his book *The World Turned Upside Down*, Ronald Tagney, explains:

In May 1775, when a report from "Congress's eminent engineer," Col. Richard Gridley, informed General Washington that defense works on Cape Ann were insufficient, "the General Court commissioned its own committee to examine the country coast." They were "attuned to a solid defense line north of Boston...

Salem Willows, Mass.
Bird's Eye View, Salem Willows Park from Old Fort Lee

Postcard of the view from Fort Lee, looking toward Marblehead, ca. 1975.

In Salem, they found three forts: Fort William on Winter Island; breast-works on Juniper Point at the Willows;* and a third, Fort Lee on the Neck (constructed by the poor, working out their taxes), perched upon a summit overlooking Beverly and Salem harbors "in a very advantageous Manner."

The latter was named for General Charles Lee, who came to Salem in 1775 with Jonathan Peele, a Salem merchant, and selected the site. 'This Fort,' the committee members reported, 'does credit to the Gentm of the Town,' but they recommended additional 'heavy pieces and Ordinance stores.'

Salem's Samuel Curwen provides this contemporary account:

Richard Ward, Esq., of Salem, son of Joshua Ward, one of the justices for Essex county, first appointed on the establishment of republican government in Massachusetts, was born in Salem, April 5, 1741. He ardently espoused the popular cause with his father, and opposed the arbitrary measures of parliament. He was a member of the committee of safety and protection during the entire period of the Revolution, and under direction of Gen. Charles Lee constructed at the neck the fort bearing his name, for the defence of the harbor and town of Salem.

* The Salem Willows, named for its trees, is still a Salem neighborhood.

What's interesting about these accounts is that when nineteenth-century historians began writing about Fort Lee, its namesake was never mentioned. Instead, in 1877, for example, C. H. Webber and W. S. Nevins, in their book *Old Naumkeag: An Historical Sketch of the City of Salem*, wrote:

In 1775 Gen. Henry Lee, commanding the north-eastern division of the country, came to Salem, and with Jonathan Peele, merchant of this place, selected this hill as the place to erect a formidable fort. It was called Fort Lee. Barracks were also built at Juniper point. In 1787 there were three forts here known as Forts William, Lee and Juniper.

In her 1948 book, Frances Robotti repeated this misstatement word for word. Since then, at least within Salem, later local history writers have trusted these two usually trustworthy sources until scholars in recent years have corrected the record. Why? Because Charles Lee was quite despised during and after the war. Some considered him a traitor. In the book of essays titled *George Washington's Generals and Opponents*, John W. Shy calls Charles Lee "Washington's worst enemy."

Charles Lee (ca. 1731-1782) was a "complicated" man who, John Shy suggests, would have benfitted greatly from a psychiatrist. He was known to be "unbalanced," perhaps a "military adventurer." Even Washington himself once called him "fickle"—a word he would later realize was a gross understatement.

Charles Lee was born near Chester, England, to a prominent family, and at the age of fourteen began to create an "impressive military record," Shy writes. By the time Lee bought a plantation in Virginia in 1773, he had fought against France in Canada and North America and against Spain in the Iberian Peninsula. He was present in Poland twice during "civic unrest" and a revolt against the king, and he fought alongside Russian troops.

Lee was sympathetic to the cause of the American Whigs, and wished to offer his military expertise. As John Shy explains, "Between his books, travels, and combat experience in irregular warfare, he had become something of a military radical, prone to doubt the accepted practices of his day." Lee fully expected to be named Commander in Chief of the Continental Army in 1775; instead, Congress chose George Washington of Virginia. As a nod to Massachusetts, they chose Artemus Ward as second in command; Charles Lee was promoted to

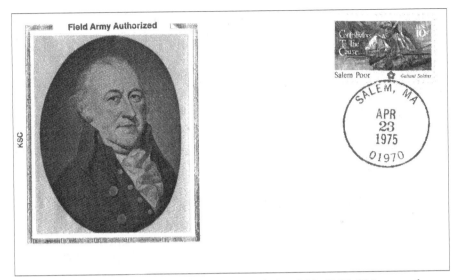

First day cover with a portrait of Artemus Ward, April 23, 1975, 200 years after Washington refused his resignation from the Continental Army.

General and named third in command—although, due to Ward's poor health, Lee became *de facto #2*.

Generals Washington and Lee journeyed to Cambridge, Massachusetts, in June where Washington assumed command. Washington "divided his army into three divisions," Shy explains, "giving Lee the northernmost command." Lee's men fortified the coast with remarkable haste—including at Salem. John Shy acknowledges, "there can be no question that Lee lived up to the highest expectations of his supporters ... he brought the organizational, tactical, and engineering skills that were so badly needed. There are glimpses in the records of Lee working tirelessly to improve the new American army." Because of his impressive leadership in fortifying Salem's coastline, town officials named their new-and-improved fort for him.

But Lee's career soon began to spiral downward, as a result of his vocal criticism of George Washington and Congress. He acted on his own initiative and disobeyed the orders of his commander, having no confidence in Washington after losses in New York in 1776. Lee was captured by British troops that December, but he was released a little over a year later in a prisoner exchange. He then proposed new military strategies to Washington and Congress that were ignored. Washington's council of generals dismissed his ideas as well. Lee refused to join

Washington's campaign after Valley Forge until Washington gave the command of detached forces to the young Marquis de Lafayette. Lee changed his mind, but he continued to argue with Washington and demanded an explanation for how he had been treated. He insisted on a court-martial to be heard.

John Shy writes: "Lee was tried on three charges: 'disobedience of orders by not attacking; making an unnecessary, disorderly, and shameful retreat'; and 'disrespect toward the commander-in-chief.'" Lee was found guilty on all three counts. Sadly, as John Shy puts it, "The rest of the story is not pretty." Lee and his supporters lobbied Congress unsuccessfully to overturn the findings. Retreating to his estate in Virginia, Lee "was dismissed from the army for a disrespectful letter written to Congress and had to fight a duel ... for his public attacks on Washington." He denounced Alexander Hamilton as responsible for ruining him. His last few years were "pathetic," Shy explains, living in a windowless sort of barn and "drawing up Utopian plans for a military colony in the West."

Charles Lee died in 1782, not living to see the U. S. Constitution ratified. By then, he was being denounced. George Washington became the universally beloved "Columbian Hero" and the first American President. Anyone who thought or wrote negatively about Washington was considered a traitor. A 1792 biography of Lee by a supporter from Georgia did nothing to alter the prevailing opinion of him, especially in the North where nineteenth-century historians did not even mention him by name. Some changed his name to "Henry Lee," whose reputation as "Light-horse Harry Lee" had made him a hero.

Even the premiere Salem historian James Duncan Phillips, writing in 1854, chose not to include Charles Lee's name. He provides this account from the committee of the Provincial Congress appointed to report on seacoast defense: June 19, 1776:

There are two forts erected on the Point of Land in Salem Harbour, No. 1 and No. 2 or old Fort. No. 1 contains 10 ambozeurs, has twelve pounders with three small pieces, fit for use which with the Cannon in the No. 2 or old Fort we judge sufficient as these forts are now overlooked by another Fort which is now erecting on an eminance not far distant—This fort we must own does credit to the gentm of the Town of Salem and with the addition of some heavy pieces and ordinance stores would enable them to make no dispicable figure in the common Defence.

From Shy's account, it seems that Charles Lee made good decisions:

Fort Number One was a battery erected on Juniper Point; Number Two was the old fort on Winter Island which had been variously called Fort Ann, Fort William, and later Fort Pickering, while the new fort was christened Fort Lee. It may well be that the strength of these defences saved Salem from some of the marauding expeditions later carried out by the British.

Fort Lee was used again during the War of 1812 as a lookout point to spot invading British ships and alert Fort Pickering. Cannon were added during the Civil War to coordinate with Fort Pickering in

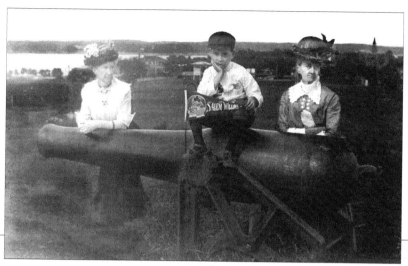

Visitors to Fort Lee, ca. 1910.

Fort Lee, ca. 1865.

fending off Confederate raiders. That was the last time the fort was used for defense purposes.

And so, Salem has an interesting "situation" on its hands! Charles A. Benjamin, writing in 1877 for *History of Essex County*, politely implies that Fort Lee's name is problematic by simply stating: "In the Revolutionary War it was called Fort Lee—and perhaps still retains the name." The implication is that he hoped future generations would change the name. John S. Shy would likely disagree, writing in defense of Charles Lee:

The contribution of Charles Lee to the Revolution was substantial, though perhaps difficult to measure. His services should not be minimized in the light of what finally happened to his career. As the partisan [Benjamin] Rush recalled, "He was useful in the beginning of the war by inspiring our citizens with military ideas and lessening in our soldiers their superstitious fear of the valor and discipline of the British army..."

Intellectual that he was, Lee tried to see the Revolution as a consistent whole, with every aspect in rational harmony with every other. It was a fight by free men for their natural rights. Neither the fighters nor the cause were suited to the military techniques of despotism—the linear tactics, the rigid discipline, the long enlistments, the strict separation of the army from civic life that marked Frederick's Prussia.

Lee envisioned a popular war of mass resistance, a war based on military service as an obligation of citizenship. He sought a war that would use the new light-infantry tactics already in vogue among the military avant-garde of Europe, the same tactics the free men at Lexington and Concord had instinctively employed.

★ The Forts are Ceded to the City of Salem

In 1921, Secretary of War John W. Weeks "recommended to Congress that more than 60 obsolete forts and military posts of no further value to the government from a military stand point, be abandonned," according to the *Salem Evening News* of May 10, 1921. These included Forts Lee and Pickering in Salem. Fort Lee's earthworks "add much to the picturesque appearance of appearance of The Neck, as well as a place for sight seeing all over the Willows along the North Shore and in Massachusetts Bay," the article continues. Fort Pickering, the reporter felt, "would make an ideal public park location on the water front."

In January of 1922, Fort Pickering, acquired by the U. S. Government in 1794, was ceded to the City of Salem "for perpetual use as a public park, and other public uses," so states the Congressional record. Fort Lee, ceded to the Government in 1867, was deemed of "historic interest" but, like Fort Pickering, "not needed for the purposes of defense."

During the American Bicentennial in 1975 and 1976 the City conducted a massive clean-up of both forts, adding interpretive signs and trails—most of which are long gone.

In 1994, Fort Lee was added to the National Register of Historic Places. While the fort has become overgrown and neglected, the original star-shaped earthworks remain intact and many residents and officials are working to clean it up once again.

In 2016, through funds provided by the Community Preservation Act and other sources, the restoration of Fort Pickering commenced.

DEDICATE OAK GROVE TO MEMORY OF SALEM HEROES OF LATE WAR

Exercises Held Saturday in Shadow of Fort Lee Mark Creation of Memorial Grove; Mayor and Legion Commander Laud the Thoughtfulness of Park Board

Arbor day was observed in a most auspicious manner in Salem, Saturday under the auspices of the Salem Park commission. The planting of a Memorial Grove of 59 red oaks on the easterly side of Fort Lee, with ceremonies conducted by the local Legion post in the mid-afternoon, featured the day. A tree was set out for each of the known Salem world war veterans who gave up their lives during the period the United States was at war with the Central Powers, or from the spring of 1917 until July 4, 1919. Fifty-nine trees were thus planted.

Despite the threating skies, there was a very good attendance upon the ceremonies, several hundred persons being present. The gathering included a goodly number of gold star mothers and fathers and members of the families of the deceased heroes, park commissioners, Mayor Denis J. Sullivan, city council members, G. A. R. post and J. C. R. Peabody camp, U. S. W. V. representatives, American Legion post officers and members, and a goodly gathering of Salemites interested in seeing the honor done the late war heroes.

Following is the list of deceased service men from Salem for whom trees were planted in the Memorial Grove. Each tree bears a number which corresponds with a list of the men whose names will be kept on file at the office of the park commission and the home of the American Legion. Later, when the trees grow to some size, each is to be labelled with

Continued on Tenth Page

➡ *Follow Memorial Drive along the right side of Fort Lee. There you will see what is left of the World War I Memorial of fifty-nine red oaks planted in honor of the fifty-nine Salem men who perished in the war. Salem dedicated the Memorial on Arbor Day of 1923.*

— End of trail. ★

Colonial Salem

In 1930, on the 300th anniversary of the arrival of Governor John Winthrop and the *Arbella* fleet in Salem, the City commissioned a replica of his flag ship and created "Pioneers' Village" to portray how Salem might have looked in 1630. Now called "Pioneer Village," this living history museum is still owned by the City and open to the public. Above: "English wigwams," the colonists' version of what their Native American neighbors used. These were the easiest homes to build before timber-frame, thatched-roof cottages could be constructed as shown below. In the foreground, note the pillory and stocks used for public punishment.

★ Salem Military Units ★

*The units described in this section, in chronological order, were either found-
ed in Salem or have a strong identification with the City. It wasn't until the
Spanish-American War that America's military was centralized within the
federal government. Independent units either ceased to exist or chose to join
the larger command structure. The Second Corps of Cadets chose the latter.*

Salem Company

As English colonists arrived to settle the Massachusetts Bay Colony in
the seventeenth century, they completely disrupted the way of life of
the people who were already there. Those who were native to the area
now called "Salem," originally, "Naumkeag," spoke the Algonquian
language and were Pawtucket. With a completely different belief
system about the ownership of land, the English systematically set
about "purchasing" (swindling, really) or taking away the land on
which the indigenous people depended to survive. For them, no one
could "own" the Earth. In the English system, though, owning property
and church membership allowed men to be citizens and vote.

For the 300th celebration of the *Arbella* fleet arriving in Salem, residents
dressed in colonial garb and posed for photographs onboard the replica ship.

Despite early attempts to live together in peace, the result of the English "land grab" from Native Americans was suspicion, fear, and violence on both sides. In addition, France wanted as much English colonial land as it could acquire. Their colonists, in Canada, oftentimes working with Native Americans, posed an additional threat.

In his article *Massachusetts Militia Roots: A Bibliographic Study* (National Guard Bureau, 1986), Capt. Robert K. Wright Jr. describes the Salem colonists' earliest formation of a defense force:

On 4 March 1628/9 the Bay Colony received its charter, which included total control over internal military and political organization. The governing body (then still located in England) issued its "First General Letter" of instructions on 17 April of that same year (ref. Records Mass. 1:37i-39, 386-398) to CPT John Endecott appointing him "governor" of the "plantation" at Naumkeag (Salem) and directing him to undertake the military organization of the trading post and settlement, which had been established the previous year. Endecott had travelled to Salem in 1628. At his request weapons and uniforms for 100 men were shipped over in 1629 to outfit a company organization which corresponded to contemporary European norms and included 1 captain, 1 lieutenant, 1 ensign, 3 sergeants, 3 drummers, possibly 1 corporal, and 90 or 91 privates.

Uniforms were extensive, and included most noticably 100 green coats bound with red tape, deliberately copying a pattern common in contemporary operations in Ireland where a form of camouflage was required. Weapons for the company included 8 cannon for the defensive fortification; 100 firearms (80 snaphances which were primitive flintlocks; 10 long fowling pieces; and 10 larger caliber matchlocks, again an arms mix of very modern content); 100 swords; 83 pole arms (3 halberds for the sergeants; 60 pikes; and 20 half-pikes); plus 60 corselets (upper torso body armor) (ref. Records Mass. 1:23-6, 31).

No exact date for implementation of this organizational table is preserved, but the absence of detail implies strongly that it was adopted in 1629, and, since the instructions from internal evidence indicated that they were merely approving Endecott's recommendations, the date 17 April 1629 can be considered acceptable as a starting date for the Salem Company. B y 1634 Endecott had been succeeded as company commander by Captain William Trask.

This poster, titled *The First Muster*, is part of the National Guard Heritage Series. It depicts the East Regiment's muster on Salem Common in the early spring of 1637—the origin of today's National Guard. Today, the image appears on the granite "First Muster Marker" on Salem Common (near the flag pole) and in every Armory used by the National Guard.

East Regiment, Massachusetts Volunteer Militia
(today's U. S. National Guard)
Capt. Robert Wright's history continues:

In December 1636, with the colony facing war with the Pequots, a regimental organization was adopted for the colony's approximately 1,500 men. Under the overall command of the Governor as "chiefe general" three geographically-based permanent regiments were set up, each commanded by a colonel and a lieutenant colonel, and each with a paid training officer (mustermaster). All regiments and companies were directed by the General Court to hold elections of officers prior to the next Court session and to report the results. Note that these units predate by six years the regiments of England. The act to execute this organization was passed on 13 December 1636 (ref. Records Mass. 1:186-187).

The organization of 13 December 1636 with the results of commissions issued on 9 March 1636/7 (ref. Records Mass. 1:186-187) was as follows:

SOUTH REGIMENT (101st Field Artillery)
COL John Winthrop, Sr.; LTC Thomas Dudley
Mustermaster CPT John Underhill
Boston: CPT John Underhill
Dorchester: CPT Israel Stoughton
Roxbury: (Note: Commander unidentified)
Weymouth: (Note: Commander unidentified)
Hingham: (Note: Commander unidentified)

EAST REGIMENT (101st Engineer Battalion)
COL John Endecott; LTC John Winthrop, Jr.
Mustermaster CPT William Trask
Salem: CPT William Trask
Saugus (Renamed in 1637 as Lynn): CPT Daniel Patrick
Ipswich: CPT Daniel Dennison
Newbury: CPT John Spencer
(NOTE: Missing is Marblehead which had town status in 1633)

NORTH REGIMENT (181st & 182d Infantry)
COL John Haynes; LTC Roger Herlakenden
Mustermaster CPT Daniel Patrick
Charlestown: CPT Robert Sedgwick
Watertown: CPT William Jennison
Newtown (Renamed in September as Cambridge): CPT George Cooke
Concord: LT Simon Willard
Dedham: (Note: Commander unidentified)
(NOTE: Missing is Medford which had town status in 1630)

BG Leonid Kondratiuk, Director of Militia Affairs for The Adjutant General of Massachusetts, concludes:

While December 13, 1636, is often cited as the "birthday" of the National Guard, it was on that day that the Massachusetts militia was organized into three regiments. Prior to that date, each town had its own militia company (also known as "trained bands") which was commanded by an officer with the rank of captain. The militia companies were nominally under the command of the colonial governor, but, in practice, operated as independent units. The regimental organization did much to improve the organization and leadership of the militia.

1st Essex Regiment, "Regular Militia," Minutemen, and the Continental Army

An outgrowth of the East Regiment was the formation of more militia units in Essex County. By 1774, there were six Essex County regiments. Brig. Gen. Len Kondratiuk explains:

Prior to the American Revolution, Massachusetts' armed citizens were organized into two major elements. There was the "regular" militia which consisted of all white males age 16 to 60, and the Minutemen who were better trained and equipped and who could react more quickly to an emergency—theoretically on a minute's notice.

Before the Revolutionary War, the 1st Essex Regiment was led by Col. William Browne, one of Salem's most distinguished citizens. But in the early days of 1775, all militia officers who were identified as loyalists to the King were removed from position. This included Col. Browne, paving the way for his successor, Col. Timothy Pickering to assume command of the 1st Essex Regiment (also known as "Minutemen"). They were present at Salem's North Bridge on February 26, 1775, for the near-engagement with British troops now known as "Leslie's Retreat" that could easily have started the war two months before the Battles of Lexington and Concord (see pp. 192-201).

Kondratiuk continues:

In the early morning hours of April 19, 1775, the militia company of Lexington, commanded by Captain John Parker, confronted British forces heading to Concord to search for stores of munitions. This led to the "shot heard 'round the world" and the beginning of the American Revolution. While the Lexington militia retreated in the face of superior British forces, militiamen continuously engaged the British as they retreated from Concord back to Boston later the same day.

After the battles of Lexington and Concord in April 1775, Massachusetts militia units were called into service, along with militia units from New Hampshire, Connecticut and Rhode Island, to form the Army of Observation whose purpose was to ensure that the British did not travel to locations outside of Boston which they occupied.

Charles A. Benjamin adds that after the Battles of Lexington and Concord, Salem men "arranged their affairs and joined the Army [of Observation], now gathering near Boston." Kondratiuk adds:

The Army of Observation fought the British at the Battle of Bunker Hill in June 1775. General George Washington assumed command of the Army of Observation at Cambridge in July 1775 and the militia units then became units in the newly-formed Continental Army. Massachusetts regiments were a major component of the Continental Army throughout the Revolution.

In 1776, Col. William Mansfield of Salem assumed command of the 1st Essex Regiment when Timothy Pickering was appointed Quartermaster General. Charles Benjamin adds that Captain John Felt "commanded a company of artillery in service this year, his lieutenant being John Butler, both of Salem. Captain John Symonds and Lieut. Benjamin Ropes Jr. commanded a "company of men ... stationed at Fort Lee as its garrison."

Benjamin continues:

In 1777 forty-four men were raised in Salem as her quota for the army, presumably under a Captain Greenwood, for we read that he marched from Salem on public service with his company, on November 11, 1777. Fifty-four additional men were also drafted to act as body guards for Burgoyne's surrendered army, under Captain Simeon Brown. Another company, under Captain Benjamin Ward, also marched to join the army at New York December 17, 1777 ... In July [1778] Captain Samuel Flagg commanded a small company raised for special service in Rhode Island.

During the Revolutionary War, Salem contributed hundreds of men to the Continental Army and newly-created Navy. Others became privateers to help disrupt British trade at sea.

Salem Independent Cadets/Second Corps of Cadets

In her history of the Second Corps titled *Merchants, Clerks, Citizens, and Soldiers: The Second Corps of Cadets in Salem, Massachusetts*, Park Service historian Emily A. Murphy explains that the "unrest" from Shay's Rebellion in 1786/7 and elsewhere prompted the Massachusetts legislature to pass a law "that would allow the formation of independent companies within the regular militia." At a meeting in Boston in 1785, she continues, "successful merchants and businessmen met ... to discuss the creation of an elite company in Salem, and "on July 10, 1786, the Salem Cadet Company was officially raised, and the first officers were commissioned." Murphy continues:

Like the "Boston Cadets" [nickname for the Independent Corps of Cadets] who were founded in 1741 and later redesignated "First Corps of Cadets," the Salem Cadet Company was an "independent" company, because the commander of the company reported directly to the commander of the Second Division, one of the three divisions of the Massachusetts Militia. One reason for this was that the cadet companies were intended to be training companies for officers, and thus the corps received special privileges.

During the War of 1812, with the threat of a British naval invasion, the Corps "had watch duties ... in Salem and Beverly," according to Murphy. After the war, she continues, "the corps began to go on 'annual campaigns,' or encampments, in order to train in camp routines, target shooting or other military maneuvers ... Some years the encampment would occur on Winter Island in Salem and include other units from the Second Division."

The Cadets also performed ceremonial duties in Salem, such as escorting "visiting dignitaries" through the streets of Salem—including President George Washington on his tour of the New England states in 1789. Washington called them "one of the handsome Corps in Uniform" (see photo, p. 92). Murphy continues: "After a parade in his honor, the Cadets escorted Washington from the Court House down what is today Wash-ington Street to the home of Mr. Joshua Ward."

The Salem Cadets were "an important part of the social life of Salem" as well, Murphy writes. "Their armory, usually a few rented rooms, was not large enough to host large gatherings, so in the 1830s, the Cadets began hosting regular dances in Hamilton Hall. These balls began as part of the annual dinner after the fall review and then became a spectacular annual ball to honor Washington's birthday. In 1855, the Cadet Ball on Washington's birthday was held in the large new armory they had just rented in the Franklin Building ... It was in this building that they held sociables, where members of the corps would demonstrate infantry drills and then hold a dance or soirée."

Unfortunately, the Franklin Building burned down in 1860; the

The Massachusetts Militia Law of 1840

... brought significant changes to the Massachusetts Militia. The first change was that it drew a distinction between the enrolled militia and the volunteer militia. The enrolled militia was simply a list of able-bodied men age 18 to 45 which would only be called upon in time of war. There was no military training requirement for members of the enrolled militia.

The volunteer militia, named the Massachusetts Volunteer Militia (MVM), were those individuals who joined MVM and conducted regular training. The MVM was organized into three divisions with two brigades each. Each brigade consisted of two or three regiments. Regiments were organized into companies, which would be from one or more municipalities.

—*BG Leonid Kondratiuk*

Front and back of an 1840 rental agreement between the "Salem Artillery Company," (a municipal company of the Massachusetts Militia located in Salem) and the City for rooms in an as-yet-to-be-identified building; Col. Francis Peabody, Cdr. "Col. Peabody's Artillery" is mentioned as early as 1824 by the *Salem Gazette*, when they participated in General Lafayette's visit to Salem.

Cadets would have to find new space. Meanwhile, though, Murphy writes, "the Salem Independent Cadets had an enviable reputation. They (along with the Boston Independent Cadets) were one of only two cadet companies in Massachusetts and were known for the high quality of training their men received...

In April 1861, only days after Fort Sumter was fired upon, the Cadets 'admitted about eighty members, it being necessary that the corps should be in a condition to respond to the call of the government, at a moment's notice, for the enforcement of the Laws and Constitution,' as company clerk R. G. Skinner recorded."

While many Cadets remained at home to train officers for militia units (the primary function of the Second Corps which, at the time, did not have federal designation), others joined the Army or Navy "mostly as commissioned officers," Murphy Emily explains. Col. J. Frank Dalton, in an article about the Corps, estimated that "approximately 500 former Cadets had volunteered for service." The Corps itself "was called into service to do garrison duty at Fort Warren in Boston Harbor," Murphy continues, "guarding Confederate officers who were prisoners of war."

Stereo view (and detail) showing Major General Benjamin Butler (to the right of the child) visiting the Second Corps on Winter Island, ca. 1880. "Beast Butler," a Civil War general, served as Governor of Massachusetts from 1883 to 1884.

Murphy describes the post-Civil War years as "one of stability and expansion," and "after a century of being known variously as the Salem Cadets, the Salem Independent Cadets, or the Cadet Company of Salem, in 1874 the company was officially designated the Second Corps of Cadets" of the Massachusetts Volunteer Militia (MVM). Boston's Independent Cadets were designated the First Corps of Cadets at the same time.

In 1890, the Second Corps purchased the grand mansion of Col. Francis Peabody on Essex Street to use as their headquarters, or "head house." Soon, they added on a massive drill shed where they could train during inclement weather (see photo, below). Once again, the Second Corps Armory became a center of Salem social life as well as for the Corps' military preparedness.

The Joseph Peabody House, ca. 1820, was sold by his descendant, Col. Francis Peabody, to the Second Corps of Cadets in 1890 for use as an Armory "head house," or headquarters. The drill shed in the rear was added in 1894. The Peabody House was replaced by a magnificent building that opened in 1908 and, sadly, burned down in 1981. Today, the site is Armory Memorial Park. The old drill shed serves as the Salem Regional Visitor Center. On the rear of the Visitor Center, you will find a plaque in honor of the 8th Regiment, Massachusetts Volunteer Militia.

Stereo view (detail) of Mechanic Hall, 285 Essex Street. It burned down in 1905 after a "moving picture machine" caught fire.

Above, left: Before they could build a new armory, the Second Corps hosted events in various buildings throughout downtown Salem—including Mechanic Hall. This is the program for an 1892 staged version of the book *Robinson Crusoe*.

Col. J. Frank Dalton (standing) visiting the Second Corps, ca. 1880s/1890s, either on Winter Island (if pre-1896) or at the Second Corps' new camp in Boxford after it opened in 1896 (see next page).

In 1896, the Second Corps Cadets Camp Association was formed to purchase a campground in Boxford, Massachusetts, where the men could train outdoors for long periods of time on their own land. There, Emily Murphy tells us, "they could set up rifle ranges, obstacle courses, and other facilities for training. This ... became even more important for the Cadets in the years leading up to World War I, as weapons became more powerful, accurate, and complex, and therefore dangerous to train on in an urban area."

Postcard of the camp at Boxford that opened in 1896—just in time for the Second Corps to train for service in the Spanish-American War.

Facing possible threats from the Spanish Navy in 1898, the Second Corps "was mobilized to provide coastal defense," Murphy writes.

They were garrisoned at Fort Miller in Marblehead where they repaired the old fort, installed modern guns, and helped mine Salem Harbor.

Military-themed souvenir card of a Second Corps Cadet in the 1890s. Produced by the Kinney Tobacco Co. of New York, the cards were enclosed in the pack to promote their "Sweet Caporal" brand of cigarettes.

The Second Corps parading in Newburyport, Massachusetts, ca. 1905.

Just like the Salem Armory back home, the Camp at Boxford was a place for social gatherings. This is a ticket to an event held in 1908.

> HEADQUARTERS
> SECOND CORPS CADETS,
> M. V. M.
>
> Camp at BOXFORD.
>
> I. Guards will pass the bearer and ladies, July 18th to 25th, 1908.
>
> By order of Major ROPES,
> L. W. JENKINS, *Adjutant,* *Commanding.*
> *2nd Corps Cadets.*
>
> *Compliments of* ....

1909 order for members of the Second Corps to report to the Armory for their annual inspection.

> HEADQUARTERS SECOND CORPS CADETS, M. V. M.
>
> SALEM, Jan. 12, 1909.
>
> General Order }
> No. 1. } Last Number Series 1908, — 9.
>
> I. In accordance with G. O. 24, A. G. O., Series 1908, the annual Inspection by an officer of the Regular Army will be held on Friday, Jan. 29, 1909, at 8 P. M.
> II. Company Commanders are hereby ordered to report to the Adjutant at the Armory at 7.45 P. M. with their Companies in dress uniform, light marching order, without leggings. Haversacks and canteens will be worn.
> III. Field, Staff and N. C. O. Staff will report to the Adjutant at the same time and place.
>
> By order of Lieut. Colonel JOHN E. SPENCER,
> L. W. JENKINS, *1st. Lieut. and Adjutant.*
> *2nd. Corps Cadets.*

In the summer of 1914, the Second Corps assisted with the devastating effects of the Great Salem Fire. They worked alongside members of the Massachusetts National Guard (whose designation had been changed from Massachusetts Volunteer Militia in 1907).

The following year, Emily Murphy explains, it was clear that "there were few roles that an independent infantry corps could play in the newly restructured National Guard ... Would they maintain their independence and be relegated to ceremonial appearances in their red and blue uniforms, or would they become a fully operational unit of the National Guard, with soldiers who were ready and able to serve in combat?" The Second Corps chose to "integrate into the command structure of the Massachusetts National Guard. They became the Second Battalion of the First Field Artillery, Massachusetts National Guard, Batteries D, E, and F." In 1916, when the "political turmoil" of World War I required the protection of the Mexican border, the battalion was stationed down there for five months.

Shortly after their return home, the Second Corps was called up as part of the 26th Division of the U. S. Army. Comprised mostly of men from New England, they became known as the "Yankee Division," or, the "YD." Massachusetts was better prepared than other states, and the YD was the first to go over to France. Murphy explains: "The Second Corps was officially called up on July 25, 1917. Their regimental designation was changed from the First Massachusetts Field Artillery to the 101st Field Artillery, and after about six weeks of training at the ... camp in Boxford, the 101st arrived in France in late September ...

[they] served in France for the last thirteen months of World War I."

The Second Corps and National Guard used the Salem Armory as Relief Headquarters after the Great Salem Fire of 1914.

The Camp at Boxford in 1917, newly named Camp Curtis Guild after Curtis Guild Jr., who died in 1915. Guild was a graduate of Harvard College (1881) where he became a Lieutenant in Harvard's rifle corps and an expert fencer. He joined the Massachusetts Volunteer Militia in 1891. While there, Guild researched the latest techniques in riflery and was appointed Inspector General of Rifle Practice by Governor Roger Wolcott.

Guild saw active duty in Cuba during the Spanish-American War, when he was commissioned Lieutenant Colonel. He retired from military service after the war, in 1899, at the rank of Brigadier General. Curtis Guild went on to become a State Representative, Lieutenant Governor, and Governor of Massachusetts from 1906-9. He was also a member of the National Lancers for several years, an elite, ceremonial mounted unit in Massachusetts that is today affiliated with the Guard.

Soldiers taking a break at Camp Curtis Guild in 1917.

Jean Missud's Salem Cadet Band, a civilian band, at Camp Curtis Guild, ca. 1918. They were the official band of the Second Corps of Cadets.

After the war, writes Brig. Gen. Kondratiuk, "the Regiments were inactivated in April 1919. In 1920, the 102nd Field Artillery was reconstituted a unit of the Massachusetts National Guard with the Second Corps of Cadets ... as its Second Battalion. Its designation was changed in September of that year to Second Field Artillery, Massachusetts National Guard and again in 1921 to the 102nd Field Artillery, Massachusetts National Guard."

On June 26, 1927, two large stables were moved across Highland Avenue to land owned by the Almy Trust for the Artillery to quarter 125 horses. The buildings were expanded and renovated with "modern improvements," making the facility "among the best in the National Guard," according to the *Salem Evening News*. The move was accomplished between 1:00 and 6:00 a.m. to minimize the impact on automobile traffic and the trolley line. For those five hours, traffic was stopped, while trolley, telephone, and other electric lines were dropped.

In January 1941, before Pearl Harbor, the Second Corps "was actually inducted into federal service with the rest of the 26th Division," Emily Murphy explains. Their designation was changed once again, to the 102nd Field Artillery Battalion. The 26th, or the YD, arrived in France in September 1944 to serve as part of General George S. Patton's Third Army. Murphy notes that "as in World War I" they were "involved in some of the heaviest fighting of the last year of the war ... in France, Luxembourg, Belgium, Germany, Austria, and Czechoslovakia, including the Battle of the Bulge, when German forces tried to drive the Allies back from the borders of Germany during the winter of 1944-1945."

Eleven members of the Second Corps died overseas during World War II. Two earned Distinguished Service Crosses. Others received Silver Stars and Bronze Stars. The Service Battery of the 102nd received the Meritorious Unit Commendation for outstanding service and recognition by the Belgian Army.

Postscript: In the years after World War II, the Second Corps was not called into federal service for the conflicts in Korea or Vietnam. In 1982, when their beloved Armory suffered a devastating fire, they were reassigned to the Lynn Armory. In 1988, the Second Corps "was consolidated with the 101st Field Artillery, headquartered in Lynn, Emily Murphy explains. "It was the end of an era. After two centuries, the Second Corps of Cadets left the city where they had been founded."

In 1996, the Second Corps was designated again as the 1st Battalion, 102nd Field Artillery, Massachusetts Army National Guard, and sent to Iraq. In 2004, they served as a Security Forces Unit in Baghdad, leaving the force structure in September 2006.

The progression of Second Corps dress uniforms, from 1785 (rear) through the Civil War (right) and up to 1876 (left). You may see replicas of Second Corps uniforms at the Salem Regional Visitor Center (see p. 108).

Salem Light Infantry

The Salem Light Infantry first paraded on July 4, 1805, under Captain John Saunders. The unit, according to Charles A. Benjamin, was, "from the outset a select body of men, numbering in its ranks in every period some of the most substantial citizens of the town, and actuated always by a strong *esprit de corps* that showed in its invariable excellence in drill and discipline." He continues:

Captain John Saunders, First Commander S. L. I., 1805

Silhouette of Captain
John Saunders

It did some slight service as coast guards during the War of 1812, and at the breaking out of the Civil War in 1861, went to the front with the Eighth Regiment Massachusetts Militia, and served three months. One incident of this service was its voyage from Annapolis to New York as guard for the old frigate "Constitution," which relic of our former naval prowess, the government was determined should not fall into the hands of the enemy. It subsequently served nine months, in 1862-63, as part of the 50th Mass. Militia, in the service of the United States, seeing plenty of war work in the Department of the Gulf. And in 1864 it again volunteered for another three months' service ... *The war record of this company is remarkable. Doing much service as an organization, and repeatedly, when at home, filling its ranks and as often depleting them in the manner alluded to, it seemed a never failing conduit for the augmentation of our armies in the field. The company still endures as part of the Eighth Regiment, Massachusetts Militia, and is a credit to the city.*

Salem Light Infantry becomes the Salem Zouaves

Arthur Forrester Devereux (1838-1906) is credited with transforming the Salem Light Infantry into an elite Zouave unit just before the outbreak of the Civil War. Devereux was born into a wealthy and military-minded Salem family. His father, George H. Devereux, served as the Adjutant General of Massachusetts from 1848 to 1851. Arthur attended Harvard College and the U. S. Military Academy at West Point, leaving before graduating to pursue business interests in Chicago. There, Devereux served in the Illinois Militia and as Adjutant to Major Simon Bolivar Buckner (who was later a Confederate General and Governor of Kentucky). Devereux also met Elmer E. Ellsworth, a close friend of President Lincoln's, who had initiated the Zouave movement in this country. Zouave units, named for the French Army units that fought in North Africa during the Crimean War, were known for their precision drill, the use of the bayonet, elaborate uniforms (in Algerian style), and showmanship. Ellsworth placed Devereux in charge of the Zouave unit he started in Chicago—the Chicago Cadets.

In 1855, when Devereux returned to Salem, he joined the Salem Light Infantry and became its Captain in 1859. It was then that he transformed the Infantry into the elite Salem Zouaves. In 1860, during an exhibition drill for Massachusetts Governor John Andrew, the Zouaves were described in a Boston newspaper as "a marvel of precision and exactness."

> *The war record of this company is remarkable.*
> —Charles A. Benjamin

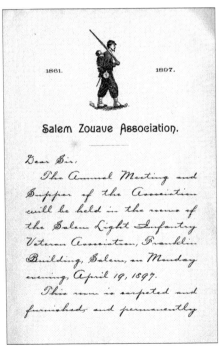

Invitation to an unknown recipient to attend the 1897 annual meeting and supper of the Salem Zouave Association, to be held "in the rooms of the Salem Light Infantry" in the Franklin Building on Essex Street (see p. 152).

Salem Light Infantry Joins the 8th Regiment, MVM

Devereux was with the Zouaves as Company J of the 8th Massachusetts Regiment, MVM from April 12 to August 1, 1861. Near Baltimore, they repaired railroads and performed guard duty.

It was during these months that the men successfully towed the USS *Constitution* from Annapolis, Maryland (where she was being used as a training vessel for the Navy) to New York and away from the Confederates who could have destroyed this all-important federal symbol.

Devereux mustered out of Company J on August 1, 1861, but he was soon commissioned Lieut. Col. of the 19th Massachusetts Regiment under the command of Col. Edward W. Hinks. Devereux served with distinction throughout the war, and was awarded the rank of Brevet Brigadier General by President Andrew Johnson.

The Salem Light Infantry remained a company of the 8th Regiment until 1921, when it was redesignated as Battery D, 102nd Field Artillery.

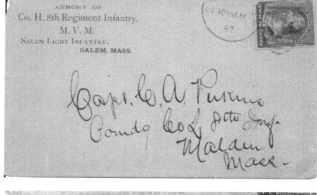

Cover (envelope) for an 1887 letter from an unknown officer in Co. H, 8th Regiment Infantry in Salem, to Capt. Clarence A. Perkins, Co. L, 8th Regiment Infantry, Malden, Mass.

Cover to an 1887 letter to Capt. John P. Reynolds of the Salem Zouaves while they were attached to the 8th Massachusetts. Reynolds was Captain in 1868, and became an active member of the Salem Light Infantry Veteran Association.

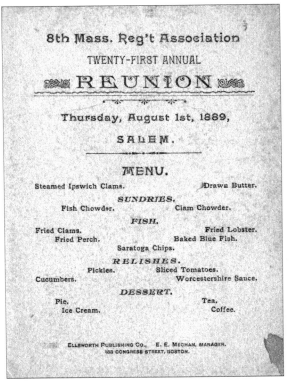

Instruction manual, published in 1901, for the 8th Massachusetts Regiment. See excerpt on opposite page.

Menu from the 8th Massachusetts Regiment's twenty-first reunion, held at at the Salem Armory in 1889.

Color postcard of the Salem Armory, ca. 1908.

The 8th Regiment, MVM in Lynnfield, Massachusetts, 1915.

My general orders are:
To take charge of this post and all government property in view;
To walk my post in a military manner, keeping constantly on the alert,
*   observing everything that takes place within sight or hearing;*
To report every breach of orders or regulations that I am instructed
*   to enforce;*
To repeat all calls from posts more distant from the guard house than
*   my own;*
To quit my post only when properly relieved;
To receive, transmit and obey all orders from, and allow myself to be
*   relieved by the commanding officer, officer of the day, an officer or*
*   non-commissioned officer of the guard only;*
To hold conversation with no one except in the proper discharge of
*   my duties;*
In case of fire or disorder to give the alarm;
To allow no one to commit nuisance in the vicinity of my post;
In any case not covered by instructions, to call the corporal of the guard;
To salute all officers and colors and standards not cased;
At night to exercise the greatest vigilance. Between (—o'clock) and broad
*   daylight challenge all persons seen on or nearby my post, and allow no*
*   person to pass without proper authority.*

(from *Duties of a Private On Guard*)

Salem Mechanic Light Infantry

Writing in 1898, Charles A. Benjamin explains: "The Mechanics' Light Infantry first paraded under Capt. Perley Putnam, July 4, 1807. As its name implies, it was composed originally of young mechanics and was always a most excellent company, as it is to-day, although its numbers are somewhat reduced … It went to the front with the Fifth Militia Regiment in April, 1861, for three months; and few companies have ever had fuller ranks than it showed on that occasion." (At this time, the word "mechanic" referred to a skilled tradesman.)

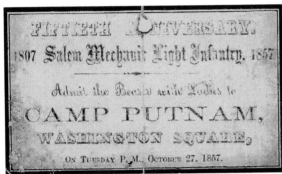

Ticket to the 50th anniversary celebration of the Salem Mechanic Light Infantry held on Salem Common in 1857. For the occasion, the Infantry named their encampment "Camp Putnam" after their founder, Capt. Perley Putnam.

Cover of sheet music for the "Salem Mechanick Light Infantry Quick Step" (or march). The illustration is by the artist Fitz Henry Lane. Note the Washington Arch on Salem Common on the far left (see p. 89).

In 1854, Boston's Winthrop Light Guard arrived at the Salem Depot where they were met by the Salem City Guard and escorted to Lowell Island (today, Children's Island in Salem Harbor) for "drill and exercise" and to camp overnight. The following morning, they departed for Marblehead, returning to Salem that evening when they "expressed themselves highly pleased with the courteous treatment they received," according to an account of the day.

Salem City Guard

Formed about 1848, Charles Benjamin writes, the City Guard "was said to be a good company in its prime, though it no longer exists. Certainly its old members may feel that though dead, it is on the field of honor, as it is the only militia company of Salem that enlisted as such for the three years' service in the War of 1861 ... [But the City Guard did not die. Instead, it volunteered as a company of the] 40th Massachusetts Volunteer Infantry, where it saw plenty of service."

In 1861, the Salem City Guard "left Salem and went direct to the City of Washington as part of the Fifth Militia Regiment, Captain Henry Danforth commanding," according to Benjamin. With them went the Mechanic Light Infantry, under Captain George Pierson, after a rousing send-off by the mayor, leading citizens, and friends. Benjamin describes the day:

They were bid God-speed, and urged to remember the high duty they were called upon to perform, while at every step of their march through the streets they were cheered by enthusiastic crowds, many of whom only regretted that circumstances prevented their being also in their ranks. The city was a unit

*in their enthusiasm, and while there was plenty of "gush," if the word may
be pardoned, and an exaltation of sentiment greater than our national
temperament has been usually given to, the occasion justified it, and it was
hearty and genuine to the last degree. In these companies over two hundred
men left Salem for Washington within five days from the call of the President.*

Fitzgerald Guards and Andrew Light Guard

The Salem units responding to President Lincoln's call for troops to
defend Washington, D. C. had all departed by mid-April 1861. But,
as Charles Benjamin explains:

*The Governor of Massachusetts, and other far-seeing men in the State, were
fully persuaded that the immediate and pressing need for soldiers would not
be confined simply to the protection of the National Capital; that the South
was making no mere demonstration, and that to preserve the integrity of
the nation there might be required another and different army from the
militia regiments now hastening to Washington. The tread, therefore, of
the marching troops was still sounding in Salem's streets, when recruiting
offices were opened at the suggestion of prominent citizens, to provide for
the unknown contingencies of the future.*

*Captains [William] Coggswell and [Edward] Fitzgerald began at once to
enlist men for three years' service, and had but little difficulty in doing so.
At an Irish patriotic meeting forty men were enlisted on the spot. The City
Council of Salem had, meantime, voted $15,000 at its first meeting after
the surrender of Sumter, to be used in aid of the families of absent soldiers.*

*The Fitzgerald Guards, as they were called, went into camp on May 10 as
part of Colonel Cass's Irish Regiment, afterwards the Ninth Massachusetts
Infantry. On Sunday, May 12th, Captain Coggswell's company, then styled
the Andrew Light Guard [named for Governor John A. Andrew], marched
from their barracks on Winter Island to attend church in a body, and two
days later they left the city for Camp Andrew, in Roxbury, where they were
incorporated with the Second Massachusetts Volunteers. The company
was presented with a color on its departure. Both of these companies were
uniformed by the city and private subscriptions, supplemented by the
personal work of the patriotic women of Salem.*

Short-lived Units

The Salem Artillery (formed in 1787) and "two juvenile organizations formed of boys under eighteen, the Washington Rangers and the Washington Blues, both first parading about 1807, were short-lived, neither surviving after about 1815," according to Charles A. Benjamin. (See p. 298 for conflicting information about the Salem Artillery.)

Salem High School Battalion

According to Brig. Gen. Len Kondratiuk, military high school training in Massachusetts began in 1865, the closing year of the Civil War. It was a "big movement," he says, and Salem "had one of the longest cadet programs in the U. S." The Salem High School Battalion became the Army Junior ROTC in the 1920s. "I remember watching [them] march in Boston Veterans Day parades through 1966," Kondratiuk recalls. While the group was inactivated in the early 1970s, they have since made a comeback.

The 1892-3 *Salem City Directory* includes an entry for the Salem High School Battalion in its "Salem Societies, Etc." section without any information about its founding. The entry reads: Salem High School Battalion. Major, Robert P. Smith; Senior Captain, Charles H. Odell; Junior Captain, D. O'Callaghan; Senior 1st Lieutenant, A. G. Reynolds; Junior 1st Lieutenant, S. A. Goodhue; Senior 2nd Lieutenant, A. N. Rantoul; Junior 2d Lieutenant, F. S. Burke; Adjutant, L. B. Goodrich; Sergeant Major, H. W. Northey.

This photograph is labeled "Pickering Cadets of Salem marching in Newburyport." It appears to be the same parade as shown in the photo on p.303.

I LOVE A PARADE — At just about the same time Robin Damon, founder of The Salem Evening News, was putting together Volume I, No. 1, give or take a few days, the above scene was being enacted in Town House Square. The year was 1880. Presumably the soldiers were veterans of the Civil War which had ended only a decade and a half earlier. It was a beautiful day, as the shadows indicate. Umbrellas were carried in those days under all conditions — to keep off the rain and to be used as a sun shade. A horse-drawn street car may be seen in the center of the photo, while the depot's Norman towers are visible in the distance.

Clipping from the *Salem Evening News* showing Civil War veterans marching through Town House Square in 1880. Note the Train Depot in the background.

American Legion first day cover, October 6, 1930.

★ Salem Veterans Organizations ★

Since the Revolutionary War, veterans have formed organizations to support each other and their families and work toward securing veterans' benefits from the federal government. Salem formed local posts, camps, and auxiliaries of national organizations, as well as veterans' groups out of active Salem units.

American Legion, Post 23

According to American Legion literature, the American Legion was "chartered by Congress in 1919 as a patriotic veterans organization. Focusing on service to veterans, service members, and communities, the Legion evolved from a group of war-weary veterans of World War I into one of the most influential nonprofit groups in the United States." That same year, the Legion became the chartering agency for the Boy Scouts of America.

Among their achievements over the years: creating the U. S. Veterans Bureau (today, the Veterans Administration or "VA") and the GI Bill; providing funds to help create the American Heart Association, National Association for Mental Health, American Legion Child Welfare Foundation, and National Emergency Fund; making the largest donation ($1 million) to the Vietnam Veterans Memorial in Washington, D. C., and sponsoring studies on the effects of the chemical Agent Orange used during Vietnam. In 1989, The Legion succeeded in raising the VA to Cabinet-level status in the federal government. They have also led the charge to account for all POWs and those missing in action.

Salem's Post 23 purchased the home of Frank Balch at 329 Essex Street in 1921 for their headquarters. Today, the group usually meets at the VFW Hall on Derby Street to continue their work and they participate in annual patriotic events (see p. 238).

American Legion events, such as this dinner, were an important part of Salem's social scene.

> *You are most cordially invited*
> *to attend the*
> ### Fourth Annual Armistice Ball
> *of the*
> *American Legion of Salem, Post 23*
> *to be held at the*
> *State Armory, Friday Eve., November 10, 1922*
> *Dress: Military and Formal*
> *Subscription: One dollar and fifty cents*

12th Annual Armistice Dance

of

Salem Post 23, The American Legion

To be held at the

Now & Then Hall :: Salem, Mass.

Tuesday Evening, November 11, 1930

Mal Hallett Orchestra   Admission 75 cents

Invitation postcard to an American Legion dance at the Now & Then Hall.

Now and Then Club, Salem, Mass.

The Now & Then Hall/ Club House was located at 102 Essex Street. Today, the site is the Hawthorne Hotel parking lot.

American Veterans / AMVETS, Post 53

According to their website: AMVETS' "commitment to service traces its roots back to 1948 when veteran volunteers first began helping veterans of World War II obtain the benefits promised them by the federal government. As the number of returning veterans swelled into the millions, it was evident that some sort of nationally organized assistance for them would be needed. The older established national groups wouldn't do; the leaders of this new generation of veterans wanted their own organization. With that in mind, eighteen of them, representing nine veterans clubs, met in Kansas City, Missouri, and founded The American Veterans of World War II on Dec. 10, 1944. Less than three years later, on July 23, 1947, President Harry S. Truman signed Public Law 216, making AMVETS the first World War II organization to be chartered by Congress."

In Salem, Post 53, located at 13 Beckford Street (see photo, p. 170), started in 1948.

Disabled American Veterans / DAV, Chapter 84

DAV was founded in the aftermath of World War I as "Americans saw the grim cost of the fighting in Europe," according to the DAV's website. It continues: "Veterans returned without arms and legs. They were blind, deaf, or mentally ill. Their battle scars told the story of massive, pounding artillery and warfare mechanized to levels no one had dreamed possible. Chemical warfare, used extensively during the war, left men with gas-seared lungs, gasping for each breath. Prolonged and chronic illnesses would forever hamper the lives of hundreds of thousands of veterans returning from the horror of rat-filled disease-ridden trenches." To make matters worse, "not only was the government at a loss about what to do with those it had sent off to war, it had very little to spend on programs for the veterans." A recession, severe disabilities, and prejudice against those disabled veterans who could work prevented thousands from being employed. Medical help was difficult to find.

Disabled veterans of World War I began to meet socially to support each other, including financially. At the same time, the Ohio Mechanics Institute (OMI) was founded in Cincinnati to train disabled veterans. Out of that organization, the OMI Disabled Soldiers was formed and attracted the attention of Captain Robert S. Marx of Cincinnati, a Superior Court judge with a "flair for organizing," wealth, and influence. Marx is credited with leading the effort "to form an organization through which disabled veterans could make themselves heard in the halls of government." The organization called itself the Disabled American Veterans of the World War (DAVWW). In 1920, Marx contacted the War Department and learned that 741,000 veterans would qualify for membership. The DAVWW held its first national convention on June 27, 1921, with Judge Marx serving as the first National Commander.

Over the years, the DAV absorbed disabled veterans from succeeding wars and they shortened their name. Today, the DAV "remains a vibrant, powerful leader in veterans' rights, services, and programs."

Franco-American War Veterans, Post 10

This veterans organization traces its roots to March 1932, when seven French-Canadian World War I veterans set in motion plans to form a veterans group for others of the same cultural background. By September, they had recruited more veterans to join them and declared themselves "La Légion Franco-American des Etats-Unis d'Amérique." By the early spring of 1933, one hundred and forty-four veterans had joined as incorporators. They were granted corporate status in May. Post #1 formed in Lawrence, Massachusetts. Salem's French-Canadian community formed Post 10 in 1946. They met in the Klondike Club building at 96 Lafayette Street.

Pvt. Frank (François) LeBrun

According to D. Michel Michaud of the Franco-American Institute of Salem, there were several Franco-American "firsts" during World War I: François Morin (1896-1969) was the first Salem resident drafted in 1917; Ovila J. Bouffard (1894-1918) was "the first Salem soldier to die for his country;" Gertrude L. Bastien was the first Salem-trained nurse to join the Army Nursing Corps; and Desneiges Sénéchal (1865-1939) was "the only mother in New England who had five sons serving overseas during the war."

Grand Army of the Republic, Post 34 / GAR

The GAR, founded in 1866 in Decatur, Illinois, was composed of Civil War veterans of the Union Army, Navy, Marines, and Revenue Cutter Service (later, the U. S. Coast Guard). Initially a fraternal organization, the GAR wielded considerable political power within the Republican Party. The GAR made Memorial Day a national holiday to mark the graves of American soldiers "with floral tributes in honor of what they did and what they dared," writes the *Salem Evening News*. The GAR also advocated for African American veterans' benefits, and helped establish veterans' pensions. According to their website, "The GAR was organized into Departments at the state level and Posts at the community level. Members wore military-style uniforms. There were posts in every state in the U. S., and several posts overseas."

In Salem, General Phil Henry Sheridan, Post 34 was founded on December 10, 1867. While Sheriden had no direct ties to Salem, he was a beloved hero of the Civil War. His decisive actions in the Shenandoah Valley helped bring victory to the Union forces. At one time, Post 34 was the second largest in Massachusetts after Lynn. But by 1922, as veterans passed away, membership had dwindled to sixty-six. The GAR disbanded nationally in 1956, after its last member died (see pp. 105-7 for more on Post 34).

Top: Salem Willows Pavilion; above: GAR reunion at the Pavilion, ca. 1900.

5,000 Recruits and 1,000 Reinstatements.

HEADQUARTERS
DEPARTMENT OF IOWA, G. A. R.,
DES MOINES, Dec. 12, 1888.

The comrades of this Department are to be most heartily commended on their deportment as Grand Army men in the late presidential campaign. By no single act or word has reproach been brought upon the order. By no possible pretext can any one accuse the order of partizanship. Yet a presidential campaign does disturb our work and progress, as it of necessity does interfere with business and social enterprises. Now, comrades of Iowa, let us "make up for lost time." Let every one take hold with a new zeal to build up the posts. Don't miss a meeting this winter. Don't let a worthy old soldier remain out of the order if you can induce him to join. Send prudent comrades to see the suspended members and get them back into line. Let us have 5,000 recruits and 1,000 reinstatements.

Yours in F., C. and L.,

E. A. CONSIGNY,
A. A. G.   *Department Commander.*

Above: Photo postcard of members of the Salem GAR parading down Washington Street in 1907.

Left: Salem GAR membership recruitment postcard, 1888.

Harriet M. Maxwell Auxiliary, U. S. Women Veterans / USWV, No. 27

Named for one of the first nurses from Salem to serve during the Spanish-American War, Harriet Maxwell was known throughout Salem as "one of the best nurses in this section, whose skill has been the means of saving many a life, alleviating pain, and whose cheerfulness has transformed the sick room into a haven of rest," according to a history of the Salem Hospital. A graduate of the Hospital's nursing school, during the war Maxwell worked in Sternberg General Hospital, Camp Thomas, Chickamauga, Georgia, one of the Army field hospitals. After the war, when No. 27 was named for her, the group held meetings once a month at the GAR Hall on St. Peter Street (see pp. 115-17).

Polish Legion of American Veterans / PLAV, Post 55

According to the Salem Maritime National Historic Site's website:

Polish-Americans often proudly point to the service of American Revolutionary War heroes Tadeusz Kosciuszko and Casimir Pulaski as models for later Polish military service in America. At times during the twentieth century, wars in Europe have complicated the allegiances of American Poles.

During World War I, for instance, some first-generation immigrants saw themselves primarily as fighting to free their homeland, a position that sometimes created tensions with America's own war effort.

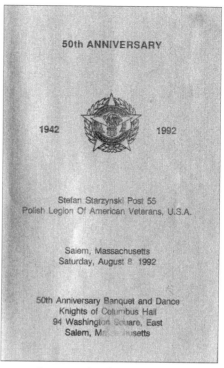

Program for the Post's 50th Anniversary banquet and dance. Post 55 formed in 1942.

By the time of the Second World War, the generation of young Polish-American men who served felt themselves to be more unambiguously American, fighting in part to help their ancestral homeland but always intending to return home to the U. S.

After World War I, the Polish American Veterans Association [PAVA] occupied more than one location in the Derby Street neighborhood, including the fire-house at 128 Derby Street and a waterfront building that was vacated after the creation of Salem Maritime NHS in the 1930s. PAVA was one of many different groups of Polish World War I veterans, several of which amalgamated in 1931 to form the Polish Legion of American Veterans. The PLAV met for many years at the old firehouse. After it burned in the 1960s, they relocated to 9 Daniels Street, the former home of the city's Polish citizenship organizations. The PLAV is still based in this location, the last active Polish organization in the Derby Street neighborhood (see p. 238).

Salem Light Infantry Veteran Association / SLIVA

According to a history published by the organization: "In 1862 the Veteran Association was organized under command of Colonel George Peabody, composed of past members, to fill the gap while the Company was in the service of the United States, which always paraded with full ranks on the various homecomings of the active Company, and rendered much valuable service, individually and collectively in many ways."

In 1905, on the Centennial Anniversary of the founding of the Salem Light Infantry, the Veteran Association held an impressive two-day celebration. It began on Sunday, September 10, 1905, at the Tabernacle Church on Washington Street. The images and quotations on the opposite page are from the 1905 program.

Today, reenactors carry on the drilling tradition of the original unit.

Envelope and letter from William C. Endicott of Salem, then Secretary of War, to Major John P. Reynolds, 1887. Reynolds served as Captain of the Salem Light Infantry in 1868. In 1887, he was Adjutant of the Veterans Association. In 1905, during the Association's Centennial Anniversary, Reynolds was its Chief of Staff.

Right: A parade of past members took place in 1873. This broadside urges all past members to meet at Hamilton Hall on the designated day. The helmet, part of the active Company's uniform at one time, became the Veteran Association's logo.

SALEM

Light Infantry Veteran Association.

1805.   1873.

A Parade of the Past Members of the Salem Light Infantry will take place on Friday, October 17th.

You are hereby notified to meet at Hamilton Hall at Two o'clock, P.M., on that day.

Uniform and equipments will be ready for delivery at the Hall on the forenoon of the above-named day.

It is earnestly desired that every old member will be present on this occasion.

Per Order of the Commander.

Captain James A. Farless, Commander S. L. I., 1855

Captain William H. Perry, Commander S. L. I., 1905

Pages from the 1905 Centennial program, showing past and present Cdrs. Capt. James A. Farless, 1855 (above, left) and Capt. William H. Perry. A silhouette of Capt. John Saunders, the SLI's first Commander, appears on p. 309.

At the present writing, [the Infantry] *returns from its camp duty, from the manoeuvres at Westfield, Mass., including all the troops of the state ... with merited honors under the present commander, Capt. Wm. H. Perry, who took his full complement to Camp, and earned the distinction of being one of the best Companies on the field.* —excerpt from Centennial program

PROGRAMME, MONDAY SEPTEMBER 11, 1905

.00 a. m.	Reveille by Bugle Corps. Salute by "Hart's Battery (2nd Corps Cadets).
.00 a. m.	Active Company will decorate the grave of its first commander, Major John Saunders.
0.00 a. m.	Parade of active Company led by Stiles' 8th Regiment Band and honorary staff.
2 m.	Lunch will be served to active Company at the Armory.
.00 p. m.	Parade of active Company, Veterans and Invited Guests.
.30 p. m.	Prize drill by active Company for medal to be awarded to "best drilled man" by the Helmet Club.
.30 p. m.	Evening Parade and Review. Retreat will be sounded during Parade. Salute by "Hart's Battery".
.00 p. m.	Banquet at the Armory.

Left: Schedule of events.

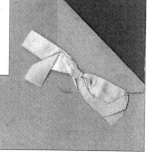

Right: Cover of the exquisite Centennial banquet program in grey and dark blue with hand-tied ribbon.

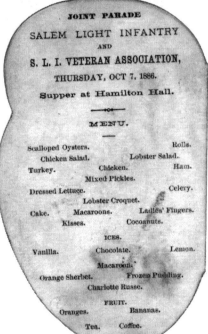

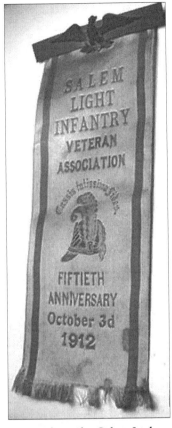

Banner from the Salem Light Infantry Veteran Association's 50th anniversary in 1912.

Top: Front of the die-cut invitation to an 1886 dinner at Hamilton Hall showing (in vivid blue) the SLI uniform cap. Middle: The back of the invitation, with the dinner menu.

Right: Hamilton Hall on Chestnut Street (detail), where the dinner took place.

Second Corps of Cadets Veterans Association / SCCVA

Organized on October 11, 1866, the Association "provided assistance for active duty members of the Corps," according to National Park Service historian Emily A. Murphy in her book on the Second Corps. She continues: "Some members of the Veterans Association helped to form the Second Corps of Cadets Camp Association to buy the camp in Boxford, which was known as Camp Curtis Guild by World War I. The Veterans Association was also very active during the World Wars, raising money to send Christmas packages to the Cadets overseas and hosting Bond Drives to raise support for the troops in the Salem area. The network of personal and family connections which has always been an important part of membership in the Second Corps was and still is reflected in the activities of the Veterans Association."

Meetings of the SCCVA took place at the Salem Armory before it burned down. They continued to meet in various locations in and around Salem—and they still do. Today's SCCVA marches in local parades in their bright red uniform jackets, and participates in ceremonial military events. Since their central role in Armory Park Dedication Day in 2003, the SCCVA works with the Massachusetts Army National Guard each spring to produce "The First Muster" event in Salem.

Their Latin motto, *Sic itur ad astra*, means "This ... way to the stars."

Top: SCCVA membership pin; below that: spouse pin.

Right: Front and back of "The First Muster" challenge coin, a military tradition.

United Spanish War Veterans / USWV
Capt. Jacob C. R. Peabody Camp, No. 22

Formed in 1904 in the aftermath of the Spanish-American War (1898–1899) and the Phillippine Insurrection (1899–1902), the USWV represented the merger of the Spanish War Veterans, the Spanish-American War Veterans, and the Servicemen of the Spanish War. Their main purpose was to help these veterans maintain contact with each other. Salem's Peabody Camp, No. 22 held its institutional

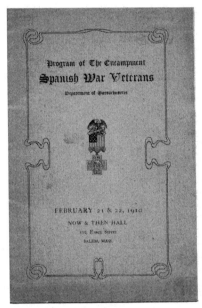 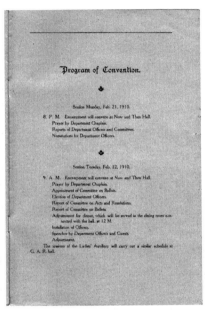

USWV 1910 Encampment program cover and schedule of events.

Dr. Laura A. C. Hughes, department president of the Auxiliary, is well known to the members of the order. During the Spanish war she was an army nurse.

Tribute appearing in the 1910 Encampment program.

Dr. Laura A. C. Hughes of Boston received her medical degree from Tufts Medical College in 1895. She was known as the "Angel of Montauk" for her work as a nurse at Camp Wyckoff, Long Island. She was a teacher, public health inspector, and American Red Cross official. In 1914, after the Great Salem Fire, Dr. Hughes supervised the Red Cross-trained nurses.

ceremony on May 2, 1901, at the OUAM (Order of United American Mechanics) Hall at 175 Essex Street, next to the Salem Armory. It was named for Col. J. C. R. Peabody, the popular commander of Co. H of the 8th Massachusetts Infantry at the end of the war. Most of the members of the Peabody Camp had served in this unit, as well as in the Civil War. They included some of Salem's most prominent citizens and political leaders. The Camp met twice a month, and held annual encampments (conventions) or reunions. Its Ladies Auxiliary was headed by Dr. Laura A. C. Hughes (see opposite page).

Capt. Jacob C. R. Peabody, for whom this camp was named is dear to the hearts of every Co. H, Eighth Mass. Infantry boy. Although entitled to the rank of "colonel" through services after the war, "the boys" love best to call him "captain."

Above: Tribute to the Peabody Camp's name-sake from the 1910 Encampment program.

Right: Spanish-American War Medal; far right: Spanish-American War Medal (with bright red and gold ribbon) worn for the 1943 veterans' reunion in Salem.

Spanish-American War veterans parading on Essex Street in 1918, a traditional part of their annual convention.

Veterans of Foreign Wars / VFW, Post 1524

According to their website, "the Veterans of Foreign Wars of the United States is a nonprofit veterans service organization comprised of eligible veterans and military service members from the active, guard and reserve forces." They trace their roots "back to 1899 when veterans of the Spanish-American War ... and the Philippine Insurrection ... founded local organizations to secure rights and benefits for their service...

Many arrived home wounded or sick. There was no medical care or veterans' pension for them, and they were left to care for themselves. In their misery, some of these veterans banded together and formed organizations that would eventually become known as the Veterans of Foreign Wars of the United States. After chapters were formed in Ohio, Colorado, and Pennsylvania, the movement quickly gained momentum. Today, membership stands at nearly 1.7 million members of the VFW and its Auxiliary ... [Their] voice was instrumental in establishing the Veterans Administration."

Salem's Post 1524, located at 95 Derby Street, formed in 1899 to fulfill the VFW's original Congressional charter mission:

The purpose of this corporation shall be fraternal, patriotic, historical, and educational; to preserve and strengthen comradeship among its members; to assist worthy comrades; to perpetuate the memory of our dead and to assist their widows and orphans; to maintain true allegiance to the government of the United States of America, and fidelity to its constitution and laws; to foster true patriotism; to maintain and extend the institution of American freedom and to preserve and defend the United States from all her enemies whomsoever.

—Congressional charter, 1899

Today, the VFW Post 1524 continues to support veterans and their families and participates in local military ceremonies. Their hall on Salem's waterfront is a popular gathering place for veterans, city officials, and neighbors (see p. 333).

> *[Their] voice was instrumental in establishing the Veterans Administration.* —VFW website

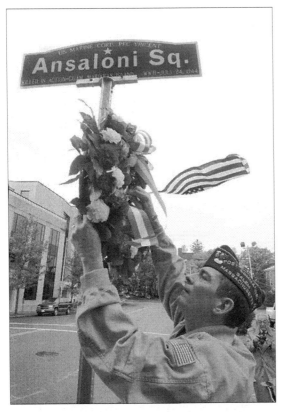

On Memorial Day of 2013, the City of Salem launched an initiative to replace faded signs marking Veterans' Squares and install new ones. Shown here is Kim Emerling, Director of Veterans' Services, at the corner of Norman and Crombie Streets.

His office is eager to gather as much information as possible about the veterans on this list, and to continue replacing all damaged signs and markers that honor veterans.

Veterans' Services may be contacted at:

Mayor Jean A. Levesque
Community Life Center
401 Bridge Street
Salem, MA 01970
978-745-0883
www.salem.com/veterans-services

★ Veterans' Squares ★

This list comes to us from Salem's Veterans' Services Office. For the most current information, please visit their website: www.salem.com/veterans-services—and let them know if you can contribute! The description of each veteran listed here is brief. Each one deserves a biography.

Abbot Square, corner of Brown and New Liberty Streets. Named in honor of Major General Stephen Abbott, Captain in the Continental Army during the American Revolution and founder of the Second Corps of Cadets. Buried in St. Peter's Church Cemetery, Salem. (Rev. War)

Arnold Square, corner of School and Dunlap Streets. Named in honor of Army Private Frederick W. Arnold, who died of disease on April 12, 1918. (WWI)

Ansaloni Square, corner of Norman and Crombie Streets. Named in honor of Marine Corps Private Vincent Ansaloni, who was killed in action on Guam on July 25, 1945. (WWII)

Biros Square, corner of Orange and Curtis Streets. Named in honor of Navy Aviator Lieutenant Commander Edmond Biros, who was killed in action on July 8, 1944, in the Pacific. (WWII)

Bouffard Square, corner of Loring Avenue and Lafayette Street. Named in honor of Army Private Oliver J. Bouffard, who died by accident in France. (WWI)

Bourgeault Square, corner of Washington and Canal Streets. Named in honor of Army Private Paul Bourgeault, who was killed in action on October 15, 1918, in France. (WWI)

Buckley Square, corner of Bridge and North Streets. Named in honor of Army Private John J. Buckley, who died of disease on September 28, 1918. (WWI)

Butler Square, corner of Hanson and Ord Streets. Named in honor of Army Private John J. Butler, who died of disease on September 23, 1918. (WWI)

Charette Square, corner of Salem and Leavitt Streets. Named in honor of Navy Seaman Ulric Joseph Thomas Charette, who went down with the USS *Ticonderoga* when she was sunk by an enemy torpedo on September 30, 1918. (WWI)

Coletti Square, corner of Pratt and Endicott Streets. Named in honor of Milano W. Colletti, an Army soldier who died of cancer in 1944. (WWI)

Corrigan Square, intersection of Bridge, Boston, Proctor, and Goodhue Streets. Named in honor of Army Corporal Henry J. Corrigan, who was killed in action on September 15, 1918, in France. (WWI)

Couture Square, corner of Cabot and Cedar Streets. Named in honor of Army First Class Joseph Couture (aka Goodhue), who died of disease on July 4, 1920. (WWI)

Coyne Square, Bay View Avenue near Chaput Beach. Named in honor of Charles Coyne who enlisted in the Merchant Marines on September 19, 1942. He was killed in action on May 4, 1943, when his ship, the USAT *Oneida*, was sunk by a Japanese submarine. (WWII)

Cravata Square, corner of Hawthorne and Essex Streets. Named in honor of Army First Class Frederick J. Cravata, who was killed in action on March 15, 1945. (WWII)

Dooley Square, corner of Essex and Summer Streets. Named in honor of John Joseph Dooley. (WWI)

Dowdell Square, corner of Cabot, Hazel, and Roslyn Streets. Named in honor of Army Private Charles R. Dowdell, who was killed in action on October 5, 1918, in France. (WWI)

Febonio Square, corner of Winthrop and Margin Streets. Named in honor of Staff Sergeant Henry C. Febonio, who was assigned to Camp Campbell, Kentucky, at the prisoner of war camp for German soldiers. He died in 1966. (WWII)

Fowler Square, corner of Boston and Fowler Streets. Named in honor of Navy Ensign Francis M. Fowler, who died from an accident on May 17, 1919, at Pensacola, Florida. (WWI)

Griffin Square, at Bay View and Columbus Avenues. Named in honor of Robert Griffin, who enlisted in the Navy after graduating from high school in 1943. He was assigned as a "belly gunner" in a Navy aircraft that was lost on a mission over the Phillippines on July 9, 1945. (WWII)

Grindal Square, corner of Pickman and Pleasant Streets. Named in honor of Navy Yeoman Leroy Hosford Grindal, who died of disease on December 8, 1919, in Salem. (WWI)

Groves Square, at Beach and High Streets. Named in honor of C. Dexter Groves, who enlisted in the Marine Corps on January 5, 1942. Private Groves was killed in action on October 25, 1942, during the invasion of Guadalcanal in the Pacific Theater. (WWII)

Harkins Square, corner of Grove and Mason Streets. Named in honor of Army Private Edward F. Harkins, who was killed in action May 14, 1918, in France. (WWI)

Hennessey Square, intersection of Hanson and Varney Streets. Named in honor of Navy Quartermaster First Class John E. Hennessey, who died of disease on June 26, 1919. (WWI)

Hix Square, corner of Cross and Saunders Streets. Named in honor of Army Corporal Oscar A. Hix, who was killed in action at Mezy-Sur-Seine, France on July 15, 1918. (WWI)

Howell Square, corner of Oakland and Balcomb Streets. Named in honor of Percy M. Howell, who died of disease on October 24, 1918, in France. (WWI)

Iwaniki Square, corner of Derby and Daniels Streets. Named in honor of Louis Iwaniki. (WWI)

Jodoin Square, at Jefferson Avenue and Wheatland Street. Named in honor of Henry Jodoin, who enlisted in the Army on March 18, 1944, and was killed in action on December 16, 1944, while fighting in Germany. (WWII)

Joly Square, corner of Charles Street and Pacific Avenue. Named in honor of Army Private Freddy J. Joly, who died in an explosion on November 4, 1918, in France. (WWI)

Jordan Square, Flint Street at the railroad crossing. Named in honor of Army Corporal Marcus A. Jordan, who died of disease on October 2, 1918, in France. (WWI)

Joy Square, corner of Canal Street and Ocean Avenue. Named in honor of Army Private Francis Joy, who was killed in action in France in 1918. (WWI)

Koen Square, corner of Hanson and South Streets. Named in honor of Navy veteran James J. Koen Jr., who died in the line of duty as a Salem firefighter on February 23, 1981. (Korea)

Larkin Square, corner of Larkin Street and Memorial Drive. Named in honor of Army Nurse Corps Lieutenant Catharine M. Larkin, who was killed in a plane crash on March 4, 1947, in India. (WWII; see also p. 82)

Larrabee Square, corner of North and Symonds Streets. Named
in honor of Army Lieutenant Edward A. Larrabee, who was killed
in action in France. (WWI)

LaVallee Square, corner of Congress and Palmer Streets. Named in
honor of Army Private Arthur G. LaVallee, Massachusetts National
Guard, who was killed in action on September 13, 1918, in France.
(WWI)

Leger Square, corner of Glover and Leach Streets. Named in honor
of Hector Leger, who died of disease on September 27, 1918, in
France. (WWI)

Lehan Square, corner of Emmerton and Forrester Streets. Named in
honor of Army Private Arthur Joseph Lehan, who died of disease
on September 30, 1918. (WWI)

Lemire Square, corner of Broad and Hawthorne Streets. Named in
honor of Army Corporal George E. Lemire, who was killed in
action on July 17, 1944. (WWII)

Leonard Square, intersection of Ward, Peabody, and Congress
Streets. Named in honor of Army Private Peter Joseph Leonard,
who was killed in action on November 12, 1918, in France. (WWI)

Levesque Square, intersection of Lafayette and Derby Streets.
Named in honor of Army Private Remi J. Levesque, who was killed
in action on October 14, 1918, in France. (WWI)

Little Square, corner of Margin and Summer Streets. Named in honor
of Army Corporal Norman Albert Little, who was killed in action
on July 15, 1918, in France. (WWI)

Lockman Square, junction of Bridge, Lynn, and River Streets.
Named in honor of Navy Aviation Lieutenant Dean E. Lockman,
Jr., who was killed in an airplane accident while serving at Coco
Solo, Panama, on May 19, 1919. (WWI)

Lynch Square, corner of Congress and Lynch Streets. Named in
honor of Army Private Patrick Lynch, who died of disease in
France on September 24, 1918. (WWI)

Malionek Square, at Blaney and Derby Streets. Named in honor
of Chester Malionek, who enlisted in the Army on March 24,
1943. He was killed in action on December 22, 1944, during the
Battle of Hurtgen Forest in Grosshau, Germany. (WWII)

Marc-Aurele Square, corner of Jefferson and Lawrence Avenues.
Named in honor of Army Private Noel Marc-Aurele, who died
in France on August 4, 1918. (WWI)

McDonald Square, corner of Essex and Webb Streets. Named in honor of Army Private John V. McDonald, who died of disease on September 2, 1918. (WWI)

McDonough Square, intersection of Broad, Flint, and Phelps Streets. Named in honor of Army Private Peter A. McDonough, who died in Baltimore, Maryland, on August 25, 1918. (WWI)

McGee Square, corner of Dearborn and Walter Streets. Named in honor of Army Corporal John McGee, who died from disease on February 19, 1919. (WWI)

McKinnon Square, corner of North Street and Liberty Hill Road. No further information is available at this time.

McManus Square, junction of Collins, Spring, and Webb Streets. Named in honor of Army Private Louis Ward McManus of the Massachusetts National Guard, who died May 11, 1918, near Vignot, France, of an accident. (WWI)

McSwiggin Square, corner of North, Liberty Hill, and Symonds Streets. Named in honor of Navy veteran and Salem firefighter Raymond McSwiggin, who was killed in the line of duty on February 20, 1982.

Miaskiewicz Square, corner of Bridge and Arbella Streets. Named in honor of Army Air Force Staff Sergeant Mecelaus "Mashie" T. Miaskiewicz, who was killed in action over Europe. (WWII)

Moody Square, intersection of North, School, and Appleton Streets. Named in honor of William H. Moody. (WWII)

Morency Square, corner of Salem and Dow Streets. Named in honor of Navy Fireman First Class Omer Morency, N.R.F., who died of disease on September 18, 1918. (WWI)

Murphy Square, corner of Charter, Front, and Lafayette Streets. Three Star Sign named in honor of brothers Army Private Henry G. Murphy, Mass. National Guard, who was killed in action on July 12, 1918, in France; Army Private John T. Murphy, Mass. National Guard, who was killed in action at Chateau-Thierry, France, July 20, 1918; and Army Private Joseph F. Murphy, who died of disease at Camp Devens, Mass., on Sept. 10, 1918. (WWI)

J.J. Murphy Square, at Juniper and Star Avenues. Named in honor of John J. Murphy, who enlisted in the Navy on February 27, 1941. While flying on a mission out of Pearl Harbor as a Navy pilot, his plane was reported missing on March 28, 1943. He was declared officially dead the next day. (WWII)

Nichols Square, intersection of Federal and Washington Streets. Named for Navy Captain Henry C. Nichols (1897-1977), who led the effort to create the William Driver Memorial (WWI, II, Korea; see pp. 156-57).

O'Brien Square, intersection of Jefferson, Jackson, and Hawthorne Streets. Named in honor of Patrick J. O'Brien. (WWI)

O'Donnell Square, corner of Boston and Grove Streets. Named in honor of Army Private First Class Edward O'Donnell, who was killed in action in New Guinea on November 6, 1944. (WWII)

O'Neil Square, intersection of Liberty Hill Avenue and Appleton Street. Named in honor of Army Private George E. O'Neil, who died of disease in Camp Taylor, Kentucky, on October 17, 1918. (WWI)

Parker Square, corner of Winthrop and Broad Streets. Named in honor of Navy Aviation Quartermaster Bradford Parker, who died of disease on September 21, 1918, while assigned to the Aviation Detachment at the Massachusetts Institute of Technology. A stained glass memorial window at the First Church in Salem honors all of the Parker sons who died young. (WWI)

Pelletier Square, corner of Charter Street and Hawthorne Boulevard. Named in honor of Army Paratrooper Private Adrian Pelletier who was killed in Normandy, France, on June 8, 1944. (WWII)

Poretta Square, corner of Mill and Margin Streets. Named in honor of Army Private Anthony Poretta, who was killed in action in France in 1918. (WWI)

Prusak Square, corner of Fort Avenue and Webb Street. Named in honor of Army Private Wladislaw Prusak, who was killed by a sniper on November 11, 1918—the last day of WWI—at Hautecort, France. His death was witnessed by Salem resident Victor Matsur.

Rabbit Square, corner of Bridge and Pleasant Streets. Named in honor of Army Private Michael J. Rabbit, who was killed in action on October 12, 1918. (WWI)

Rizzotti Square, corner of Summer and High Streets. Named in honor of Army Staff Sergeant Stephen Rizzotti, Jr., who died in England on January 1, 1945, from wounds received in Germany. (WWII)

Ruxton Square, corner of Buffum and Mason Streets. Named in honor of Army Private Francis H. Ruxton, who died of disease on October 6, 1918. (WWI)

Sands Square, corner of Dalton Parkway and Essex Street. Named in honor of Army Private Maurice C. Sands, who died of battle wounds on October 31, 1918, in France. (WWI)

Sheldon Square, corner of Federal and North Streets. Named in honor of Army Private Charles W. Sheldon, who died of disease in France. (WWI)

Sheridan Square, corner of Grove, School, and Tremont Streets. Named in honor of Army Second Lieutenant Philip B. Sheridan, who was killed in action October 9, 1918, in France. (WWI)

Skinner Square, corner of Church and St. Peter Streets. Named in honor of Army Private Fred F. Skinner, who was killed in action on October 16, 1918, in France. (WWI)

Splaine Memorial Park, Essex and May Streets, named in honor of John Splaine, Jr., a veteran of WWI, Post Commander, Post 23 American Legion, and U. S. Veterans Administrator for Essex County. (WWI)

Sutherland Square, corner of Bridge and St. Peter Streets. Named in honor of Army Private Ronald Sutherland, who died of battle wounds on October 6, 1918, in France. (WWI)

Sweeney Park, corner of Flint and Oak Streets. Named in honor of Navy Petty Officer Wilfred Patrick Sweeney, who was killed in a Kamikaze attack on May 4, 1945. (WWII)

Terranova Square, corner of Margin and Norman Streets. Named in honor of Army Private Salvatore Terranova, who died of disease on April 6, 1918. (WWI)

Thomas Square, corner of Northey and Bridge Streets. Named in honor of Army Private Herbert B. Thomas, Jr., who served in the Panama Canal Zone. (WWII)

Trask Square, intersection of Chestnut, Norman, and Summer Streets. Named in honor of Army Private George Caldwell Trask, who served in the 71st Artillery, Coastal Artillery Company. He died of disease on October 4, 1918, in France. (WWI)

Tully Square, corner of Boston and Essex Streets. Named in honor of Army Private George H. Tully, who served with the Massachusetts National Guard on the Mexican border and in France. He died of shell wounds on April 14, 1918, in France. He was the first Son of Salem to lose his life during World War I. (WWI)

Twarog Square, corner of Congress and Derby Streets. Named in honor of Private John J. Twarog, who served in the Army Air Corps. He received the Air Medal with three Oak Leaf Clusters, the European-African-Middle Eastern Campaign Medal, and four Bronze Service Stars. (WWII)

Upton Square, intersection of Bridge, Northey, and Winter Streets. Named in honor of Corporal Thomas A. Upton of the Massachusetts National Guard, who was killed in action on July 20, 1918, in France. He had served earlier with the Guard in the Phillippines and on the Mexican border. (WWI)

Vasilakopoulos Square, corner of Margin and Endicott Streets. Named in honor of Army Private Speros A. Vasilakopoulos who was killed in action on October 11, 1918, in France. (WWI)

Wesolowski Square, corner of Derby and Union Streets. Named in honor of Army Private Konstanti Wesolowski, who died of disease on May 20, 1918, at Camp Devens, Massachusetts. (WWI)

Wilkins Square, corner of Buffum and School Streets. Named in honor of Quartermaster Sergeant Charles A. Wilkins, who died of disease on September 28, 1918, in France. (WWI)

Zavalia Square, corner of Prescott and Summer Streets. Named in honor of Army Private Francis J. Zavalia. No other information is available at this time. (WWII)

Zingaretti Square, intersection of Endicott and Summer Streets. Named in honor of Army Private Guilo Zingaretti, who died of disease in Camp Jackson, South Carolina, on October 16, 1918. (WWI)

★ Veterans' Memorials and Parks ★

Most of the Memorials and Parks listed here are on one of the walking trails. For those that are not, we have added a photograph and location. Information for this section comes from Salem's Veterans' Services Office. For the most current list, please visit: www.salem.com/veterans-services—and let them know if you can add information! Each honored veteran deserves a biography.

Thomas E. Atkinson Memorial

Greenlawn Cemetery. Navy Yeoman Thomas E. Atkinson was awarded the Congressional Medal of Honor "for his bravery in the naval assaults of Mobile Bay, Alabama, on August 5th, 1864." Because he is buried on the island of San Lorenzo, he has not received proper recognition in the city of his birth. This memorial was dedicated in 2017 by a grateful community (see p. 138).

Sergeant James A. Ayube II Memorial Drive

Bridge Street to Salem-Beverly Bridge. Sergeant Ayube (1985-2010) served as an Army medic during Operation Enduring Freedom. He was killed in Chehel Gazi, Afghanistan, on December 10, 2010. He was posthumously awarded the Bronze Star and Purple Heart.

Dedication program.

Our Fallen Hero

SGT James A. Ayube II
Salem, MA

SGT James Ayube II was born at Wright Patterson AFB in April of 1985, although he spent most of his life in Salem, Massachusetts. He attended St. James Church, was a proud member of Boy Scout Troop 24 and went to Salem public schools. He earned an Associate's Degree from Bunker Hill in 2007 before enlisting in the Army as a medic. He has a brother, Alex; sister, Ashleigh; mom, Christina; and dad, James. He married Lauren Foster in January of 2008. James went on two Army deployments: Iraq in 2008 and Afghanistan in 2010, where he was killed by a suicide bomber.

While James' life was short, he had a very good life. His parents and siblings were loving and supportive; James loved them with all his heart. James married a fine woman that deeply loved him, and he deeply loved her. He had awesome family and friends to whom he was very close, who he loved and with whom he thoroughly enjoyed being. James died after making a Man's Decision to support his country, join the Army, and volunteer to be with his Army comrades in Afghanistan. He died doing what he wanted to do and what he always did: helping others.

Blue Star Memorial By-Way

Hawthorne Boulevard Traffic Island. Given by the Salem Garden Club to honor veterans past, present, and future. This program was started in 1944 in New Jersey by the state Council of Garden Clubs as "a living memorial to veterans of World War II," according to National Garden Club literature. In 1945, the national organization adopted the program and initiated an effort to create "a Blue Star Highway system that covers thousands of miles across the Continental United States, Alaska, and Hawaii." The large metal blue star that adorns each memorial harkens back to World War II. The blue star "became an icon … and was seen on flags and banners in homes for sons and daughters away at war, and in churches and businesses."

Captain William Driver Memorial Park

(see pp. 156-57)

Civil War Monuments

Washington Square North and Winter Street
(see p. 87)
Greenlawn Cemetery (see p. 204)
Harmony Grove Cemetery (see p. 210)

Dalton Parkway

From Broad Street, at Flint Street, to upper Essex Street (see pp. 190-1).

Essex County Armed Services Memorial/ Armory Memorial Park

(see pp. 108-14)

First Muster Marker

(see p. 95)

Fort Pickering

(see pp. 247-67)

Furlong Memorial Park

Franklin Street. Named for William P. Furlong, veteran of the Spanish-American War and beloved Salem Fire Fighter.

Robert F. Hayes Bandstand

Salem Willows. Dedicated in 2013 in honor of World War II veteran Robert F. Hayes, Musician 2nd Class, U. S. Navy, who served on board the USS *Essex* in the South Pacific.

Immaculate Conception Parish Memorial

Traffic island, Hawthorne Boulevard, across from the Immaculate Conception Church. Honors parish members who were killed during World War I.

Irzyk Park

(see pp. 241-42)

Juniper Point Monument

Private. Honors four neighborhood men who died during World War II: Charles L. Coyne, C. Dexter Groves, Robert F. Griffin, and John J. Murphy. Each one also has a Square named for him.

Leslie's Retreat Monument

(see p. 199)

Mansell Parkway

Intersection of Pope and Proctor Streets. Named for World War II Private Benjamin F. Mansell, 432nd Anti-Aircraft Artillery Battalion. He was killed in action in Italy on September 24, 1944. His received the Purple Heart, American Campaign Medal, and World War II Victory Medal.

McGlew Park

North Street, opposite Nursery Street. Named in honor of Marine Corporal John Robert McGlew, who was killed in action on Iwo Jima on February 19, 1945. He was awarded the Purple Heart. (WWII)

Lieut. Col. Henry Merritt Camp

(see pp. 122-24)

Merritt Triangle

Intersection of Winter Street and Washington Square West. Named in honor of Lieut. Col. Henry Merritt who was killed at the Battle of New Bern in April 1862 (see pp. 87-88).

Monument to the USS *Essex*
Pickering Wharf (see pp. 276-79).

Persian Gulf Plaque
Salem City Hall. Dedicated on Pearl Harbor Day (December 7) 1991, to remember those who served in the Persian Gulf and Operation Desert Storm.

Riley Plaza
(see p. 136)

Roll of Honor
Jefferson Avenue and Lawrence Street. Located in one of Salem's historically French-Canadian communities, the memorial lists the names of the men who were killed overseas during the First World War. The original monument was erected in 1919. Due to its disrepair, this new monument was installed and dedicated in 1986.

Saint Joseph's Parish Monument
Lafayette Park, Lafayette Street. The monument honors parishioners of Saint Joseph's Church, which no longer stands, who served in both World Wars. It was dedicated in 1947.

Saint Mary's Veterans Memorial
Saint Mary's Cemetery, North Street/Route 114. Located on top of a hill and surrounded by veterans' graves, the memorial honors the women and men who served our country during times of war and peace.

Salem Teachers College World War II Plaque
Ellison Campus Center, Salem State University. As Salem Teachers College eventually became Salem State University, this plaque was moved to its current location to continue honoring the women and men of the Teachers College who served during World War II.

Sylvania World War II Memorial
Bertolon School of Business, Salem State University. A Sylvania plant was once located on this site. During World War II, the company was awarded the Army-Navy "E" Award for excellence in the production of radio tubes. However, eight of their employees served overseas and

lost their lives during the war. This memorial, recently refurbished by Salem State University, stands in their honor (see p. 78).

Sergeant Philias J. Verrette Monument
Mason Street at Flint Street. Sergeant Verette of the Massachusetts National Guard served with Company I, 119th Infantry Regiment, 30th Infantry Division, during World War II. For his many acts of bravery, he was awarded the Silver Star, Bronze Star, Purple Heart, and several campaign medals including the European Campaign Medal with 5 Battle Stars. He fought in the battles of Normandy, St. Lo, Mortain, Aachen, and The Bulge. He survived the war to return home where he worked for Salem State College and joined Salem's VFW, Post 1524. Verrette passed in 2009. Grateful friends and citizens of Salem erected this monument in 2011.

Veterans Memorial Bridge
Connecting Salem to Beverly. Dedicated on August 2, 1996, in remembrance of all Salem veterans.

War Memorial Honor Roll
Salem Common. Honors Salem citizens who gave their lives during World War II, Korea, Vietnam, Iraq, and Afghanistan.

Ward Three World War I Honor Roll
Dalton Parkway and Broad Street. The memorial lists the names of the 286 Salem citizens living in Ward Three who served in "The Great War."

World War I Memorial
Corner of Highland Avenue and Jackson Street. Honors Salem men who were killed during the First World War.

Ward Three World War I Honor Roll at Dalton Parkway and Broad Street.

Author's note: What is not included in this list are the many ways in which Salem's houses of worship, schools, and other municipal buildings have remembered the men and women who have served. Many of these places have plaques, portraits, or spaces named in honor of a veteran.

The Nelson Dionne Salem History Collection

The Nelson Dionne Salem History Collection is a rich source of material on the history of Salem. The collection focuses on the nineteenth century to the present, with an emphasis on ethnic groups, business, travel and tourism, transportation, religious and social organizations, and the built environment. Included in the collection are books, photographs and postcards, stereographs, organization and business records, trade publications, and a wide variety of ephemera. The collection is open to the public and is currently being used for scholarly projects, student and faculty work, and digital exhibits. The Archives & Special Collections is planning to scan much of the material and make it available on the Internet for all to use.

—Susan Edwards, Archivist, Archives & Special Collections, Salem State University

My collection has enough material to fill dozens of books, theses, papers, and articles. It just needs to be used! —Nelson Dionne

Salem's Forgotten Stories

This volume is the second in a series of books produced by Nelson Dionne titled "Salem's Forgotten Stories." The first book, *U. S. Coast Guard Air Station Salem, Massachusetts, 1935-1970,* appeared in 2016. Future titles on historical subjects may include *Salem's Bravest* (Salem Fire Department); *Salem's Finest* (Salem Police Department); *Salem Eats* (favorite food and restaurants); *Salem Gets Moving* (trolleys, buses, trains); *Salem's Got Talent* (inventors, artists, writers, entrepreneurs, Salem "firsts"); *Salem Plays* (theater, music, museums, social clubs, special events and celebrations). To find out "the latest" about new titles and book signings, please visit **SalemsForgottenStories.com** or **Facebook/Salem's Forgotten Stories.**

★ About Nelson Dionne ★

Nelson Dionne, age 18, at his home on 12 Sumner Road, Salem. He was just home from boot camp at Fort Dix.

By the time Nelson Dionne enlisted in the U. S. Army in 1965 at the age of seventeen, he had already started collecting Salem history—specifically, postcards about the Great Salem Fire of 1914. Members of his French-Canadian family, like so many others, had been burned out of their homes, lost their places of work, and had to rebuild their lives from scratch.

Like everyone else who enlisted in the Army, Dionne took their required battery of tests. He scored so high on the IQ test, they placed him in Army Intelligence. Dionne was sent to Fort Dix, New Jersey, for basic training, and then to Fort Devens, Massachusetts, for Intelligence School.

PFC Dionne with his father, Nelson Dionne Sr., and his sister Karen in 1966, waiting for his flight on a C119—the first step in his journey to the Far East.

PFC Dionne in Thailand.

After training, SP4 Nelson Dionne was assigned to Bankok, Thailand, and then to the "Det. D" in Udorn, Thailand, where he spent a year doing radio communications intelligence work. In 1967, Dionne was reassigned to Bad Aibling, Germany, for another two years of intelligence work.

Nelson Dionne was discharged in 1969 at the end of his enlistment, and he returned home to Salem to pursue his interest in fire science at the North Shore Community College.

In 1972, Dionne recalls, "the economy was in the tank." Luckily, having volunteered for the Red Cross and taken courses at the Massachusetts Civil Defense Academy in Topsfield, Massachusetts, while still in high school, Dionne was able to secure a position doing ambulance work.

He also spent time driving a taxi in Salem, learning the streets well.

In Bad Aibling, Nelson Dionne (first row, center, holding fire nozzle) volunteered for the post's fire department.

Nelson Dionne Sr. (kneeling) and Nelson Dionne Jr. (standing behind)
traveled to Europe in 1984 for the 45th Anniversary of D-Day.
As the Vice President of the (American) Military Vehicle Collectors Club,
the younger Dionne was able to meet many of his European counterparts.

In 1978 Dionne joined the Salem Police Department, which put him in a position to gather information about Salem during a time of massive urban renewal. Unlike most collectors of Salem history, Dionne decided to specialize in Salem's Industrial Age, post-Civil War to the present day.

Nelson Dionne served for many years as an officer of the Military Vehicle Collectors Club. He is shown here with his 1942 U. S. Army Harley Davidson WLA in 1993. The club had been invited to add "color" to the Boston port visit of the USS *John Brown,* a World War II Liberty Ship.

In 1992, an injury Dionne suffered while on duty as a police officer led to his disability retirement in 1995. This gave him the opportunity to read and expand his collection while being "Mr. Mom" at home for his two children (Nelson is an excellent cook and baker!).

Nelson Dionne was diagnosed with Parkinson's Disease in 2003 —a result of his exposure to Agent Orange in Thailand. It began to slow him down a bit physically, but he kept on collecting. In 2011 he joined with Jerome Curley, a retired social worker from Salem with a passion for his home city, to publish their first book—*Salem, Then & Now*, for Arcadia Publishing. Dionne provided the "Then" half of the book, while Curley had already been photographing "Now."

Starting in 2012, Dionne endured a series of illnesses that led to his being declared a 100% service-related disabled veteran. But he kept on rebounding, and he kept on collecting. "It was the best way for me to deal with my illnesses," he recalls.

Somehow, in between visits to the hospital, Dionne published *Salem in Stereo: Victorian Salem in 3-D* in 2012 with Hardy House Press of Salem.

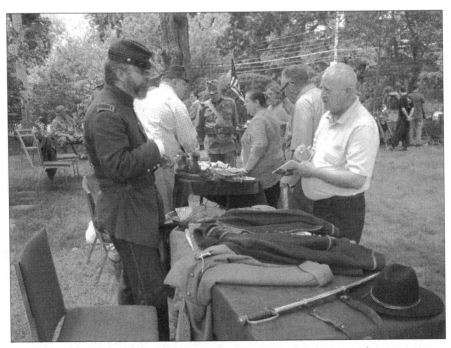

Collecting information from a Civil War reenactor at the Wenham Museum's annual Military History Day.

And, after fifty years of collecting Salem history and wanting his material to have a safe, permanent, and accessible home, Dionne turned over his archive to Salem State University's Archives & Special Collections. He donated his collection of items suitable for display to the Salem Museum at Old Town Hall. He has also donated collections to UMass/Boston (bicycle history); U. S. Army Transportation Museum (fire apparatus); National Fire Heritage Center (texts and print materials); Beverly Historical Society/Walker Transportation Collection (railroad magazines, photographs, books); U. S. Coast Guard Historian's Office in Washington, D. C.; and Massachusetts Aviation Historical Society. (Not a complete list, and he's not done!)

At Archives & Special Collections, Salem State University: Nelson Dionne consulting with Susan Edwards, Archivist; in background: Dayle Persons, Archives Assistant.

Dionne is still adding to his collection—historical material via eBay, flea markets, and antique stores, and present-day paper items from walking around Salem. He consults with Salem State to help identify and explain his collection items, and he is always happy to answer questions posed by reporters, writers, historians, City planners, and more.

At Salem State University's reception to honor Nelson Dionne for donating his material to their Archives & Special Collections are (left to right): President Patricia Meservey, Chief of Staff Beth Bower, Nelson Dionne.

With Salem Mayor Kimberley Driscoll at Greenlawn Cemetery, Memorial Day, 2016.

In 2013, Dionne co-produced *Legendary Locals of Salem* with Jerome Curley and Dorothy Malcolm. Later that year, Historic New England awarded Dionne their coveted *Prize for Collecting Works on Paper*. Dionne's third book with Jerome Curley, *Salem Through Time*, appeared in 2014.

In 2015, Dionne launched his book series "Salem's Forgotten Stories" with Bonnie Hurd Smith, the author of *Salem Women's Heritage Trail* and other books on local and women's history, and a publisher (Hurd Smith Communications). They released their first book that summer: *U. S. Coast Guard Air Station Salem, Massachusetts, 1935-1970*. That Fall, the Essex National Heritage Commission presented Dionne with a *Pioneer in Partnership Award* "in recognition of his leadership in preserving and promoting regional history."

In 2016, on the occasion of his 69th birthday on October 8, Rep. Paul Tucker (D-Salem), formerly Salem's Chief of Police, presented Nelson Dionne with a *Certificate of Congratulations* from the Massachusetts House of Representatives "in recognition of your service to the U. S. Army, Salem Police Department, and for chronicling the history of Salem and the greater North Shore."

Nelson is still collecting Salem history to add to his collection and for more books. Stay tuned! *Questions? Material to contribute? Find Nelson Dionne on Facebook, LinkedIn, at 978-532-4306, or nelson@salemsforgottenstories.com.*

Rep. Paul Tucker, bringing greetings from the Massachusetts State House.

★ Appendix ★

Was Salem the *Real* "Birthplace of the American Navy?"

At the risk of annoying our neighbors in Beverly and Marblehead (who both lay claim to this designation), in an address before the Beverly Historical Society in 1968 Donald W. Beattie assessed the "historical events from which each of the claims are drawn … and the connection between the pre-Revolutionary War skirmishes or events discussed and the emergence of the American Navy." (Just to confuse matters, Whitehall, New York, and Machias, Maine, also claim "birthplace" designation.)

As for Salem, Beattie writes, "Salem's claim to the birth of the American Navy is not nearly as vocal as similar claims from other sectors. Nonetheless, its case is significant … A factor which has received little illumination in terms of the overall Navy controversy (as pertains to the Massachusetts North Shore communities, in particular) is the fact that British officials were somewhat ignorant of or puzzled about the geography and exact names of towns in the Cape Ann region."

He goes on to explain: "The community of Salem was sometimes considered a province by the Mother Country and at other times designated Marblehead in British correspondence and official documents. These mistakes were often at the expense of Salem and with the result of crediting Marblehead with firsts in American naval history. With the enforcement of the Boston Port Bill by the British, which transferred shipping to Marblehead in Salem harbor, the confusion was intensified. In that Salem, Beverly, and Marblehead were each centers for commerce coming into Massachusetts, after 1774 … and within considerable proximity to each other … it is not unreasonable to conceive the British confusion over the names of these several towns.

As a result of this confusion, certain British documents misrepresented Marblehead for Salem, when recording American Revolutionary history along the North Shore…."

Beattie goes on to describe "the impact made by Salem when Captain John Derby of that town arrived in London, May 28, 1775, with the first report to reach the English capital concerning the Battles of Lexington and Concord." Derby had "offered his services, gratus, to the Massachusetts Provincial Congress, for the purpose of rushing the news of these events to the king. His father, Richard, donated the services of the *Quero* and its crew for expenses. Presumably the motivation behind this scheme was to vex the British and perhaps to persuade them to redress the grievances against the Americans or fight a war."

Derby reported his activities to General Washington when he returned from London in June. By then Washington had accepted the role of "Commander-in-Chief of the American forces."

Beattie observes: "It is only in connection with this naval project that Salem has any claim to being the Birthplace of the American Navy. Gardner W. Allen in *A Naval History of the American Revolution* reinforces this view when he indicates that: 'The first public service afloat, under Revolutionary authority, was perhaps the voyage of the schooner *Quero* of Salem, Captain John Derby, dispatched to England by the Massachusetts Provincial Congress with the news of the Battle of Lexington.'"

Beattie does note that all investigators of the facts agree that Beverly was "the port from which the first American armed cruiser under Continental service and pay was commissioned and sailed." She was the *Hannah*, captained and crewed by Marbleheaders and owned by Salem native John Glover who owned wharves in Beverly and Marblehead.

In 1968-69, Whitehall, New York, and Beverly, Massachusetts, presented their cases to the U. S. Navy Department in hopes of receiving the "birthplace" designation. Both failed. In light of the several communities involved in making this claim, the Navy Department chose to "not officially recognize any one place as the birthplace of the American Navy." Instead, the official Navy Day was designated October 13, 1775, when "the first naval legislation was passed by the Continental Congress in Philadelphia."

In summary, Beattie writes: "The claims made by Salem, Whitehall, and Machias must be ranked as isolated incidents of pre-Revolutionary War skirmishes ... Therefore, the contention for the claim of being the birthplace of the American Navy must be determined on the basis that the *Hannah* was the first official Continental armed cruiser of the American Revolution, and that at the same time the claim to the *Hannah* must be based on its outfitting, departure, and return to

Beverly, its port of commission (Beverly's claim), or that it was owned, captained, and manned by Marbleheaders (Marblehead's claim). It appears that whichever community can claim the armed cruiser *Hannah*, most substantially, has the better claim to being the birthplace of the first American Navy—Washington's Navy.

The claim should be shared, but Beverly's case is strongest in that it is the first naval base from which the first and five additional official Continental armed cruisers of Washington's New England fleet were outfitted, sailed, and returned with their prizes.

All the same, even if Marblehead and Beverly were to concede to share the glory of the claim ... these communities have a fight on their hands to get the Navy Department to change Navy Day from October 13, 1775, to September 5, 1775, the latter being the day on which the *Hannah* 'with the aid of a fair wind ... spread her sails and stood forth from Beverly Harbor.'"

A new annual event for the North Shore?

Beattie's assessment raises an interesting question, and provides an intriguing and amusing opportunity for an annual event:

Should Salem, Beverly, and Marblehead claim September 5
as North Shore Navy Day and plan accordingly?

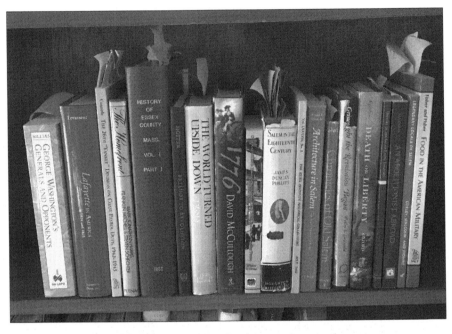

Well-worn and much-used Salem resources at home!

★ Bibliography ★

Manuscript and Archival Sources

Salem State University Archives and Special Collections:
Nelson Dionne Salem History Collection, sections on
military, railroads, social life, postcards, stereo views,
postal history, trade cards, bill heads, matchbook covers,
visitor guides, and newspaper clippings from *The Boston
Globe, The Essex Gazette,* * *The Salem Evening News/
The Salem News,* * *The Salem Gazette,* * *The Salem Daily
Gazette,* * *The Salem Observer,* * *The Valley Patriot.*

Salem Public Library
Vertical files
Salem City Directories
Reference books on Salem military units
and lists of service members
*Available here on microfilm

**Military Records of The Adjutant General of Massachusetts,
Historical Services**
McBrien, Ronald J. *The Corps: A History of the Massachusetts
Women's Defense Corps, 1941-1946.* May, 1992.
Wright, Robert K. *Massachusetts Militia Roots: A Bibliographic
Study.* July 19, 1986.

Franco-American Institute of Salem
Michaud, D. Michel. "Remembering the Great War."
La Revue de Salem, Vol. 20, No. 1, 2018.
Michaud, D. Michel. "Franco-American War Veterans." und.

Phillips Library, Peabody Essex Museum
Papers of Ralph Cowan Brown and Salem Light Infantry.

Peabody Historical Society
The Pequot Shield

Countway Library, Harvard University
"The Salem leg, under the patronage of the United States
Government for the use of the army," Center for the History
of Medicine.

Individuals
Arlander, Ben. *Scrapbook on the Life of Captain Henry C. Nichols.*
Smith, Bonnie Hurd and Dionne, Nelson. *Salem's Finest:*
A Pictorial History of the Salem Fire Department. (unpub.)
Smith, Bonnie Hurd. *Voices of Gratitude and Affection:*
Essex County Welcomes Washington and Lafayette. (unpub.)

Books

A Handbook for Messengers. Washington, D. C.: Training Section,
U. S. Office of Civilian Defense, 1941.
Americans Who Have Contributed to the History and Traditions of the
United States Merchant Marine. New York: Education Unit,
U. S. Merchant Marine Corps, 1943.
Annual Report of The Adjutant General of the Commonwealth of
Massachusetts for the Year Ending December 31, 1914.
The Adjutant General of Massachusetts, Charles H. Cole.
Boston: 1914.
Bentley, William. *Diary of William Bentley, D.D., Pastor of the East*
Church, Salem, Massachusetts. Gloucester: Peter Smith, 1962.
Connole, Dennis A. *The 26th "Yankee" Division on Coast Patrol Duty,*
1942-1943. Jefferson: McFarland & Company, Inc., 2008.
Converse, Florence. *Wellesley College: A Chronicle of the Years 1875-1938.*
Wellesley: Hathaway House Bookshop, 1939.
Curley, Jerome, Malcolm, Dorothy V. and Dionne, Nelson L. *Legendary*
Locals of Salem. Charleston: Arcadia Publishing, 2013.
Curwen, Samuel. *Journal and Letters of the Late Samuel Curwen, Judge of*
Admiralty, etc. George Atkinson Ward, ed. New York: Leavitt,
Trow & Co., 1845.
Doherty, Richard P. *History of the Massachusetts Committee on Public*
Safety, 1940-1945. Washington, D. C.: Commission on Admini-
stration and Finance, 1945.
Dow, George Francis. *Old Wood Engravings: Views and Buildings in the*
County of Essex. Salem: Essex Institute, 1908.

Farwell, Byron. *Over There: The United States in the Great War, 1917 1918*. New York: W. W. Norton & Company, Inc., 1999.

Felt, Joseph B. *Annals of Salem, from its first settlement*. Salem: W[illiam] & S[tephen] B. Ives, 1827.

Fisher, John C. and Fisher, Carol. *Food in the American Military: A History.* Jefferson: McFarland & Company, Inc., 2011.

Harris, Mark Jonathan, Mitchell, Franklin and Schechter, Steven. *The Homefront: America During World War II. New York:* G. P. Putnam and Sons, 1984.

Hoffer, Perry Charles. *Prelude to Revolution: The Salem Gunpowder Raid of 1775*. Baltimore: Johns Hopkins University Press, 2013.

Hurd, D. Hamilton, ed. *History of Essex County, Massachusetts.* Philadelphia: J. W. Lewis & Co., 1888.

Hutchinson, T. J. and Son, comp., *Patriots of Salem: Roll of Honor of the Officers and Enlisted Men, during the late Civil War, from Salem, Mass.* Salem: Salem Publishing Company, 1877.

Johnson, Allen and Malone, Dumas, eds. *Dictionary of American Biography, Vol. III.* New York: Charles Scribner's Sons, 1930.

Kaufman, J. E. and Kaufman, H. W. *Fortress America: The Forts that Defended America, 1600 to the Present.* Cambridge: Da Capo Press/Perseus Books, 2014.

Levasseur, Auguste. *Lafayette en Amérique, en 1824 et 1825.* Paris: Baudouin, 1829; translated by Alan R. Hoffman as *Lafayette in America in 1824 and 1825: Journal of a Voyage to the United States.* Manchester: Lafayette Press, Inc., 2006.

Maritime Salem in the Age of Sail. National Park Service, Division of Publications. Washington, D. C.: Department of the Interior, 1987.

McCullough, David. *1776.* New York: Simon & Schuster, 2005.

Murphy, Emily A. *Merchants, Clerks, Citizens, and Soldiers: The Second Corps of Cadets in Salem, Massachusetts.* Salem: Salem Maritime National Historic Site; available at www.nps.gov/sama.

Ohly, John H. *Industrialists in Olive Drab: The Emergency Operation of Private Industries During World War II.* Washington, D. C.: Center of Military History, U. S. Army, 2000.

Orbanes, Philip E. *The Game Makers: The Story of Parker Brothers from Tiddley Winks to Trivial Pursuit.* Boston: Harvard Business School Press, 2003.

Osgood, Charles Stuart and Batchelder, Henry M., *Historical Sketch of Salem, 1626-1879.* Salem: Essex Institute, 1879.

Phillips, James Duncan. *Salem in the Eighteenth Century.* Boston: Houghton Mifflin Company/The Riverside Press, 1937.

Phippen, Walter G. *From Charter Street to The Lookout: The Salem Hospital, A Brief History.* Salem: Essex Institute, 1966.

Pocket Guide to Salem, Mass., 1885. Salem: H. P. Ives, 1885.

Pynchon, William. *Diary of William Pynchon of Salem: A Picture of Salem Life, Social and Political, a Century Ago.* Edward Oliver, ed. Boston: Houghton Mifflin Company/The Riverside Press, 1890.

Report to Accompany H. R. 9057. Washington, D. C.: U. S. House of Representatives, Committee on Military Affairs, 1922.

Reynolds, John P. and Hart, William F. *Summary of the Salient Points in the History of the Salem Light Infantry.* Salem: Newcomb & Gauss, 1927.

Robotti, Frances Dianne. *Chronicles of Old Salem: A History in Miniature.* New York: Bonanza Books, 1948.

Tracy, Cyrus M., Graves, William E. and Batchelder, Henry M. for Wheatland, Henry. *Standard History of Essex County, Massachusetts.* Boston: C. F. Jewett & Company, 1878.

Salem Gazette. Historical Sketch of the Salem Lyceum. Salem: *Salem Gazette,* 1879.

Salenius, Sirpa. *Abolitionist Abroad: Sarah Parker Remond in Cosmopolitan Europe.* Boston: University of Massachusetts Press, 2016.

Sargent, Emma Worcester, arr., and Sargent, Charles Sprague. *Epes Sargent of Gloucester and His Descendants.* Boston: Houghton Mifflin Company/The Riverside Press, 1923.

Smith, Bonnie Hurd. *Salem Women's Heritage Trail.* Salem: Salem Chamber of Commerce, 2000.

Smith, Bonnie Hurd. *U. S. Coast Guard Air Station Salem, 1935-1970.* Salem: Hurd Smith Communications, 2016.

Stark, James H. *The Loyalists of Massachusetts and the Other Side of the American Revolution.* Clifton: Augustus M. Kelley, 1972.

Stevens, William B. *History of the Fifth Regiment of Infantry.* Boston: Griffith-Stilling Press, 1907.

Tagney, Ronald N. *The World Turned Upside Down: Essex County During America's Turbulent Years, 1763-1790.* West Newbury: Essex County History, 1989.

The North Shore on Parade. Salem: Lavender Printing Co., August, 1941.

Tolles, Bryant F. Jr. *Architecture in Salem: An Illustrated Guide*. Hanover: University Press of New England, 1983.

Trustees of Harmony Grove. *Harmony Grove Cemetery and Blake Memorial Chapel*. Salem: privately printed, und.

Unger, Harlow Giles. *Lafayette*. Hoboken: John Wiley & Sons, Inc., 2002.

War Duty Suggestions for Police. Washington, D. C.: U. S. Department of Justice, July, 1942.

Webber, Carl and Nevins, Winfield S. *Old Naumkeag: Historical Sketch of the City of Salem and the Surrounding Towns*. Salem: A. A. Smith & Company, 1877.

Webber, Harry E. *Greater Salem in the Spanish-American War*. Lynn: Perry & Searle, 1901.

Whipple, George M. *History of the Salem Light Infantry*. Salem: Essex Institute, 1890.

White, Stephen P. *Inaugural Address of Stephen P. White, Mayor of the City of Salem*. Salem: T. J. Hutchinson, printer, 1862.

Articles, book chapters, and brochures

Annual Report, 1972-1973. Essex Institute Historical Collections, October, 1973.

Bay State Monthly. "On August 12th, General Henry Kemble Oliver died...," *Bay State Monthly*, August, 1885.

Bishop, Eleanor C. "Hooligan's Navy: Coastal Pickets at War," *Naval History*, Summer, 1992.

Blackwell, Wally. "The Amazing Story of Miss X," *FlakNews*, und.

Brooks, Henry M. "Some Localities About Salem," *Essex Institute Historical Collections*, Vol. XXXI, 1894.

Carroll, Thomas. "Bands and Band Music in Salem," *Essex Institute Historical Collections*, Vol. 36, No. 4, October, 1900.

Dalton, Arthur Treadwell. "Military Service of Col. Arthur Treadwell Dalton, 1898-1932," *Essex Institute Historical Collections*, Vol. 88, January, 1952.

Day, Jacque. "I Will Try," *The Norwich Record*, March, 2014.

Edmands, Thomas F. "The Massachusetts Militia," *New England Magazine*, February, 1985.

Felt, Joseph B. "Historical Sketch of the Forts on Salem Neck,"
Essex Institute Historical Collections, Vol. V, 1863.

Fried, Stephen. "Saved by the Bell: How the Liberty Bell Won the
Great War," *Smithsonian,* April, 2017.

Goss, David. "Salem's Forgotten Soldiers of Freedom," *Salem Gazette,*
February 28, 2012.

Harwood, Reed. "The History of Misery Island," *Essex Institute
Historical Collections, Annual Report,* 1966-1967.

Houston, Alan Fraser and Houston, Jourdan Moore. "The 1859
Lander Expedition Revisited," *The Magazine of Western History,*
Summer, 1999.

Hudgins, Bill. "The Origins of the Purple Heart," *American Spirit,
November/December, 2014.*

Kolakowski, Chris. "General Ward and the Ever Victorious Army,"
Emerging Civil War, July 21, 2017.

Lee, Jack. "Jack Lee's Search for Miss X," *Salem Evening News,* via
FlakNews, und.

Massachusetts Archives, Vol. 137. "The Seacoast Defences of Essex
County in 1776," *Essex Institute Historical Collections,* Vol. XLIII,
1907.

McAllister, Jim. "Many Scenic Vistas were Once Employed for
Coastal Defense," *Salem News,* June 18, 2007.

McAllister, Jim. "Salem and the Civil War," *Salem Evening News,*
May 26, 1999.

National Guard Magazine. "What States Are Doing: Massachusetts,"
National Guard Magazine, January, 1911.

"Pencils on Street Corners: The History of the DAV," DAV.org, und.

Pitcoff, Rita L. "Greenlawn Cemetery: Salem's 'Botanical Garden,'"
Essex Institute Historical Collections, January, 1981.

Porter, Dorothy Burnett. "The Remonds of Salem, Massachusetts:
A Nineteenth-Century Family Revisited," *Proceedings of the
American Antiquarian Society,* 1985.

Putnam, Eben. "Report of the Commission on Massachusetts'
Part in the World War" (chapter), *The Gold Star Record
of Massachusetts.* Boston: Commonwealth of Massachusetts,
1929.

Rantoul, Robert S. "A Historic Ball Room," *Essex Institute Historical
Collections,* Vol. XXXI, Nos. 7-12, August-December, 1894.

Rantoul, Robert S. "The Cruise of the Quero," *Essex Institute Historical Collections,* Vol. XXXVI, 1900.

Reynolds, John P. "Narrative of the Salem Light Infantry," Program booklet for the Centennial of the Salem Light Infantry, 1905.

Salem Maritime National Historic Site. "Bowditch's Salem: A Guide to the Great Age of Sail" (brochure), National Park Service, und.

Scott, Lloyd N. "Inventive Accomplishments of Members," Publication of the Naval Consulting Board of the United States, U. S. Navy, 1920.

Seltzer, Frank R. "Famous Band Masters in Brief," *Jacobs' Band Monthly,* January 1919.

Shy, John W. "Charles Lee: The Soldier as Radical" (chapter), *George Washington's Generals and Opponents: Their Exploits and Leadership* by George Athan Billias, ed. Cambridge: Da Capo Press, 1994.

Streeter, Gilbert L. "The Story of Winter Island and Salem Neck," *Essex Institute Historical Collections,* Vol. XXXIII, 1898.

Tuoti, Gerry and Dowd, William. "Mass. was key to U. S. effort in WWI," *Salem Gazette,* April 7, 2017.

The V. F. W. Story (pamphlet), National Headquarters, Veterans of Foreign Wars of the U. S., und.

Welch, William L. "Salem Neck and Winter Island," *Essex Institute Historical Collections,* Vol. XXXIII, 1898.

Websites and Blogs

American Battlefields Trust

American Legion

American Veterans / AMVETS

Ancestry.com

Black Past (articles by Shirley Yee)

boston1775.blogspot.com (hosted by J. L. Bell, author of *The Road to Concord,* and noted scholar on the start of the American Revolution in and Around Boston)

City of Salem Veterans' Services

Essex County Veterans

Essex Lodge, The Masons

Find A Grave Memorial

FlakNews/398th Bomb Group Memorial Association
Fort Pitt Society
Friends of Greenlawn Cemetery
Gravematters.com
Historic Salem, Inc.
The Gilder Lehrman Institute of American History
    "Civilian Defense on the Home Front, 1942."
Newspapers.com
Newspaperarchives.com
Alanrothschild.com. "This is the Reason the Civil
    War Changed the Field of Military Surgery,"
    December 11, 2016.
Rootsweb.com
Salem Common Neighborhood Association
Salem Marine Society
Salem Public Library/Reference
Streetsofsalem.wordpress.com (hosted by Donna Seger,
    Chair, Department of History, Salem State
    University)
Phillips House, Historic New England
Schooner Fame
Traces of War
Trustees of Harmony Grove Cemetery
U. S. Army
U. S. Coast Guard Historian's Office
U. S. Merchant Marine Academy
U. S. Naval Shipbuilding Museum
U. S. Navy
USS *Salem*
Veterans of Foreign Wars / VFW
Washington's Crossing Historic Park
Wikipedia.com (with verification)

Physical objects
Salem Police Department and Salem Fire Department badges and
patches; Salem Police Auxiliary night stick; military medals, badges,
patches, lapel pins, buttons, dog tags, and WWI Liberty Bond Drive
rubber stamp; Civilian Defense armbands; card game by Parker
Brothers. Private collection of Nelson Dionne.

★ Index ★

Please look under "Salem" for Salem streets where historic sites in the book are located, buildings, cemeteries, neighborhoods, schools, places of worship, veterans' posts, City services and officials, newspapers, etc., as well as for organizations and businesses with the word "Salem" in their title. Missing information is noted with [?].

Abbott, Stephen, 91, 113-14, 335
Acton (Mass.), 122
Adams, John, 6, 186, 215, 249-50, 277
Afghanistan, 108, 343, 347
Africa (North), 310
Agent Orange, 352
Air-Sea Rescue (ASR), 69, 271
Alabama, 138, 343; Mobile Bay, 138, 205, 343
Alaska, 344
Alert (ship), 279
Alexander, Col. [?], 251
Algeria, 310
Almshouse, *see* Salem
Almy Trust Company, 307
Amberjack (ship), 82
Ambulance service; first in the U. S., 18
American Campaign Medal, 345
American Legion, Post 23, *see* Salem
American Red Cross, *see* Red Cross
American Veterans/ AMVETS, 170; Post 53, 320-21
Ansaloni, Vincent, 335
Andrew, John A., 19, 106, 122, 208, 211, 310, 316
Andrew Light Guard, 253, 316
Andrews, George L., 122, 173
Andover (Mass.), 277
Annals of Salem (Felt), 3, 12, 248-51
Annapolis (Md.), 309, 311

Arbella (ship), viii, 247, 290-91
Arlander, Ben, 157
Arlington (Menotomy), (Mass.), 5; *see also* Revolutionary War
Armistice Day, 38
Armory Memorial Park, *see* Salem
Arnold, Frederick W., 335
Aronson, Lillian, 60
Asbury Grove (Hamilton, Mass.), 15
Ashland (Mass.), 90
Assembly Hall/House, *see* Salem
Atkinson, Thomas, 205, 343
Atlantic Fleet/Reserve, 228
Atlantic Ocean/North Atlantic, 266-67, 269, 272
Austria, 307
Averill, Anna G., 59
Ayube, James A. II, 108, 343

Babbage, Martha Silsbee, 159
Bacall, Mrs. Channing, 165
Bachelor, George, 184
Bad Aibling (Germany), 350
Baghdad, 308
Baker's Island, *see* Salem
Balch, Frank, 169, 319
Ballou, Sarah S., 59
Baltimore (Md.), 311
Bands and band music, 97-106

Bands and Band Music in Salem (Carroll), 97-102
Bankok (Thailand), 350
Banks, Nathaniel Prentice, 208
Barbary War, 276
Barnard College, 202
Barnard, Thomas Jr., 167, 193, 196-97
Barron, William, 279
Barton, Clara, 120, 163
Barton, Samuel, 163
Bastien, Gertrude, 151, 322
Batchelder, Henry M., 96, 125-26, 145
Bates, George, 228
Bates, William H., 240
Bay State Monthly (magazine), 172
Bearss (destroyer), 81
Belgium, 307
Benjamin, Charles A., 2-3, 6, 12-13, 15, 17, 22, 216, 218, 281, 288, 296, 309-10, 314-17
Bentley, William, 156, 252; Bentley School, *see* Salem
Berlin Crisis, 240
Berry, Scott, 15
Bertram, John, 150, 212
Bethlehem Steel Company, 227
Beverly (Mass.), 59, 68, 172, 198, 231, 347
Airport, 83-85, 269-70, 275
Harbor, 220, 246, 282, 297, 355-57
Historical Society, 355
Bicentennial (American), 90, 115, 192, 281-82, 289

Bigelow, Frederick E., 104
Biros, Edmond, 335
Bishop, Eleanor C., 41, 269
Blockhouses, 2, 124, 186
Blue Star Highway System, 344
Bond, Richard, 127
Boscawen (N.H.), 235
Boston, (Mass.), viii, 6, 10, 29, 58, 99, 100, 123, 126-27, 133, 135, 194, 216, 224, 234, 275, 296
  Boston & Maine Railroad, 134; *see* also Salem Train Depot
  Boston Brass Band, 154
  Boston Globe, 144
  Boston Independent Cadets, 297, 299-300; *see* also First Corps of Cadets
  Boston Latin School, 172
  Boston Light Artillery, 175
  Boston Tea Party, 4
  Boston-Worcester Telegraph Line, 235
  British troops in, 4-5, 117, 295
  Fire alarm system, 235
  Harbor/Port, 40, 195, 351
  Lafayette in, 177
  North Station, 154, 240
  Port Bill, 4, 355
  Trade/shipping, 4
Bouffard, Oliver J., 335
Bouffard, Ovila J., 322
Bounty (ship), 159
Bourgeault, Paul, 335
Bowden, Samuel, 140
Bowditch, Nathaniel, 155, 223, 234-35, 244
Boxford (Mass.), *see* Camp Curtis Guild
Boy Scouts of America, 30-31, 90, 169, 319
Boyce, David, 195
Boys & Girls Club, 157
Bracket, George Clark, 60
Bradford (Mass.), 211
Bradstreet, Simon, 149
Bratu, Cecil V., 270

Brave Black Regiment (Emilio), 211
Breadcake, Thomas, 248
Breed, Col. [?], 91
Bridges, David N., 19
Bridgman, Lewis Jesse, 196
Briggs, Enos, 276; Shipyard, 275-78
Briggs, George N., 172
Britain, *see* Great Britain
Bronze Star, 307, 239, 347
Brookhouse for Women/ "Old Ladies' Home," 144
Brown, John, 16
John Brown (ship), 351
Brown, Ralph C., 114, 236
Brown, Simeon, 91, 296
Browne, John W., 120
Browne, William, 11, 295
Bryant, Gridley J. F., 133
Bryn Mawr College, 202
Brunswick (Me.), 271
Buchanan, James, 100
Buckley, John J., 335
Buckner, Simon Bolivar, 309
Buczko, Thaddeus, 81, 113
Buffum, Robert, 137
Bunker Hill, Battle of, *see* Revolutionary War
Bunker Hill Monument, 181
Burgoyne, John, 296
Burke, Alan, 269
Butler, Benjamin, 191, 246, 253, 299
Butler, John, 296
Butler, John J., 335

Cabot, Francis, 11, 179
Cadmus (ship), 181
Cahill, Francis D., 24
Calcutta (India), 244
California Gold Rush, 205
Cambridge (Mass.), 146, 203, 210, 219, 236, 284
Camp Curtis Guild, 277, 301-6, 329
Camp Peabody, 330-31
Camp Putnam, 314
Camp Thomas, 324
Camp Wykoff, 330

Canada, 69, 271, 283;
  Colonists from, 292
  Halifax, 6, 10
  Louisburg, 3
  Montreal, 3
  Quebec, 3
Cape Cod, 216, 274
Cape of Good Hope, 279
Cape Horn, 279
Cape Verde Islands, 25, 262
Caron, Eugene, 61
Carpenter, Benjamin, 244
Carroll, Thomas, 97
Casablanca (Morocco), 226
Cass, Col. [?], 316
Castle Hill, 31
Castle William, 195
Cate, Mary R., 202-3
Centennial (American), 176, 193
Cervera, Pascual, 262
Challenge coins, 95
Chandlery shop, 234
Channing, William F., 235
Chapman, Mary 179
Charles Doggett (ship), *see* William Driver
Charlestown (Mass.), viii, 100, 181
Charlestown Navy Yard, 212-13
Charette, Ulric Joseph Thomas, 335
Chelsea Soldiers' Home, 209
Chesapeake (frigate), 13-14
Chester (England), 283
Chicago (Il.), 309-10
Chicago Cadets, 310
China, 159, 231-33, 213, 244
Choate, Rufus, 16
Christmas Day, 117
Cincinnati (Oh.), 321
Citizen soldiers, 250;
  see also Massachusetts Militia, Massachusetts Volunteer Militia, Massachusetts National Guard, and Massachusetts Army National Guard

Civil War
16-22, 24, 87-88, 100, 115-17, 121-24, 133, 137-40, 154-55, 159-60, 163, 204-5, 317, 331
Ambulance service in (first in the U. S.), 18
And GAR, 323-34
And Mass. 54th and 55th Regiments and Salem, 20-21, 175-76
And Salem City Guard, 315-16
And Salem Light Infantry, 309-11
And Second Corps of Cadets, 299-300
Battles (other than listed here), 87, 138-40, 154, 190, 205-6, 208, 211, 345
Emancipation Proclamation, 19, 175, 211
Fort Sumter, 17, 299, 316
Freedmen's Aid Societies, 22
Gettysburg, 126
Mobile Bay, 138, 205, 343
New Bern, 345
In Salem, 252-61, 286, 288
Salem Field Hospital Corps volunteers, 18
Sanitary Commission, 173-74
Shenandoah Valley, 323

Clements, George F., 76
Cleveland, George, 244
Cleveland, Grover, 212
Cloutman, Capt. (?), 182
Cloutman, Mrs. Fred, 165
Coast Guard, *see* United States Coast Guard
Coffey, Edward A., 83, 135-36
Coffey, Mary G., 227
Cogswell, William, 211, 253, 316
Cold War, 229, 240
Cole, Charles, 187
Coletti, Milano W., 336
Collins, Francis X., 157

Colonial Wars, 1-3
Colonists (European), *see* Massachusetts
Colorado, 333
Community Preservation Act, 289
Compromise of 1850, 16
Conant, Roger, 108
Concert Hall, *see* Salem
Concord (Mass.), *see* Revolutionary War
Confederacy, 253, 299, 311; *see also* Civil War battles
Connecticut, 194, 295
Connors, Jeremiah, 21
Concord (destroyer), 81
Constitution (frigate), 13, 106, 309, 311
Continental Congress, *see* Revolutionary War
Conway, Edward, 113
Conway, James, 113
Conway, John, 113
Conway, Richard, 113
Conway, William, 113
Cooke, Harriet, 160
Copson, Edward, 25
Corrigan, Henry J., 336
Council of Garden Clubs, 344
Cousins, Frank, 145, 192
Couture, Joseph, 336 (aka Goodhue)
Cox, Francis, 11
Coyne, Charles, 336, 345
Cramp, William and Sons, 226
Cravata, Frederick J., 336
Crimean War, 232, 310
Croix de Guerre, 239
Crombie's Tavern, 125
Crowninshield, Benjamin, 182
Crowninshield, George, 179
Crowninshield, George Jr., 14
Crowninshield, Jacob, 244
Cuba, 253, 262; *see also* Spanish-American War
Curaçao, 175
Curley, Jerome, 67, 137-42, 186, 207-8, 252, 352, 354
Curtis, Kenneth G., 221
Curtis, Mabel, 165

Curwen, Samuel, 11, 282
Cushing, Caleb, 15
Czechoslovakia, 307
Czechoslovakian War Cross, 240

Dabney, Nathaniel, 11
Dalgleish, Andrew, 11
Dalton, Arthur Treadwell, 191
Dalton, J. [Joseph] Franklin, 191, 299, 301
Dalton, Eleazer Moses, 190
Dalton Parkway, *see* Salem
Dalton, Samuel A., 101, 190-91
Dalton, Tom, 240-42
Danforth, Henry, 315
Daniel, J. C., 227
Danvers (Mass.), 75, 198, 277
Darby Fort, 248
Dartmouth College, 172
Daughters of Union Veterans, 22
Davenport, Jean Marie, 155
Davies, Norman Edward Jr., 113
Davis, Jefferson, 253
Day, Jacque, 232
Deblois, George, 11
Decatur (Il.), 206
Dearborn, Charles L. Jr., 205
Dee, Katherine I., 59
Deering, Bessie G., 151
Delaware River, 117-18
Democratic Party, 16
Dennison, Daniel, 294
Derby, Elias Hasket, 215, 234
Derby, John, 5, 194, 219, 355-56
Derby, Richard, 219, 356
Devereux, Arthur F., 309-11
Devereux, George H., 309
Devereux, James, 244
Dickinson, Elizabeth M., 151
Dictionary of American Biography, 235-6
Dionne, John, 38

Dionne, Nelson L. Jr., iv,
1, 61, 70, 131, 147, 155,
238, 243, 274, 349-54
Dionne, Nelson L. Sr., 70,
349, 351
Nelson Dionne Salem
History Collection,
1, 117
Disabled American
Veterans/DAV, 321-22
Distinguished Service
Cross, 239-40, 307
Dodge, Pickering, 182
Dolphin (ship/privateer),
217
Dominican Republic, 224
Donlon, Lawrence A., 113
Dooley, John Joseph, 336
Douglass, Frederick, 120,
175
Dowdell, Charles R., 336
Driscoll, Kimberley, 241,
254
Driver, Mary Jane, *see*
Roland, Mary Jane
Driver
Driver, Ruth Metcalf, 158
Driver, William, 156-62;
Captain William Driver
Memorial Park, 156-57
Dutch, *see* Holland
Duties of a Private On Guard
(manual), 313
Dyer, Perley, 262

Earle, Capt. [?], 252
East Church, 156, 252
East India Marine Society,
234
East India Trade, 244; *see
also* Salem/maritime trade
East Regiment, Massachu-
setts Militia, vi, 2, 95,
113, 293-95
Eastern Railroad, 123, 136,
154; *see also* Salem Train
Depot
Eastern Sea Frontier, 270
Eastman, Mrs. Roger, 165
*An Easy Plan of Discipline for
a Militia* (Pickering), 185
Edison, Thomas, 236
Ellsworth, Elmer E., 310

Embargo of 1807, 12
Emerging Civil War
(Kolakowski), 232
Emerson, Ralph Waldo, 120
Emilio, Luis F., 20, 106,
113, 211
Emilio, Manuel, 106
Emmerton, Caroline, 213
Endecott/Endicott, John,
2, 95, 248, 292, 294
Endicott, Charles Moses,
198
Endicott Junior College,
231
Endicott, William
Crowninshield, 211-12,
326
England, 1, 3, 10, 67, 120,
144, 154; *see also* London
and Great Britain
And Civil War
(American), 253
And War of 1812, 213
Colonists from, viii, 1,
248, 283, 291-94
Militia system, vi, 293
Threats from, 249, 252
Trade with, 132
Wars with France, 12
Espionage Act of 1917, 40
Essex (frigate), 12, 157,
276-79
Essex (USS, CV-9), 345
Essex Agricultural School
and Nursing School, 82
Essex Agricultural Society,
186
Essex Bridge, 94
Essex County, 4, 113
1st Essex Regiment, 185,
195, 295-96
Court of Common Pleas,
185
First District Court, 147;
Probate Court, 20
Register of Deeds, 185
Essex Gazette (historical
newspaper), 185, 219
Essex Institute, 115, 160,
168, 191, 196, 198, 208,
247, 276
Essex Lodge (Masons), 121
Essex National Heritage
Commission, 108, 354

Europe/Europeans, 41,
213, 217, 288, 351
And southern cotton,
175-76
And World War I, 321
And World War II, 239;
see also, individual
countries
European Campaign Medal,
347

Fame (schooner), 217
Faneuil Hall, 133
Farless, James A., 327
Farragut, David G., 138-39
Farwell, Byron, 236
Father Mathew, 147-48
Febonio, Henry C., 336
Federalists, 277
Felt, John, 296
Felt, Jonathan, 196-97
Felt, Joseph B., 181, 248-50
Fenno, Mrs. Thomas, 165
Fenollosa, Ernest F., 106
Fiji, 159
Fillmore, Millard T., 16
First Church in Salem,
see Salem
First Corps of Cadets,
300; *see also* Boston
Independent Cadets
The First Muster (event),
vi-vii, 96, 114, 293, 329
The First Muster (marker),
vi-vii, 293
The First Muster (painting
by Troiani), vi-vii, 293
First Universalist Society
of Salem, *see* Salem
Fisher, George A., 115
Fisher, Mr., 188
Fisk, Brig. Gen. [?], 91
Fitzgerald, Edward, 316
Fitzgerald Guard, 316
Flag Day, 32
Flagg, Samuel, 296
Fletcher, Edward H., 117
Florida, 226
Flying Cloud III (schooner),
71-72
Flynn, Arthur L., 136
Fontainebleau (France),
210

Foote, Caleb, 120
Ford, George, 20
Fore River Shipyard, 224,
    227
Forest River Lead Co., 207
Fort Ann/e, *see* Salem/Fort
    Pickering
Fort Devens, 240, 242, 349
Fort Dix, 349
Fort Drum, 242
Fort Knox, 240
Fort Lee, *see* Salem
Fort Juniper, *see* Salem
Fort Miller, 302
Fort Naumkeag, *see* Salem
Fort Pickering (formerly
    Fort Ann and Fort
    William), *see* Salem
Fort Pitt Society, 124
Fort Warren, 299
Fort William, *see* Salem/Fort
    Pickering
Forten, Charlotte, 19
Foster, Capt. [?], 194
Foster, William H., 216
Fowler, Francis M., 336
France/French, 96, 106,
    213, 232, 240, 283
    And Civil War
    (American), 253
    And Lafayette, 181
    And World War I, 29-30,
    202-3, 304
    And World War II, 307,
    347
    And Zouaves, 310
    Colonists from, 1
    French Revolution, 277
    Garde National de Paris,
    vi
    In Salem, 249
    Isle de France, 244
    Threats to Mass. Bay
    Colony/America, 95,
    124, 194, 249; Quasi-
    War, 277-79, 281
    Wars with Great Britain,
    3, 12
Franco-American/French
    Canadian community in
    Salem, *see* Salem
Fraser, S. B., 246
Fred J. Dion Yacht Yard,
    71-72

Frederick II of Prussia
    (Frederick the Great),
    288
Freedmen's Aid Societies,
    22, 121
Frye, Peter, 11
Frye, Peter Pickman, 11
Fugitive Slave Law of 1850,
    16
Fulda (Germany), 240
Fullinwider, S. P., 236
Furey, Tom, 241
Furlong, William P., 344

Gage, Thomas, 4, 9-10,
    132, 146, 194-95, 198
*The Game Makers: The
    Story of Parker Brothers
    from Tiddley Winks to
    Trivial Pursuit* (Orbanes),
    27
Gannon, Fred, 219-20
Garrison, William Lloyd,
    175
Gates, Thomas S., 228
Gedney, Bartholomew, 149
Gedney, Benjamin, 113
General Motors Institute
    of Technology, 206
Gentlemen's Magazine
    (British publication), 198
Germany/Germans, 29, 38,
    40-41, 236-37, 239-40,
    267, 307, 350; *see also*
    World War I and World
    War II
General Pickering (privateer),
    53-54
George I, 248
Georgia (state), 285
Gerry, Elbridge, 14
GI Bill, 319
Gifford, Mrs. Harry, 165
Gifford, Mrs. Josiah H., 165
Gilmore, Patrick S., 99-100
Glory (movie), 211
Gloucester (Mass.), 25, 57,
    108, 249, 262, 314
Glover, John, 5, 117-18,
    356
Gold Star families,
    280

Goodale, Mr. [?], 177-78,
    180
Goodale, Nathan, 11
Gordon, Mrs. John, 165
Goucher College, 202
Gould, Capt. [?], 250
Grand Army of the
    Republic (GAR), 22,
    33, 115-17, 155, 208;
    Museum, 155; Post 54,
    145-46, 204, 280, 322-
    24; Women's Relief
    Corps, 117
Grant, James, 11
Great Britain, *see also*
    England
    64th Regiment of Foot,
    4, 146, 195
    And Civil War
    (American), 253
    And Leslie's Retreat, *see*
    Revolutionary War
    Government, 3-5, 11,
    146, 167, 198, 201,
    219, 248-50, 282, 295,
    355-57
    In War of 1812, 252, 276
    In World War I, 29-30,
    236, 267
    In World War II, 269
    Royal Navy, 248
    Wars with France, 3, 12
Great Salem Fire of 1914,
    see Salem
*Greater Salem in the Spanish-
    American War* (Webber),
    144
Greece, 227
J. S. Green (transport ship),
    174
Greene, Lieut. [?], 252
Greenlawn Cemetery, *see*
    Salem
Griffin, Robert, 336, 345
Grindal, Leroy Hosford, 336
Groves, C. Dexter, 337, 345
Grush, Benjamin, 205
Guam, 226
Guild, Curtis Jr., 305-6,
    329; Camp, 277, 301-6,
    329
Gun Powder Raid, 193; *see
    also* Revolutionary War/
    Leslie's Retreat

Haiti, 24, 224
Halifax (Nova Scotia), 10
Hamilton (clipper ship), 231
Hamilton, Alexander, 252,
    285
Hamilton (Mass.), 157
Hamilton Hall, *see* Salem
Hammond, Natalie Hays,
    57
Hancock, John, 4, 146
Hannah (brig), 117, 355-57
Haradan, Jonathan, 151,
    153-54
Harding, Warren G., 144
Harkins, Edward F., 337
Harley-Davidson, 351
Harmony Grove Cemetery,
    see Salem
Harris, Mrs. Alfred S., 165
Hart, John W., 205
Harvard College/University,
    104, 172, 184, 211, 305,
    309
Harvard Law School, 211
Hathorne, John, 149
Hawaii, 240, 344
Hawthorne Hotel, 81, 90,
    151-52, 169, 273, 320
Hawthorne, Nathaniel, 16,
    120, 149
Hayes, Robert F., 345
He Rode Up Front for Patton
    (Irzyk), 239
Hennessey, John E., 337
Henry (brig), 14
Henthorne, John R., 83-84
Highland Athletic Club,
    225
Hill, Edwin, 113
Hinks, Edward W., 311
Historic Naval Ships
    Association, 229
Historic New England
    (SPNEA), 174, 354
Historical Sketch of Salem
    (Osgood and
    Batchelder), 145
*Historical Sketch of the Salem
    Light Infantry* (Whipple),
    119-20
History of Essex County
    (Hurd), *see* Benjamin,
    Charles A.
Hitchins, William S., 227

Hix, Oscar A., 337
Hoffer, Peter Charles, 198-
    99, 201
Hoffman, Alan, 181, 183
Holland/Dutch, 248
Holyoke, Edward Augustus,
    11
Honduras, 226
Hovey, Lieut. [?], 91
Howard, John, 182
Howell, Percy M., 337
Hoyt, Margery L., 59
Hughes, Laura A. C., 330-
    31
Hull Lifesaving Museum,
    216
Huntington, Asahel, 174
Huntington, Caroline L.,
    173-74
Hurley, John, 22
Hutchinson, Thomas, 4
Hygrade Lamp Co., 37, 79
Hytronic Laboratories, 79

Iberian Peninsula, 283
Illinois, 206, 309
Impressment, 12
Independent Corps of
    Cadets/First Corps of
    Cadets, 208
India, 159
"Indian Wars," 130
Indians, *see* Salem/Native
    Americans in
Institute of Electrical
    Engineers, 237-8
Ionian Islands, 227
Iraq, 308, 347
Ireland/Irish, 99, 244, 248,
    292, 316
Irzyk, Albin F., 113, 239-43;
    Irzyk Park, 241-42
Irzyk, Evelyn, 241
Isles of Shoals, (N. H.), 3,
    71-72
Italian Band, 106
Italy, 226, 345
Iwaniki, Louis, 337
Iwo Jima (Japan), 345

Jacobins, 277
Jacobs' Band Monthly, 104

Japan, 60, 223, 226, 244,
    269; *see also* World War II
Jefferson, Thomas, 12, 186;
    Embargo of 1807, 217,
    252
Jeffrey, James, 179
Jewett, George Baker, 23
Jodoin, Henry, 337
Johnson, Andrew, 311
Johnson, Samuel, 120
Joly, Freddy J., 337
Jones, John Paul, 218
Jordan (country), 228
Jordan, Marcus A., 337
Joshua Ward House, 90, 132
Joy, Francis, 337
J. S. Green (transport ship),
    174
Julius Caesar (ship), 154

Kaiser Company, 231
Kaiser William II, 267
Kansas City (Mo.), 170, 320
Kansas-Nebraska Bill, 16
Kehrhahan, Louis, 100
Kemble, Elizabeth, 172
Kentucky (ship), 35
Kentucky (state), 240
Key, Albert L., 225
Kimball, Clara Bertram,
    212
King, John G., 182
"King Philip's" War, 2
Klondike Club, 322
Kolakowski, Chris, 232
Kondratiuk, Leonid, vi, 30,
    59, 294-95, 298, 307, 317
Korea, 153, 274, 307, 347

Lafayette Coffee House, 183
Lafayette in America
    (Hoffman), 181
Lafayette, Marquis de/
    General, vi, 127, 149,
    171; in Boston, 177; in
    Revolutionary War, 219-
    20, 285; in Salem, 176-
    83, 207, 220, 288
Lakeman, John R., 117
Lander, Frederick W., 19,
    113, 122, 154-55, 186
Lane, Fitz Henry, 314

Lane, Lillian G., 145, 150
Laner, Edward, 182
Larcom, Paul S., 41, 69, 275-77
Larivee, Samuel, 25
Larkin, Catharine Marie, 60, 82; Larkin Square, 337; *see also* Salem/Larkin Lane
Larkin's Market, 82
Larrabee, Edward A., 337
Laurier Guard, 110
LaVallee, Arthur G., 338
Lawrence, James, 14
Lawrence (Mass.), 172, 322
Leach, Julia May, 145, 150
Lebel, Lena, 62
LeBrun, François (Frank), 322
Lee, Charles, 132, 282-86; *see also* Salem/Fort Lee
Lee, Henry ("Light-Horse Harry"), 283, 285
Lee, Jeremiah, 117
Lee, Joseph ("Jack"), 83-85
Leger, Hector, 338
Legg's Hill, 13
Legion of Merit, 239
Lehan, Arthur Joseph, 338
Lemire, George E., 338
Leonard, Peter Joseph, 338
Leslie, Alexander, *see* Revolutionary War
Leslie's Retreat, *see* Revolutionary War
Levesque, Alfred J., 82
Levesque, Raymond August, 82
Levesque, Remi J., 338
Levasseur, Auguste, 183
Lexington (Mass.), 58; *see also* Revolutionary War
Liberty Bell, 32
Liberty Bonds, 33-34, 38
Liberty Ship, 351
Liberty Tree, *see* Salem 107
Little, David M., 212-13
Little, Norman Albert, 338
Lloyd, Edna Mae, 270
Lincoln, Abraham, 16-17, 19, 159, 205, 211, 254, 310, 316
Lincoln (Mass.), *see* Revolutionary War

Lockman, Dean E., 338
London, 5, 96-97, 355
Long (destroyer), 223
Long Island/Sound, 69, 118, 271, 330
Low, Charles, 244
Low, Daniel & Co., 130, 145
Loyalists (in Salem), *see* Salem
Ludlow, Augustus C., 14
Lusitania (ocean liner), 29
Luxembourg, 307
Lyceum Hall, *see* Salem Lyceum
Lynch, Patrick, 338
Lynde, Benjamin, 11
Lynn (Mass.), 25, 117, 154-55, 262, 323
Lynn Armory, 155, 307
Lyons, Thomas, 138
Lynnfield (Mass.), 313

MacDermaid, Emma C., 151
Machner, Jean I., 231
Madison, James, 186
Maine (state), 69, 235, 271
Maine (ship), 24, 27, 127, 144
Malcolm, Dorothy V., 190, 354
Malden (Mass.), 311
Malionek, Chester, 338
Manhattan, (N.Y.), 14
Manley, John, 218
Mansell, Benjamin F., 345
Mansfield, William, 296
Marblehead (Mass.), 3, 13-14, 117, 122, 218, 242, 245-46, 251, 260, 275, 302, 315
And U. S. Navy, 355-57
And USS *Constitution*, 216
And Leslie's Retreat, 195-98
Trade/shipping, 4
Marc-Aurele, Noel, 338
Marden Construction Co., 275

Maritime Salem in the Age of Sail (National Park Service), 153, 217-18
Martineau, Jean-Guy, 242
Marx, Robert S., 321
Maryland, 122, 311
Massachusetts
Adjutants General of, 172, 187, 294, 309
As Massachusetts Bay Colony, vi, vii, 1, 289, 292; English colonists in, viii
As Commonwealth of Massachusetts, 112; birthplace as, 5, 146
Bureau of Labor Statistics of, 172
Civil Defense Academy of, 350
Committee on Preparedness of, 151
Committee on Public Safety of, 57
Constitution of, 6
Department of Veterans Affairs of, 209
General Court of, vi, vii, 4-5, 95, 146, 185, 248, 293
Governors of, 4, 38, 57, 59, 106, 111, 146, 157, 191, 209, 211, 263, 299, 305, 310, 316; *see also* individual names
Legislature of, 21, 296, 305, 354
Military Commission of, 194

Military of (in chronological order)

Massachusetts Militia
vi-vii, 1-3, 5, 106, 113
117, 149, 157, 184-85, 207, 293-96
Salem Artillery Company, 298
Salem Company, 291-92

1st Essex Regiment, 185, 195, 295-96

Massachusetts Volunteer Militia 298, 305

Civil War Units
1st Regiment of Cavalry, Mass. Vols., 208
1st Mass. Vol. Infantry Regiment , 15
2nd Mass. Vol. Infantry Regiment, 21, 316
5th Mass. Vol. Infantry Regiment, 174, 314-15
8th Mass. Vol. Infantry Regiment, 25-26, 309, 312-13, 331*
Co. H, 25, 108, 188, 311; Co. J, 134
9th Mass. Vol. Infantry Regiment, 316
19th Mass. Vol. Infantry Regiment, 311
21st Mass. Vol. Infantry Regiment, 117
23rd Mass. Vol. Infantry Regiment, 87-88, 122, 124, 211
24th Mass. Vol. Infantry Regiment, 100
32nd Mass. Vol. Infantry Regiment, 205
40th Mass. Vol. Infantry Regiment, 148, 205, 315
50th Mass. Vol. Infantry Regiment, 309
54th Mass. Vol. Infantry Regiment, 19-21, 106, 175-76, 211
55th Mass. Vol. Infantry Regiment, 20, 175-76, 211
57th Mass. Vol. Infantry Regiment, 206
5th Mass. Light Artillery, Battery, 1st Brigade, 1st Division, 106
1st Mass. Vol. Heavy Artillery Regiment, ("Heavies"), 25, 190-91, 205, 262-63*

*Also present in Salem during the Spanish-American War

Unattached Civil War Units Stationed on Winter Island
3rd Mass. Volunteer Infantry (unattached), 254
12th Mass. Volunteer Heavy Artillery (unattached), 253

Massachusetts National Guard
vii, 58-59, 96, 114, 209
101st Field Artillery, 175, 304, 307
102nd Field Artillery Band, 111, 307-8, 311
119th Infantry Regiment, 30th Infantry Division, 347
215th Army Band, 106
And the Great Salem Fire, 187-89
And U. S. Army, Yankee Division, 304, 307
Museum and Archives, vii
Naming of, 304
see also First Corps of Cadets and Second Corps of Cadets

Massachusetts Army National Guard
see First Muster (event)

Massachusetts (cont.)
Militia Law of 1840, 298
Pine Tree Flag, 157
State Marshal of, 92, 94
State Police of, 242
Supreme Judicial Court of, 168, 211
Volunteer Aid Association of, 150
Women's Defense Corps of, 57-58, 111, 774
Massachusetts Bar, 184

Massachusetts Historical Society, 186
Massachusetts Institute of Technology (MIT), 206
Massachusetts Militia Roots (report), 292
Mason, David, 113, 194-96, 213
Mason, Hannah, 113
Mason and Slidell Affair, 252
Mason, James, 253
Maxwell, Harriet M., 144-50; Auxiliary, 324
McAllister, Jim, 13, 113, 232
McClellan, George B., 154
McCullough, David, 118
McDermott, Mrs. William V., 165
McDonald, John V., 338
McDonough, Peter A., 339
McGee, John, 339
McGlynn, Edna, 68
McIntire Brothers, 132
McIntire, Samuel, 89-90, 114, 149, 154, 172, 179
McKinley, William, 28, 144
McKinnon Square, 339
McManus, Louis Ward, 339
McSwiggin, Raymond, 339
Mechanic/k Light Infantry, *see* Salem
Medal of Honor, 136-42, 205
Mediterranean Sea, 227-28
Memorial Day, 238, 322
Merchant Marine, 244, 272
Meritorious Unit Commendation, 307
Merritt, Henry, 19, 87, 122-24, 154-55, 204, 345
Mexico, 15, 29, 213, 224, 304
Mexican-American War, 15-16, 232
MIAs (Missing in Action), 19; *see also* Office of Missing Soldiers and Red Cross/Searchers
Miaskiewicz, Mecelaus ("Mashie"), 339
Michaud, J. Alex, 113, 206
Middleton (Mass.), 207

Military Vehicle Collectors Club (MVCC), 351
Mill Prison (England), 213
Mines/Mine sweepers, 236-38
Minton, Chester G., 135
Missouri, 205, 320
Missud, Jean, 96, 112, 213, 306
Monroe, James, 181
Montague, Marion P., 151
Montauk (N. Y.), 330
Moody, William H., 339
Morency, Omer, 339
Morin, François, 322
Morris, Robert, 20-21
Morse, Francis W., 98-99
Mount Auburn Cemetery, 203, 210
Mount Holyoke College, 202
Mount Vernon (ship), 215
Murphy, Emily A., 96, 108, 296-7, 299-300, 302, 304, 307, 329
Murphy, Henry G., 339
Murphy, John, 244
Murphy, John J., 339, 345
Murphy, John T., 339
Murphy, Joseph F., 339

Nahant (Mass.), 262-63
Nanjing (China), 233
Nashville (Tenn.), 159-161
Nashville (ship), 25, 136, 141-42
National Guard, *see* U. S. National Guard
National Guard Magazine, 144
National Lancers, 305
National Register of Historic Places, 154-55, 289
National Park Service, 88, 108, 112, 153, 155, 215, 218; *see also* Salem Maritime National Historic Site
Native Americans, viii, 1-2, 95, 124, 290; land taken from, 140, 291-92; wars with, 140, 292

Algonquian, 291
Kiowa, 140
Pawtucket, 291
Pequot, 2, 293
Wampanoag, 2
Naumkeag (place name), 1, 95, 291-92
"The NC-4" (march), 104
Neutrality Patrols, 41
Nevins, W. S., 283
New American Practical Navigator (Bowditch), 155, 234-5, 244
New England, 30, 249, 271
New England Guard, 100
New Hampshire, 235, 295
New Jersey, 118, 349, 344
New Orleans, 139, 174, 253
New York, 118, 123, 174, 284, 296, 309, 311
New York National Guard, vi
New Zealand, 159
Newburyport (Mass.), 15, 25, 262, 303, 317
Newport (R. I.), 153, 236
Nice (France), 213
Nichols, Henry C., 156-57, 340
Nichols, James W., 113
North America, 1, 283
North Carolina, 100-1
North Church (Salem), *see* Revolutionary War/ Leslie's Retreat and Salem
North Sea, 236
North Shore Community College, 350
North Shore Sunday, 29
Northern Air Patrol, 270
The Norwich Record (magazine), 232
Norwich University, 232-33
Noska, Jane E., 59
Now & Then Club/Hall, *see* Salem
Nurses, *see* Salem Hospital Nursing School

O'Brien, Patrick J., 340
O'Connor, Mrs. John C., 165

O'Donnell, Edward, 340
O'Neil, George E., 340
Office of Missing Soldiers, 163, 170
Ohio, 321, 333
Ohio Regiment, 160
Old Glory (American flag), 33, 156-62
Old London Coffee House, 146, 201, 230
Old Naumkeag: : Historical Sketch of the City of Salem and the Surrounding Towns (Webber and Nevins), 283
Oliver, Daniel, 172
Oliver family, 173
Oliver, Henry Kemble, 113, 127, 167, 172-73
Oliver, Peter, 11
Operation Desert Storm, 346
Order of United American Mechanics (OUAM), 331
Oregon, 231
Orne, Joseph, 179
Orne, Timothy, 11
Osgood, Capt. [?], 94
Osgood, Charles, 162
Osgood, Charles S., 96, 125-26, 145
Osgood, Joseph, 179
Otis Air Base, 274
Over There: The United States in the Great War (Farwell), 236

Page, S [?]., 180
Park Street Church (Boston), 173
Parker, Bradford, 340
Parker Brothers, 27, 80
Parker, John S., 295
Parker, George S., 27
Parker, Mrs. John S., 165
Parkinson's Disease, 352
Parks, Sarah Jane, 159
Joseph R. Parrott (ship, aka USS *Salem* #2), 226
Parsons, John, 101
Patrick, Daniel, 294
Patrick, Deval, 209

Patton, George S., 239, 241, 307
"Patriots," 5
Peabody, Elizabeth, 149; and Lafayette, 182
Peabody, Francis, 108, 207-8, 210, 213, 298, 300
Peabody, George, 326
Peabody, Capt. Jacob C. R., 144; Camp, 280, 330-31
Peabody, Joseph, 109, 182, 207, 213, 330
Peabody, Mary (m. Mann), 149
Peabody (Mass.), 75
Peabody, Sophia (m. Hawthorne), 149
Peabody Essex Museum, 89, 112-14, 154-55, 171, 233; Phillips Library, 114, 60-62; *see also* Salem/Armory Memorial Park and Essex Institute
Pearl Harbor Day, 346
Peele, Jonathan, 282-83
Peele, Willard, 182
Peirson, Edward Brooks, 23
Pelletier, Adrian, 340
Pequot Mills, 66
Pennsylvania, 118, 333
Pensacola (ship), 138-39
Pequot House, 273
Perkins, Clarence A., 311
Perkins, Joseph, 216
Perry, Oliver Hazard, 14
Perry, William H., 327
Persian Gulf War, 127, 346
Pfaff, Charles A., 262
Phalen, Edward A., 117
Philadelphia, 32, 102, 184, 224, 226, 229
Philippines, 191, 206, 330, 333
Phillips family and House, 174-75:
  Anna
  Charles Appleton
  Edward W.
  Stephen Clarendon
  Stephen Willard
Phillips, James Duncan, 4, 8, 10-11, 95, 154, 167, 185, 194-98, 218-19, 285-86

Phillips, Wendell, 120
Pickering Cadets, 317
Pierson, George H., 315
Phippen, Walter G., 151
Phippen, Mrs. Walter G., 165
Pickering, John, 180, 182
Pickering, Timothy, 5, 184-86, 195, 250, 295; House, 184-85
Pickering Wharf, *see* Salem
Pickering's Hill, 186
Pickman, Benjamin, 11
Pierce, Benjamin, 113, 115
Pierce, Franklin, 16
Pinnock, Lorna, 224
Pioneer Village, viii, 290
Pirates, 3, 248
Pitman and Brown, 37
Plum Island (Newburyport), 262
Poland/Polish, 283
Polish-American community in Salem, *see* Salem
Poppe, Cheryl L., 209
Poretta, Anthony, 340
Portland (Or.), 231
Port Royal (S. C.), 248
Porter, David, 279
Portsmouth (N. H.), 180, 220, 222
POWs (Prisoners of War), 319
Powder Houses, *see* Revolutionary War
Poynton, Thomas, 11
Prelude to Revolution (Hoffer), 198-99, 201
Prescott, James, 123
Prince, John, 11, 179
Privateers, 3, 117, 125, 151, 213, 215, 217-18, 249, 296
Proctor, John, 163
Prusak, Wladislaw, 340
Prussia, 288
PT boats, 206
Purbeck, D. P., 126
Purple Heart, 239, 345, 347
Putnam, Col. [?], 182
Putnam, Perley, 314; Camp, 314
Pynchon, William, 11, 180

Quasi-War with France, 12, 215, 276
Queen Victoria, 96
Quero (ship), see Revolutionary War
Quigley, William, 242
Quincy (Mass.), 208, 224, 227, 229
Quonset Point (R. I.), 271

Rabbit, Michael J., 340
Radcliffe College, 202
Radiology, 236
Raney, Roy L., 41, 230
Ranney, Stephen, 250
Ration stamps/books, 62-65; coins, 65
Rantoul, Robert S. Jr., 4-5, 146
Rantoul, Mrs. William G., 121
Raymond, Josephine, 24
Red Cross (American), 31, 60, 120-21, 129, 143, 151, 163-66, 202-3, 213, 330, 350; Junior Red Cross, 30; Searchers, 203
Reeves, Robert W., 117
Rehoboth (Mass.), 244
Reignor, Mrs. Lee, 165
Remond, Charles Lenox, 20-21, 175
Remond family, 22, 121
Remond, John, 175
Remond, Sarah Parker, 20, 121, 175-76
Republican Party, 16, 322
Repulse at the North Bridge, 196-97; *see also* Revolutionary War/ Leslie's Retreat
Reserve Officers Training Corps, 239
Revere, Paul, 112
Reynolds, John P., 117, 311, 326
Reynolds, Joseph P., 212

Revolutionary War
vi, 1, 4-11, 32, 81, 117-18, 151, 153, 247
And Tadeusz Kosciuszko, 325

And Lafayette, 171, 175-81
And Casimir Pulaski, 325
And Salem Forts, 280-88
Army of Observation, 295
Articles of Confederation, 6
Banishment Act, 10
Beginning of, 193, 198, 199-219, 295
Boston Port Bill, 4, 230, 355
Boston Tea Party, 4, 167, 230
Bunker (Breed's) Hill, 5-6, 126, 296
Committee of Safety, 282
Concord, 5, 115, 146, 185, 198, 201, 219, 288, 295-96, 355
Confiscation Act, 10
Conspiracy Act, 10
Continental Army, 118, 215, 283-84, 296
Continental Congress, 356
Declaration of Independence, 176
First blood shed, 196
Leslie's Retreat, 5, 10, 167, 185, 213, 249, 295; Centennial of, 199; story of, 192-201; Letters of Marque, 215; *see also* Privateers
Lexington Alarm, 5, 113, 185, 198, 201, 219, 288, 295-96, 355
Loyalists in Salem, *see* Salem
Menotomy (Arlington), 5, 115, 185
Mandemus Counsellors, 11
Minutemen, 195, 198, 295
Powder Houses, 275
Privateers in, *see* Privateers
Provincial Congress, 4-5, 146, 184-85, 219, 249, 355

Quero (ship), 5, 219, 356
Saratoga, 201
Siege of Boston, 117
Sons of Liberty, 9
Treaty of Paris, 181
Trenton, 118, 201
Valley Forge, 285
Veterans of, 191
Yorktown, 201

Rhode Island, 69, 271, 295-96
Richardson, J. M., 253
Richmond (ship), 138
Richmond, Katherine, 165
Riley, John Phillip, 25, 113, 136, 141
Riley, John Phillip II, 142
Riley Plaza, 133-36, 141-42
Rizzotti, Stephen Jr., 340
Robinson Crusoe (play), 301
Robotti, Frances, 2, 16, 18-19, 24-25, 29, 31, 38, 112, 133-34, 262, 267, 283
Roland, Mary Jane Driver, 160
Roosevelt, Franklin D., 40-41, 43, 60, 151, 230-31, 269
Roosevelt, Theodore, 25-27, 144
Ropes, Benjamin Jr., 281, 296
Ropes, George, 114, 167-68
Ropes, Joseph, 182
Ropes, Margaret L., 121
Ropes, Nathaniel, 179
Ross, Eleanor, 173
ROTC (Reserve Officers Training Corps), 317
Row, Thomas, 107
Roxbury (Mass.), 316
Ruff (submarine), 220
Rush, Benjamin, 288
Russia, 232, 283
Ruxton, Francis H., 340

Sabine (ship), 213
Saigon (Vietnam), 240

Salem
Abolitionists in, 22
African American community in, 22; *see also* Remond and Shearman families
American Legion, Post 23, 318-20
Almshouse of, 186
Almshouse Road, 84
AMVETS, Post 53, 320-21
Appleton Street, 204
Armory, *see* Salem Armory
Armory Memorial Park, 5, 90, 136, 206, 241, 300
Assembly Hall/House, 9, 90, 171-72, 179
Back Street, 178
Baker's Island, 216, 246
Bands/Band music in, 97-106; *see also* George Washington/ in Salem
Bayview Avenue, 280
Beckford Street, 170, 238
Benevolent institutions in, 234
Bentley School, 241-42
Bicentennial Commission of, 90
Blockhouses in, *see* Blockhouses
Block House Square, 84
Blue Star Memorial By-Way, 344
Board of Selectmen of, 92-93
Boston Street, 82
Bowker Block, 117
The Bridge at 211/ Murray Hall, 163
Bridge Street, 343
British troops in, 4-5, 146, 185, 194; *see also* Revolutionary War/ Leslie's Retreat
Broad Street, 172, 184-86, 190, 347; forts and common, 186
Broad Street Cemetery, 154-55, 186-87

Brown Street, 108, 114
Buffum Street, 195
Castle Hill, 31
Cat Cove, 242, 275
Cemeteries in, *see*
 individual cemeteries
Central Hall, 145
Central Street, 117, 145-
 47, 183; Custom
 House on, 230
Central Wharf, 220
Charter Street, 149-50
Charter Street Cemetery,
 149, 186
Chestnut Street, 41, 71,
 173-75, 328
Children's Island (aka
 Lowell's Island), 315
Church Street, 118-120,
Churches in, 53, 121,
 130, 156, 163, 167;
 see also individual
 churches
City Council of, 82-83,
 123, 241, 280, 316
City Hall of, 89
Civil Defense/Office of
 Civil Defense (OCD)
 in, 42-56, 148
Cogswell School, 211
Colonial defense of, 186;
 see also Massachusetts
 Militia
Colonial legislature in,
 184
Committee of Arrange-
 ments of, 92-94
Common, *see* Salem
 Common
Concert Hall, 94, 178-
 79, 181
Constable, 260
Corwin House/Witch
 House, 156
Courts in, 147
Court House/Court-
 house, 93
Court Street, 91
Crombie Street, 125
Custom Houses, on
 Derby Street, 41; on
 Central Street, 230
Dalton Parkway, 190,
 347

Daniels Street, 325
Dearborn Street, 202
Derby School, 30
Derby Street, 215
 20, 230-33, 238-39,
 319, 325, 333; *see*
 also Waterfront and
 Derby Street (Trail),
 215-43
Derby Wharf, 219
Driver Park (Captain
 William Driver
 Memorial Park),
 156-57
Downtown of, *see*
 Salem Common and
 Downtown (Trail)
Draft Board in, 60
East India Square, 114
Essex House, 155
Essex Street, 108-9,
 117, 124-28, 145, 153,
 156, 163, 167-169,
 183, 190, 194, 197,
 300-1, 310, 320, 331
Federal Street, 91-92;
 121, 171-72, 238
Fire Department of, 56,
 119-121, 136, 142,
 170, 176, 344;
 Auxiliary, 56, 119; fire
 alarm service in, 235
Fires in, 112, 125, 130;
 see also Great Salem
 Fire of 1914
First electrified rooms in
 America in, 236
First Universalist Society
 of Salem, 39, 163
Fish Street, 94
Fishermen/fisheries in,
 2-3, 247
Flint Street, 190, 347
Fort Ann/e, *see* Fort
 Pickering
Fort Avenue, 84
Fort Lee, 132, 245, 249-
 51, 278, 280, 296;
 see also Salem's Coastline
 Defense (Trail), 281-89
Fort Juniper (aka "Fort
 #1"), 245, 249, 280;
 see also Salem's Coastline
 Defense (Trail), 281-89

Fort Naumkeag, 2, 124
Fort Pickering ("Old
 Fort," Fort Ann/e, Fort
 William), 25, 29, 69,
 245, 247-267, 271,
 278, 282-83, 285-86,
 288-89; *see also Salem's*
 Coastline Defense (Trail),
 281-89
Fort William, *see* Fort
 Pickering
Franco-American/French
 Canadian community
 in Salem, iv, 38-39,
 110, 187, 322, 346,
 349
Franco-American War
 Veterans, Post 10, 322
Franklin Building, 148,
 151-52, 297, 310
Franklin Street, 344
Furlong Memorial Park,
 344
GAR (Grand Army of
 the Republic) Hall,
 324
General Court in, 4-5
Great Salem Fire of
 1914, 110, 112, 151,
 187-89, 304, 330, 349
Greenlawn Cemetery,
 87, 124, 138, 343;
 Friends of, 203-6;
 Soldiers' Monument,
 126, 204
Grove Street, 210
First Church in Salem,
 121, 145, 167, 208
Forest River Park, 83
Hamilton Hall, 175-76,
 183, 297, 326, 328
Harbor, *see Waterfront and*
 Derby Street (Trail) 215-
 43
Harmony Grove Ceme-
 tery, 87, 123, 142, 210-
 13; Trustees of, 210-11
Hawthorne Boulevard,
 81, 344-45
Heritage Days, 241
Higginson Grammar
 School, 19
High Avenue, 280

High School, 106, 236, 239-40; Battalion, 317
Highland Avenue, 280, 307, 347
Historic Salem, Inc., 155
Homan's Cove, 195
Howard Street, 14
Howard Street Cemetery, 14
Howard Street Church (formerly Branch Church), 14
Horse Pasture Point, 207
Immaculate Conception Church/Memorial, 345
Industries in during wartime, World War I: 36-37; World War II: 75-79
Inventors in, 169, 208-9, 234-38
Jackson Street, 347
Juniper Point, 345; *see also* Fort Juniper
Kernwood Avenue, 207
Kernwood Mansion/ Kernwood Country Club, 207-8, 210
Lafayette Street, 82, 148, 322, 346; Lafayette Park, 346
Larkin Lane, 82; *see also* Catharine Larkin
Lawrence Street, 346
Lead mills in, 36-37
Leather industry in, 75-77
Leslie's Retreat, *see* Revoltionary War/ Leslie's Retreat
Lowell Island, 246, 315
Loyalists in, 4-5, 8-11, 132, 146
Lynde Street, 122-24, 193, 195
Mack Park, 82
Main Street, 91-92
Mansell Parkway, 345
Margin Street, 133, 143-44
Maritime trade/shipping in, 4, 158-59, 213, 217; *see also* East India Marine

Society
Ship captains, 150, 153, 186, 198, 215, 231-32, 244; *see also* William Driver
Ship's crew and sailors, 234, 244
Market Street, 94
Marshal (City), 135-36, 147, 205
Mason Street, 83, 193
Masonic Temple, 121
Mayors of, 22, 25, 38, 83, 127, 135, 157, 173, 211, 224, 228, 241, 274; *see also* individual names
McGlew Park, 345
Mechanic Hall, 98, 125-26, 301
Memorial Day in, 204
Memorial Drive, 241
Merchants in, 2-4, 12, 132, 146, 150, 167, 213, 217, 234, 244, 282-83; and USS *Essex*, 277; *see also* Maritime Trade
Merritt Square/Merritt Triangle, 87-88, 122-23, 167
Murray Hall (The Bridge at 211), 163
Native Americans in, *see* Native Americans
Naumkeag Mills, 259
New Liberty Street, 108
Newhall Building, 117
Norman Street, 133
North Bridge, 167, 192-93, 195-96, 199, 295; *see also* Revolutionary War/Leslie's Retreat
North Church, 130, 167, 173, 184, 193, 208, 210; *see also* Revolutionary War/Leslie's Retreat
North River, 93
North Salem/North Fields, 5; *see also* Revolutionary War/Leslie's Retreat and *North Salem (Trail),*

192-213
North Street/Route 114, 5, 155, 185, 193, 195, 206, 345-46
Now & Then Club/Hall, 152, 169, 320
Nursery Street, 345
Oak Grove, 280
Ocean Avenue, 83
Old Burying Point, *see* Charter Street Cemetery
Old Home Week, 224
Old Salem Train Depot, *see* Salem Train Depot
Old Town Hall/Town House, 135-36, 146
Oliver Grammar School, 172
Orne Street, 203
Orne's Point, 195
Palmer Street, 82
Parades in, 92, 241
Parks Commission/ Department of, 83, 280
Pearl Street, 235
Phillips House, 174-75
Phoenix Building, 133, 148
Pickering House, 184-85
Pickering Light, 253
Pickering Wharf, 274, 276
Pickering's Hill, 186
Pioneer Village, viii, 290
(The) Point, 187
Police Department of, iv, 54-55, 136, 147-48, 351-52; Auxiliary, 43, 54-55, 147; *see also* City Marshal and Provost Marshal
Polish-American community in Salem, 239, 241, 325
Polish Legion of American Veterans, Post 55/ PLAV, 325
Pope Street, 345
Port Security of, 42
Post Office in, 18, 60, 143
Price Acts in, 7
Proctor Street, 345

Provost Marshal (military police) of, 19
Railroad in, 123, 133-36; *see also* Salem Train Depot
Ropes Mansion, 167-68
Rust Street, 163, 165
Saint Joseph's Parish Monument, 346
Saint Mary's Veterans' Memorial, 346
St. Peter Street, 114-15, 117, 236, 324
Salem (three Navy war ships), 127, 214, 223 29
Salem Armory ("Cadet Armory," "Salem Armory," "Salem Cadet Armory"), 59, 78, 108-14, 111-114, 224, 304, 312, 329, 331; *see also* Armory Memorial Park
Salem Artillery Company (Mass. Militia), 91, 250, 298, 317
Salem Athenaeum, 234
Salem-Beverly Bridge, 343
Salem Brass Band, 98-100
Salem Cadets, *see* Second Corps of Cadets
Salem Cadet Band, 96, 98, 101-4, 112, 126, 204, 213, 225, 306
Salem Chamber of Commerce, 112
Salem City Guards, 17, 133, 148, 315-16;
Salem Common, vii, 4, 83-84, 89, 126, 151, 276, 293, 314; *see also Salem Common and Downtown (Trail)*, 87-152
Bandstand, 95-96, 213;
The First Muster (event), vi-vii, 96, 114, 293, 329
The First Muster (marker), vi-vii, 293
Liberty Tree, 107, 168
Washington Arch, 89-

90, 314
Salem Common Neighborhood Association, 87-90
Salem Company, 2, 291-92
Salem Community Concert Band, 104-5
Salem Evening News/ Salem News (historical newspaper), 24-25, 30-31, 33, 36, 38, 74, 82-85, 87, 115, 121, 131, 134-36, 143, 157, 220-22, 233, 236, 240-42, 262-63, 269-70, 273-74, 280, 288-89, 307, 318, 322
Salem Female Anti-Slavery Society, 16, 121
Salem Fire, *see* Great Salem Fire of 1914
Salem Five, 62
Salem Daily Gazette (historical newspaper), 267
Salem Gazette, (historical newspaper),122, 125, 177-80, 182
Salem Garden Club, 344
Salem Glee Club, 173
Salem Hospital, 144-45, 150-51, 324
Salem Hospital Nursing School/nurses from or in Salem, 144-45, 150-51, 324
Salem Laundry, 148
Salem Leg Company, 22-23, 291-92
Salem Light Artillery, 155
Salem Light Infantry/ Salem Zouaves, 17, 98, 125, 133-34, 146, 148, 155, 172, 182-83, 309-11; Veterans Association, 212, 311, 326-28;
Salem Light Infantry Quick Step (march), 314
Salem Lyceum, 106, 119-20,163

Salem Marine Society, 151
Salem Maritime (oil tanker), 231
Salem Maritime National Historic Site (National Park Service), 112, 215, 230-31, 234, 325
Salem Mechanic/k Light Infantry, 17, 122, 148, 182, 314
Salem Mercury (historical newspaper), 90-94, 171
Salem Neck, 249, 281; *see also Salem's Coastline Defense (Trail)*, 281-89
Salem Normal School, *see* Salem State University
Salem Philharmonic Orchestra, 106
Salem Regional Visitor Center, 90, 108-9, 112, 114, 300, 308
Salem Register (historical newspaper), 125, 252
Salem Rotary Club, 95, 107
Salem Sanitary Society, 173-74
Salem State University, 19, 346-47
Archives and Special Collections, 353
Bertolen School of Management, 346
Normal School, 19
Teachers College, 68
Salem Train Depot (Old), 22, 29, 61, 123, 129, 133-36
Salem Willows, 35, 82, 87, 104, 282, 288, 323, 345
Salem Witch Trials, 149, 163
Salem Women's Heritage Trail, 82, 354
Salem Zouaves, *see* Salem Light Infantry
Salem's Forgotten Stories (book series), 117
Sargent Pond, 209

Sargent Street, 209
Schools, 156, 172, 210, 236; *see also* individual schools
Sewall Street, 124
Sheridan School, 74
Shipbuilding in, 247; *see also* USS *Essex*
Ships, 215; *see Waterfront and Derby Street (Trail), 215-43*
South River, 149
South Salem/South Fields, 194
Summer Street, 154, 156
Sumner Road, 349
Tabernacle Church, 121, 130
Telegraph office in, 235
Temperance Movement in, 147
Town House Square, 22, 32, 38, 128-131, 163, 195, 318
Tremont Street, 83
Vessels, 2-3, 5, 71-3, 93, 221; visiting, *see Waterfront and Derby Street (Trail), 215-43*
Veterans, *see* Salem During Wartime, Salem Military Units, Salem Veterans Organizations, Salem Veterans' Squares, and Salem Veterans' Memorials and Parks
Veterans' Council of, 138, 319
Veterans' Day in, 204
Veterans' Memorials in, 39, 83-85, 87, 107-8; 343-47, 398th Bomber Memorial Group, 84
Veterans' Memorial Bridge, 347
Veterans' Services Department/Agent/Director of, 238, 242, 319, 343
VFW Post 1524, 238, 347
Victory Gardens in, 30
Waikiki Beach, 259
War Memorial, 347

Ward Three, 190, 347
Washington Square, 87, 89, 151, 183
Washington Street, 93, 120-21, 126, 127-28, 132-33, 297, 345
Water Department/System of, 205
Waterfront of, *see Waterfront and Derby Street (Trail), 215-43*
Winter Island, 12, 25, 99, 245, 297, 299, 301, 316; U. S. Coast Guard Air Station Salem, *see* U. S. Coast Guard
Winter Street, 87, 88, 124, 345
Witch City Canteen, 273
Witch House/Corwin House, 155-56
Wreaths Across America in, 204
Young people in during wartime, 30-31, 52-53, 74

Saltonstall, Leverett, 57, 127, 182
Salvation Army, 148
San Lorenzo, 343
Sanders, William H, 25-26, 113
San Francisco (Ca.), 232, 242
Sands, Maurice C., 341
Sardinia, 106
Sargent, F. Carroll, 209
Sargent, Horace Binney, 208-9
Sargent, John, 11, 194
Saugus (Mass.), 221
Saunders/Sanders, John, 91, 309, 327
Sayre, Jennie Wilson, 208-9
Schnepf, Ed, 269
Scotland, 248
Scott, Gen. [?], 15
Sea Dog (submarine), 222
Sea-fencibles, 216
Second Corps of Cadets (aka "Salem Cadets"), 90-95, 106-7, 112, 148, 151-52, 155, 190-91,

205, 211-12, 216, 246 (#7 in caption), 291, 297-308; and the Great Salem Fire, 188; Veterans Association, 95-96, 114, 209, 329
Sénéchal, Desneiges, 322
Servicemen of the Spanish-American War, 330
Shad (submarine), 220-2
Shanghai (China), 213, 232-33
Shannon (battle ship), 13
Sharpe, Samuel, 247
Shawmut (ship, formerly USS *Salem* #1), 226
Shay, Daniel, *see* Shay's Rebellion
Shay's Rebellion, 6, 296
Sheldon, Charles W., 341
Shearman, James L., 20
Shearman, Nancy Remond, 20
Shearman, William, 20
Shelby Shoe Co., 76-77
Sheridan, Philip B., 341
Sheridan, Philip Henry, 22, 115-17, 127, 323; Post 34, 115-17
Sherry, Mary C., 151
Shreve, Racket, 73
Shreve, William, 41, 71-73
Ship sponsors, *see* U. S. Navy
Shy, John W., 283-86, 288
Sibley, Clifton Abbott, 157
Silsbee, Nathaniel, 182
Silver Star, 239, 307, 347
Simpson, Mrs. James L., 121
Simsbury Iron Works, 194
Skinner, Fred F., 341
Slavery, 15-16, 19-22
  Abolitionists from/in Salem, 16, 175-76; *see also* Remond, Shearman, and Salem Female Anti-Slavery Society
  Amistad Case, 88
  Emancipation Proclamation, 19
  Fugitive Slave Law of 1850, 16
Slidell, John, 253

Smallpox, 168
Smith College, 202
Smith, Jesse, 213
Smith, Jerome H., 98-99
Smith, Laura M., 59
Smithsonian (magazine)
160-61
Sneedon, Mrs. Roger P., 165
Society for the Preservation
of New England
Antiquities (SPNEA),
174; *see also* Historic New
England
Soldiers of Fortune, 232
Sons of Union Veterans, 22,
117, 123-24
Sousa, John Phillip, 112
South America, 267
South Carolina, 155, 253
South Pacific, 345
Spain, 106, 283; pirates
from, 3

Spanish-American War
24-28, 60, 136, 141-42,
144-45, 150, 191, 212,
238, 305, 324, 331-33;
in Salem, 247, 262-67,
291, 302
Spencer, John, 294
Splaine, John Jr., 341
Springfield (Mass.), 6
St. Joseph (Mo.), 205
St. Peter's Church, 97, 114
Standley, Carolyn F., 59,
111
Stearns, Joseph Oliver, 254
Stearns, Ruth, 254
Sternberg General Hospital,
324
Stone, Laura Poor, 121
Story, Clinton R., 143
Story, Joseph, 14, 88, 175,
182-83; house, 175
Streeter, Gilbert Lewis
(G. L.), 247-50, 252-53,
276-79
Stromberg's Restaurant, 67
Stuttegart (Germany), 240
Success (ship), 217
Suez Canal Crisis, 228
Sullivan, Denis J., 280
Sumner, Charles, 120
Surrette Batteries, 79

Sutherland, Ronald, 341
Swampscott (Mass.), 212
Sweeney, Wilfred Patrick,
341
Swiniuch, Louis A., 82
Switzerland, 163
Sylvania, 29, 37, 70; Army-
Navy "E" Award, 78, 346
Symonds, John, 203, 281,
296

Taft, William Howard, 96
Tagney, Ronald, 281
Tahiti, 159
Tarring and feathering, 168
Tay, Mary, 165
Taylor, Zachary, 15-16
Telegraph, 235
Telephone, 238
Tennessee, 159
Terranova, Salvatore, 341
Texas, 15, 140
Texas Rangers, 213, 232
Thailand, 350, 352
Thomas, Herbert B., 341
Tilford, Leland, 147
Tobin, Maurice, 111
Todd, Sally, 165
Tolles, Bryant F., 112, 127-
28, 132, 143, 147
Topsfield (Mass.), 277, 350
Tories, *see* Loyalists
Town House Square, *see*
Salem
Townsend, Moses, 231
Traces of War (website), 239
Train Depot (Old), *see*
Salem Train Depot
Trask, George Caldwell, 341
Trask, William, 292, 292
Trenton (ship), 253
Trenton (N. J.), *see*
Revolutionary War
Troiani, Don, vi-vii, 95
Truman, Harry S., 170, 274,
320
Tsai Ting Kai, 233
Tucker, Paul, 354
Tully, George H., 341
Turkey (country), 248
Twarog, John J., 342
Tyburn, Henry, 15

U-boats, *see* U. S. Coast
Guard Air Station Salem
and World War I
Udorn (Thailand), 350
Underground Railroad, 88
University of Massachu-
setts, 239
University of Virginia, 234
Upton, Thomas A., 342

United States
Adjutants General of,
186
Citizens Defense Corps/
Office of Civil Defense
(OCD) of, 43
Congress, 169-70, 211,
244, 269, 285, 289,
320; House of Repre-
sentatives, 186;
Senate, 186;
see also Revolutionary
War/Provincial
Congress
Constitution of, 6, 285
Department of Transpor-
tation of, 274
Federal Bureau of
Investigation (FBI)
of, 54
Merchant Marine, 244

Military of
(in alphabetical order)

Army
18, 28, 78, 205, 349-50
26th Infantry Division
("Yankee Division" or
"YD"), 29-30, 40, 60,
304, 307
432nd Anti-Aircraft
Artillery Battalion,
345
Air Corps, 83
Cadet Nursing Corps,
151
Chaplains, 167
Field hospitals, 324
Food, 28
Horse Cavalry, 239
Non-commissioned
Officers (NCOs), 254
Nurse Corps, 60, 144-45

Quartermasters General, 186
Third Army, 239, 241, 307
Third Cavalry Regiment, 239
Women's Army Corps (WACs), 60
Women's Army Nurses Corps, 60

Coast Guard
Air Station Salem, 41, 69-70, 81, 83, 230-31, 268-75; Air-Sea Rescue designation, 271
And Nathaniel Bowditch, 235
Auxiliary, 40-41, 269, 274
Captain of the Port Program (COTP), 230-31
Historian's Office, 269
Motto of, 270
Reserve, 70, 269, 274
"SPARS"/Women's Reserve, 60, 270

National Guard
iv, vi-vii; Salem as birthplace of, iv, vi-vii, 2, 95, 106, 293-95; Origin of name, vi, 304; *see also* Massachusetts National Guard

Marine Corps
345

Navy
2, 25, 38, 71, 73, 78, 80-82, 88, 100, 117, 136, 138-42, 143, 155, 206, 213, 235
And Nathaniel Bowditch, 235
And torpedo warfare, 236
First Naval District/Ship Yard, 143; 220, 269, 351
Founding/birthplace of, 277, 296, 356-57

In Salem, 220, 223
Motto of, 279
Naval Reserve Training Center, 220-22
Navy Day, 356-57
Reserves, 222
Ship and submarine visits (to Salem), 34, 220-29, 351
Ships, 100, 138, 345; *see also USS Essex and USS Salem*
Ship sponsors, 224, 227, 229

United States (cont.)
Office of Price Administration of, 64
Post Master General of, 186
Public Health Service of, 151
Secretary of War of, 186, 212, 280, 288
Supreme Court of, 88
War Department of, 75, 321
U. S. Naval Shipbuilding Museum, 229 (non-military)
U. S. Spanish War Veterans/USWV, 330
U. S. Torpedo Station, 236 (non-military)
Usovicz, Stanley J., 241

V-Mail, 66
Vasilakopoulos, Speros A., 342
Vassar College, 207
Verrette, Philias J./ Monument, 347
Very, Lydia Louisa Anne, 200
Veterans (Salem), *see Salem*
Veterans Administration (VA), 124, 169, 319
Veterans Day, 38-39, 238, 317
Veterans of Foreign Wars (VFW), 238, 333; Post 1524, 333

Vietnam, 169-70, 240, 274, 307, 319, 347
Virginia, 190, 248, 283, 285
Volpe, Jennie, 156
Volpe, John, 156-57

Wadsworth, Alex, 210
Walker, William, 232
War of 1812, 12-14, 125, 151, 155, 276-79, 286; in Salem, 252, 297, 309; privateers in, *see* Privateers
Ward, Artemus, 283-84
Ward, Benjamin, 296
Ward, Frederick Townsend, 213, 231-33
Ward, James, 15
Ward, Joshua, 90, 132, 282, 297
Ward, Richard, 132, 282
Washington Blues, 317
Washington Crossing Historic Park, 118
Washington, D. C., 17, 64, 101, 114, 160, 163, 315-16
Washington, George, 5, 89-94, 111, 114, 117-18, 127, 132, 219
And Continental Army, 213, 283-84, 296, 356
And Timothy Pickering, 171-72, 186, 250
Body guards of, 212
Enemies of, 283-86, 288
In Salem, 89-94, 297
Washington Rangers, 317
Waters, David P., 25
Webb, Jonathan, 179
Webber, C. H., 283
Weeks, John W., 288
Wellesley College, 202
Wenham (Mass.), 352
Werner, Edward, 270
Wesolowski, Konstanti, 342
West, Benjamin, 5-6, 113
West India Fruit and Steamship Company, 226
West Indies, 244
West Point, 232, 234, 309
Westfield (Mass.), 327
Wetmore, William, 179

Wheeler, Mr. [?], 180
Whig Party, 15-16, 283
Whipple, George M., 115, 117
White, Stephen, 182
Wicher, Joseph, 196
Wilcox, J. H. & Co., 126
Wildes, George Dudley, 18, 113
Wilkins, Charles A., 342
Willoughby, Malcolm F., 271
Willson, Edmund B., 167
Wilson, Henry B., 224
Wilson, Woodrow, 38, 96, 202
Wingate, Francis, 165
Winter Island, *see* Salem/ Winter Island
Winthrop, John, viii, 247, 290
Winthrop Light Guards, 133, 315
Witch Trials, *see* Salem Witch Trials
Wolcott, Roger, 263, 305
Women's Defense Corps, *see* Massachusetts, Women's Defense Corps
Wood, Robert, 107
Woods, George, 18, 117, 206
Woods, Kate Tannat, 18, 206
Worcester (Mass.), 235, 270

World War I
7, 28-39, 60, 107, 121, 128-30, 134, 151,163, 166, 169, 304, 319
And American Legion, 318-20
And DAV, 321-32
And Food Conservation Army, 31
And Red Cross, 202-3, 213
Armistice Day Parade (in Salem), 129
Army food in, 28
Espionage Act of 1917, 230
Liberty Bond Drives, 32, 34, 38, 128
Memorials in Salem, 190, 280, 289
Mines, 236-37
Salem industries and, 36-37, 76
Special Aid Society for American Preparedness, Salem Chapter, 174-75
U-boats/submarines/sub-chasers in, 226, 236-37, 267, 269, 272-74

World War II
1, 40-85, 131, 134-36, 143, 147, 151, 155, 307, 325
And AMVETS, 320
And Coast Guard Air Station Salem, 69-70, 247, 268-75
And Red Cross, 164-66
Battle of the Bulge, 307
Captain of the Port Program, 230-31
Civil Defense, *see* Salem/ Civil Defense
D-Day, 351
"E" Award, 78, 346
Memorials in Salem, 190
Pearl Harbor, 60, 127, 239, 346
Procurement and Assignment Service, 151
Public Health Service, 151
Ration books/stamps/coins, 5, 119
Salem industries and, 75-79
V-E Day, 81, 274
V-J Day, 81, 131, 274
V-Mail, 66-67
Veterans, *see* Salem/ Veterans
Victory Bonds, 66, 74
Victory Medal, 345
Victory Parade (in Salem), 81, 274

The World's Turned Upside Down (song), 198
The World Turned Upside Down (Tangney), 281-82
Wright, Robert K. Jr., 292-93

X-ray machine, 238

Yankee Division ("YD"; 26th Infantry Division), *see* United States Army
Yost, Paul A., 272
Young Men's Christian Association (YMCA), 107

Zavalia, Francis J., 342
Zingaretti, Guilo, 342
Zoll, Samuel, 274
Zouave Movement, 310; *see also* Salem Light Infantry

"West View, Salem Mass.," from *Album of New England Scenery*
by J. B. Bachelder, 1856.

Bonnie Hurd Smith has contributed to the cultural and preservation communities of Salem, the North Shore, and Cape Ann in northeastern Massachusetts for many years as a researcher, author, speaker, event planner, promoter, and leader of nonprofits. Her work for the Peabody Essex Museum on Armory Park in Salem led to the creation of this book, recognition by the Massachusetts Army National Guard, and an honorary membership in the Second Corps of Cadets Veterans Association. In 2015, Smith teamed up with Nelson Dionne to create "Salem's Forgotten Stories," a series of books to share and promote his Salem History Collection. Smith is well known for her work in the field of American women's history, especially women (and their male colleagues) who have worked for progressive change and equal rights. As a result, *Salem Serves* includes stories about women and African Americans in Salem who served in the military or contributed "on the home front." Smith is a native of Concord, Massachusetts, the granddaughter of a Navy commander, and the current spouse of an Army veteran named Nelson Dionne. *bonniehurdsmith.com*

Nelson Dionne, born and raised in Salem's large French-Canadian community, began collecting Salem history over fifty years ago as part of a Salem High School civics class. His interest never waned throughout his career of service—as a soldier in the Army during Vietnam, as an ambulance driver, Salem Police Officer, and volunteer for numerous historical and military organizations. In fact, he considers his relentless collecting of Salem history a service to the hometown he loves. All of Dionne's material eventually found a home at Salem State University's Archives & Special Collections. For his tireless collecting, Dionne has received numerous awards and citations from city and state government and civic and cultural organizations. *See pages 348-354 to learn more about Nelson Dionne, or find him on Facebook and LinkedIn.*

salemsforgottenstories.com
Facebook/salemsforgottenstories

Made in the USA
Lexington, KY
07 December 2019